Europe's Health for Sale
The heavy cost of privatisation

Europe's Health for Sale
The heavy cost of privatisation

Copyright © Libri Publishing Ltd 2011.

Authors retain the rights to individual chapters.

ISBN 978 1 907471 18 6

The right of John Lister to be identified as the editor of this work has been asserted in accordance with the Copyright, Designs and Patents Act, 1988.

All rights reserved. No part of this publication may be reproduced, stored in any retrieval system or transmitted in any form or by any means, electronic, mechanical, photocopying, recording or otherwise, without the prior written permission of the copyright holder for which application should be addressed in the first instance to the publishers. No liability shall be attached to the author, the copyright holder or the publishers for loss or damage of any nature suffered as a result of reliance on the reproduction of any of the contents of this publication or any errors or omissions in its contents.

A CIP catalogue record for this book is available from The British Library

Design by Carnegie Publishing

Printed in the UK by Ashford Colour Press

Libri Publishing
Brunel House
Volunteer Way
Faringdon
Oxfordshire
SN7 7YR

Tel: +44 (0)845 873 3837

www.libripublishing.co.uk

Contents

Introduction	Alexis Benos, John Lister	1
Chapter 1	World champions in hospital privatisation – the effects of neoliberal reform on German employees and patients Nils Böhlke, Ian Greer, Thorsten Schulten	9
Chapter 2	Privatising the Greek health-care system – a story of corporate profits and rising health inequalities E. Kondilis, E. Smyrnakis, S. Giannakopoulos, T. Zdoukos, A. Benos	29
Chapter 3	In between Basaglia and Einthoven – the chronicle of a predictable failure of mental-health reform in Greece George Nikolaidis	45
Chapter 4	The effect of health reforms in Turkey: out-of-pocket payments are increasing Kayıhan Pala, Harika Gerçek, Alpaslan Türkkan, Hamdi Aytekin	65
Chapter 5	Working conditions of physicians employed in public institutions in Turkey Nilay Etiler, Betul Urhan	83
Chapter 6	The struggle for the right to health in Turkey: 2003 to 2009 Öztürk Osman, Çerkezoglu Ali, Ağkoç Süheyla	95
Chapter 7	Fighting privatisation in Madrid CAS Madrid	103

Chapter 8	Global Neoliberalism and the consequences for health-care policy in the English NHS *Clive Peedell*	**107**
Chapter 9	Combating health inequalities amidst the credit crisis *Dr Onteeru Reddy*	**119**
Chapter 10	'Save our hospital' campaigns in England – why do some hospital campaigns succeed? A preliminary exploration *Sally Ruane*	**125**
Chapter 11	Reducing senility to 'bare life' – are we heading for a new Holocaust at mid-twenty-first century? *Dr Andrea Capstick*	**149**
Chapter 12	The impact of the media on health policy – case studies from England and the UK *John Lister*	**159**
Chapter 13	Talking drugs at the captain's corner – an analysis of a pharmaceutical industry conference *Marisa de Andrade*	**171**
Chapter 14	A brief historical review of the British press coverage of AIDS and its role as an educator in the 1990s *Danielle Cox*	**185**
Contributing Authors		**200**

Introduction

The papers in this volume stem from a successful conference of the International Association of Health Policy in Europe[1], which was hosted in June 2009 by Coventry University. Entitled 'Condition Critical: Health care, marketising reforms and the media', the conference[2] innovatively attempted to link analysis of the evolving policies of governments with the limited discussion and public awareness of these policies which result from patchy and inadequate coverage of the key issues by the news media.

June 2009, of course, was still relatively early in the unfolding economic and financial crisis that has gripped governments over much of the world since the banking crash of 2008. Some of the impact of this was reflected in the contributions from various countries.

The colossal, multi-billion-dollar subsidies that have been paid out by governments to prop up the tottering banking sector have resulted, as we all know, in a wave of austerity programmes. These feature enormous cuts in public spending by governments, in many parts of the world, as they require the public – working people – to pay the price for rescuing the private sector.

---

1   The **International Association of Health Policy (IAHP)** is a scientific, political and cultural organisation founded in 1977. It is an international network of scholars, health workers and activists which aims to promote the scientific analysis of public health issues and to provide a forum for international comparisons and debate on health policy issues. The basic principle adopted by IAHP members is that health should be regarded as a social and political right. The main goal of the Association is the promotion of health, the struggle against health inequalities, and the development of social solidarity. IAHPE is the European section of the world-wide IAHP, and the Coventry Conference was the fifteenth European conference to be held. In addition to the papers in this volume, it also heard lively presentations from two of the historic founders of IAHPE, Hans Ulrich Deppe and Julian Tudor Hart.
2   The conference attracted over 40 papers and almost 60 participants from a variety of European countries as well as Malaysia, Taiwan, the USA and Brazil. A six-DVD record of the full conference is available from IAHPE, including many of the valuable presentations which have not been included in this Europe-focused collection: see http://www.healthemergency.org.uk/publications.php#videos.

But while public-sector budgets are facing an unprecedented squeeze, the crisis of the private sector has driven a parallel attack. In the quest for new sources of profit, the private sector is seeking to recapture a far greater share of the spending on services which, in most countries, were largely removed from the competitive market in post-war welfare states.

Since the 1980s, many governments have privatised utilities and services formerly in the public sector – water, electricity, gas, telecommunications, the postal organisations and many functions of local government. Some have gone further and privatised transport services, prisons and local government services, and have withdrawn from any commitment to social housing.

In general, however, education and health care have until now been largely excluded from this process of privatisation. In the richest OECD countries, which spend 90 per cent of the world's health budgets, most of this expenditure is controlled and delivered through public-sector bodies or social health insurance, allowing limited private-sector involvement.

Attempts in the 1980s and 1990s – notably in Sweden, the UK, the Netherlands and New Zealand – to break through this public-sector domination and open up health care to private for-profit providers[3] proved to be politically fraught with danger for governments. Outright privatisation tended to be restricted to relatively marginal areas within health care[4].

However, the mood of many governments has been changing. This is partly due to the widespread ideological capitulation of social democratic parties to the concepts and mantra of neoliberalism (notably Tony Blair's "New Labour" party in Britain; but this is a trend echoed in other traditionally social-democratic political parties). Partly also it is a result of electoral changes that have brought explicitly right-wing governments into office at regional or national level, for example in parts of Scandinavia.

Even before the economic tsunami of the banking crisis broke in 2008, governments in many European countries and global bodies shaping the development of health-care systems had begun determined moves towards remodelling services on a market basis. This involves dismissing the value of planning and stressing instead the allegedly positive role of competition and "choice" of provider. It means contrasting the claimed dynamism and efficiency of the private sector with the "bureaucracy", poor quality and indifferent staff alleged to be the inevitable consequence of publicly provided services. These

---

3 See Lister, J., *Health Policy Reform: driving the wrong way?* (Middlesex University Press, 2005)
4 For example the radical neoliberal government of Margaret Thatcher in Britain from 1979, which led the pace in Europe for the privatisation of utilities and service industries, restricted its efforts on health to privatising hospital support services (such as cleaning, catering and so on) and non-clinical services; and later (from 1989) the introduction of an "internal market" within the National Health Service. It always denied any intention to privatise clinical care. (Lister, J., *The NHS after 60: for patients or profits?*, Middlesex University Press, 2008)

INTRODUCTION

policies have a very important common factor: they are all driven first and foremost by the ideology of neoliberalism – and in each case they make no reference to evidence to show that the new approach can hope to deliver what is promised.

There is a good reason for this: there is no such evidence. A recent OECD ministerial conference in Paris on 'Health Priorities in the Aftermath of the Crisis', seeking to emphasise value for money and coordinate the drive towards market-based health care, confirmed that its teams of researchers, with access to data from all of the 33 members states over much of the last 30 years, had been unable to uncover any evidence that might offer a rational basis for such policies. Instead, the evidence – as expensively and disastrously demonstrated in the USA[5] – shows that a market-style health system is incapable of delivering universal or comprehensive care to a whole population.

Nowhere in the world can health services be delivered purely by the private sector organised as a free market[3]. Indeed, the private for-profit sector seeks to deliver only certain types of health care – those offering low risk and the prospect of high returns – and can only be drawn into providing other services if a generous premium payment is available to guarantee profits. Left to its own devices, the private sector focuses its main effort only on guaranteed high returns and low-risk services – most commonly the elective hospital care of the wealthier urban population of working-age adults. Around the world, private for-profit providers are careful wherever possible to avoid any commitment to deliver emergency services, community-based services, rural health services or care for chronic conditions.

In other words, even where they are paid for through public-sector funds, systems which make extensive use of private for-profit provision are inevitably more expensive and more bureaucratic than those which rely on public provision, collective sharing of risk and the planning of services. Recent figures in the UK show that the private health sector, with a network of small hospitals (average size just 50 beds), is accustomed to profit margins of 30 per cent on its relatively small-scale £5 billion turnover on uncomplicated elective treatment, compared with the average surplus of just 7 per cent retained by public-sector providers on the much larger number of often more complex and demanding cases[6].

To respond to a public-sector cash squeeze by adopting (or maintaining) market-style policies is thus doubly detrimental to the delivery of health care to

---

5   The US spends one dollar in six (16.6 per cent of GDP, $2.5 trillion a year) from its gigantic economy on health care whilst, at the last count, leaving one American in six (50 million) without proper health insurance and thus dependent on the minimal provision from state and federal subsidy.

6   Davie, E., 'Fair trading complaint raises competition warning', *Health Service Journal*, 21 October 2010, pp.10–11

those who need it most. On the one hand, overall resources are frozen in real terms or in some cases even reduced in absolute terms; and on the other, a greater share of the funding that is available for health care is spent not on front-line care but on new and bureaucratic systems designed to open up a competitive "market" and on the inflated costs of delivering care through for-profit providers, which function first and foremost to deliver profits to their shareholders.

The IAHPE Coventry conference set out to debate these issues, not just in the context of Europe, but also on a wider level, taking in the ways in which these same issues are reflected in developing countries through the influence of the World Bank, the International Monetary Fund and other global bodies. The opening keynote speaker was Oxfam's Anna Marriott, who outlined her important pamphlet '**Blind Optimism: Challenging the myths about private health care in poor countries**'. Other distinguished speakers also presented papers on this wider context[7].

The way in which market-style policies and the commercialisation of health care have tended to sideline public health – despite the potential gains and cost-effective solutions it offers – was also a feature of the conference, with contributions from a variety of mainly British academics.

But the centrepiece of the discussion was the drive towards privatisation and market-style policies in the developed countries. The conference heard papers on these issues from a number of European countries, as well as from a keynote speaker from the US Physicians for a National Health Program who discussed the issues and dilemmas confronting health reformers in the US since President Obama's election.

While market-style reforms and their impact have been discussed by conferences for a number of years, an innovative element of the Coventry IAHPE conference was the integration of a discussion of the role of the media in the current situation. An opening paper exposed the stark contrast between, on the one hand, the scale of the changes in health-care systems and the issues facing the wider public; and on the other, the very limited scope of press and broadcast news coverage that they attract. This issue is also linked to the lack of properly trained, specialist health journalists: in Britain, the overwhelming majority of the news seen and heard by the wider public audience is presented by journalists with little or no specialist background in health. The result is that huge sums of taxpayers' money are spent – and services which could literally mean the difference between life and death are reorganised, cut or closed – with little or no actual public debate or awareness.

This theme of limited media coverage was further developed in a paper highlighting the disproportionate reliance of the mainstream media on

---

7   All of the speeches that – for a variety of reasons – are not in this volume are available on the DVD record of the conference.

press releases and PR from the drug companies. The problems of conveying a consistent and enlightened media message on complex public-health issues such as AIDS were also emphasised.

Two areas of health care which are largely ignored by much of the mainstream press are mental health and care of older people: both have therefore been widely viewed by governments as potential soft targets for spending cuts. The conference heard a warning that older people suffering from dementia are increasingly politically excluded and regarded as a "drain on the economy". And from Greece came an account of how some of the neoliberal attempts to combine cuts in spending on mental health with the privatisation of service provision can result in disastrous failures in health care, which actually cost more or fail to deliver promised economies.

This volume has deliberately focused on European health care. It brings together important studies on German hospital privatisation; three papers on the impact of privatisation and market reforms on staff and patients in Turkey and the campaign against these policies; a study of privatisation in Greece; different aspects of the situation in England; and a contribution on Spain from a vigorous campaigning group based in Madrid. These papers have retained their immediacy and interest. The conference was held in June 2009, but the themes and issues it identified have continued and intensified in the period since, giving an added value to the analysis put forward here.

One notable example of this has been the growing crisis in health care in Ireland where, in 2009, the budget cuts arising from the government's heavy-handed austerity programme were already beginning to take effect, in the form of closed beds and lost jobs. Yet one of the conspicuous features to emerge from the analysis of the policy agenda of governments, whether in Europe or in developing countries, was the extent to which policies were in many cases being driven by ideological concerns, regardless of the potential and actual financial cost.

The Irish government, for example, has carried on cutting back on its public provision of health services – cuts which are still taking place, even to the extent of denying prostheses for amputees[8] – whilst continuing with its expensive policy of subsidising private medical insurance and private health care, estimated to cost upwards of €500 million and possibly as much as €700 million per year[9]. The latest figures as this volume is prepared show that the cuts in public spending are leading Ireland back towards recession – the dreaded so-called "double-dip" recession in which levels of unemployment rise and

---
8 See the *Connacht Tribune*, 29 July 2010, http://www.galwaynews.ie/14176-cruellest-cut-leaves-amputees-out-limb
9 Staines, A., 'HSE needs a programme of rapid, focused cost savings', *Irish Times*, 2010, http://www.irishtimes.com/newspaper/opinion/2010/1002/1224280187472_pf.html

restrictions on popular spending power prevent any new expansion of either private- or public-sector services.

Similarly in England, in June 2009, Gordon Brown's New Labour government was ignoring the evidence, and the views of senior doctors and health professionals, and driving forward with an aggressive effort to encourage private providers to deliver a growing (if still relatively tiny) share of services funded publicly through the National Health Service (NHS). These various policies, hotly challenged by campaigners and their evidence base disputed, brought rising overhead costs and an often-questionable quality of care. The diversion of public funds to private providers, even on a relatively limited scale, has squeezed public services and forced closures and cutbacks.

Worse, they have now laid the groundwork for the far-reaching health "reforms" put forward since May 2010 by the coalition Conservative and Liberal Democrat government. These could result in the privatisation of the vast majority of health-service provision in England, using the tax-funded pool of NHS finance to sponsor a new "market" in which "any willing provider" would be invited to bid for clinical services[10]. In addition to this potentially costly and wasteful exercise in building a new health market, the Con–Dem government is also pushing for £20 billion of "efficiency savings" by 2014 from the £105 billion NHS budget, as resources are frozen in real terms while demand for health care and cost pressures increase by up to 4 per cent per year.

The Turkish government, again motivated by ideology rather than evidence, has continued to drive the privatisation agenda discussed in this volume. In addition, it is now preparing to copy another failed policy that has been tested to destruction by the British NHS by signing up for a large-scale hospital development to be funded by the Private Finance Initiative (PFI). Bids are lining up for the lucrative project of building new "city hospitals" in Kayseri and five other cities, at an estimated cost of €250m per hospital[11]. In Britain, where PFI schemes have been used to fund over 90 per cent of new hospitals since 1997, official Treasury figures show that buildings costed at £11 billion are set to cost the taxpayer more than £65 billion over the lifetime of their extended contracts. PFI charges are set to increase year by year regardless of the income of the hospitals and their ability to pay[12].

Greece, of course, has also been at the epicentre of the economic crisis since the banking collapse. Its government has been bludgeoned and bullied by other EU governments to drive through staggering cuts in wages, pensions

---

10 Lister, J., 'Devastating the NHS', 2010, available http://www.healthemergency.org.uk/diary.php?rn=66

11 *Hurriyet Daily News*, 'Construction Firms compete for Turkey's "city hospitals"', 1 October 2010, http://www.hurriyetdailynews.com/n.php?n=construction-firms-compete-for-the-8216city-hospitals8217-2010-10-01

12 Lister, J., *The NHS after 60: for patients or profits?* (Middlesex University Press, 2008)

and welfare to rein in public spending. In the midst of this is a health service that has been focused on channelling a growing share of public health budgets to private providers. Hospital doctors in Greek state hospitals were among the tens of thousands of workers who staged angry strikes as part of a Europe-wide day of protest against austerity on 29 September 2010.

Across much of Europe, the private sector is moving in on a variety of fronts, including hospital services, care-home provision and domiciliary care. Crisis-ridden health services in Romania and Bulgaria are seen as ripe for private-sector expansion and more hospitals are being privatised in Poland, where private-sector hospitals (which have an average of just 27 beds) draw some 60 per cent of their revenue from the National Health Insurance Fund[13].

However, while private providers are drawn by the magnetic attraction of large pools of public and social insurance funds in European countries, the extravagant promises by the World Bank's private-sector arm, the International Finance Corporation, of a private-sector-led expansion of health care in Africa, backed by a high-profile McKinsey report, have fallen flat. McKinsey had predicted a doubling of health spending in Africa by 2016 – to what most campaigners would regard as a still-pitiful $35 billion, with the private sector share set to grow to 60 per cent.

In 2007, in a fanfare of press releases, the IFC trumpeted the launch of a £1-billion fund to meet health needs in sub-Saharan Africa. Two similarly named, relatively small equity funds – the Investment Fund for Health in Africa and the Africa Health Fund (AHF) – were established and gathered funds, to be administered by private-equity fund-managers in tax havens. Yet, more than half way through 2010, only a minuscule level of investment has taken place. The AHF's first investment, of just $2.6m, was announced in January 2010 after a "six month search". So from the 2007 talk of investing up to $1 billion, two funds totalling just over £100m have eventually been established; and in two-and-a-half years only one single investment, of just $2.6m, has been achieved.

From different parts of the world, over a timeframe of more than 30 years, the experience and evidence of neoliberal policies so far point to the same conclusions: markets in health care and private for-profit provision of health services are incompatible with either the planned allocation of resources and services on an equitable basis or universal access to care.

Markets are more expensive as a way to organise services, less efficient, with higher bureaucratic overheads, and less accountable to the wider public and service users. So why are market reforms continuing even in the midst of such a dramatic onslaught on public-sector spending and in defiance of the

---

13 Useful updates on these developments in Europe can be found in the newsletter from the pro-market website Healthcare Europa at http://www.healthcareeuropa.com.

evidence? Regardless of the evasive and duplicitous arguments put forward by neoliberal advocates of market-style reforms, who invariably attempt to brand their opponents as "ideological", these "reforms" continue because of the market system's inescapable attraction for private-sector providers: namely, that it funnels profits from the public purse and from social insurance into the hands of private providers and their shareholders.

In assembling this volume and revisiting the core issues of the debate, we hope to put fresh arguments and evidence in the hands of those who are resisting similar policies around the world.

Alexis Benos, President IAHPE
John Lister, joint Vice President

October 2010

CHAPTER 1
World champions in hospital privatisation
The effects of neoliberal reform on German employees and patients

Nils Böhlke, WSI
nils-boehlke@boeckler.de

Ian Greer, Leeds University
icg@lubs.leeds.ac.uk

Thorsten Schulten, WSI
thorsten-schulten@boeckler.de

Over the past decade, German hospitals have been privatised at a rate not seen in any other country. In response to massive public-sector debt and the resulting investment backlog, many state and local governments have been privatising hospitals. The most common arguments for privatisation are repeated in a recent study commissioned by the association of private hospital owners (Bundesverband Deutscher Privatkliniken – BDPK) namely that private hospitals manage in a more efficient manner and are economically more successful (Augurzky, Beivers et al., 2009). Indeed, in some cases, private for-profit hospital companies have invested generously and turned inefficient public hospitals into profitable private ones. Of interest to us is the cost of this trend, to workers and patients.

Assertions that privatisation has not undermined the quality of care are highly dubious. In German public opinion, there is broad scepticism about the privatisation of hospitals. While there are very few scientific studies on the effects of privatisation on patients, there are a growing number of local ballot initiatives and other campaigns to fight it. There are widespread fears that for-profit health-care provision would undermine the existing system, which provides universally accessible medical treatment at a relatively high level of quality. Even among physicians, often considered the winners of privatisation, there is scepticism (Bundesärztekammer, 2007).

We will argue below that one reason for these problems is the effect of privatisation on employees. Trade unionists and works councils in privatised hospitals have seen a severe deterioration in working conditions (Ver.di Vertrauensleute und Vorsitzende und Mitglieder von Konzernbetriebsräten und Konzern-Jugend- und Auszubildenden-Vertretungen privater Krankenhauskonzern, 2008). Since personnel accounts for about 60 per cent of hospitals' overall costs (Statistisches Bundesamt, 2008b), private for-profit hospitals can only make profits at the expense of employees. These perceptions are supported by the statistics presented in this paper, and trade unions and employees protest – in cooperation with other parts of civil society – almost every planned privatisation.

Drawing on publicly available quantitative data and qualitative interviews, we map out in this paper the trend toward the privatisation of German hospitals. We begin by showing how and why privatisation has proceeded in Germany despite the controversy. Then we examine the effects of privatisation on workers and patients. We will conclude with some implications for policy and practice.

The waves of privatisation

The privatisation of German hospitals has been well documented by the federal statistics office (Statistisches Bundesamt, 2008a) (see Figure 1). From 1991 to 2007

Figure 1: Ownership structure of German hospitals, in per cent

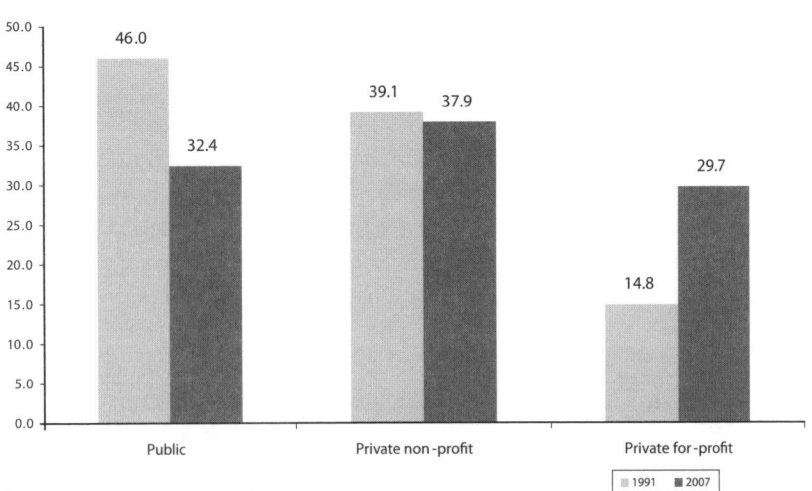

Source: Statistisches Bundesamt, 2008a; authors' own calculations

the proportion of private hospitals has almost doubled and has reached nearly 30 per cent. On the other hand the proportion of public hospitals has dropped from 46 per cent to about 32 per cent. Over this time, the proportion of private non-profit hospitals run by the churches and non-profit organisations has been relatively stable.

The total number of public hospitals has dropped from 1,110 in 1991 to 677 in 2007. In the same time the number of private hospitals has increased from 358 to 620. This decline in the importance of public hospitals has two reasons: closures of public hospitals and the sale of public hospitals to for-profit hospital chains. This latter process we call material privatisation (see Table 1).

Table 1: The German hospital sector, 1991 and 2007

	1991	2007	Change 1991–2007
Hospitals	2,411	2,087	-13.4%
Of these			
public	1,110	677	-39.0%
private non-profit	943	790	-16.2%
private for-profit	358	620	+73.2%
Hospital beds	665,565	506,954	-23.8%
Hospital beds per 100,000 inhabitants	832	616	-26.0%
Employees (total)	1,111,625	1,074,883	-3.3%
Employees (Full-time-equivalents)	875,816	792,299	-9.5%
Number of cases	14,576,613	17,178,573	+17.9%
Occupied beds in days	204,204,000	142,893,000	-30.0%
Average length of stay	14.0 Days	8.3 Days	-40.7%
Occupancy rate	84.1%	77.2%	-8.2%

Source: Statistisches Bundesamt, 2008a; authors' own calculations

Reasons for privatisation

The reasons for these changes can be found in the precarious situation of public budgets and the fundamental change in the financing system of German hospitals (Simon, 2008b). Since the early 1970s there has been a so-called "dual financing system" for hospitals, under which statutory health insurance funds pay for the operational costs, while the federal states (*Länder*) are responsible for the investments. Since the early 1990s, this system has been reformed several times in order to reduce costs, mainly by linking reimbursements to the diagnoses treated and decoupling them from the operating costs of hospitals.

The first important reform came in the early 1990s, when the principle of full-cost recovery was abolished. Previously, the costs for the hospitals were automatically covered by the health insurance funds. Thus pressures on the hospitals to reduce costs rose dramatically and drastic changes became necessary.

A system of mandatory nationwide case-based reimbursements was introduced in 2004 as the G–DRG-System (German Diagnosis Related Groups). According to this system, treatments are financed on the basis of defined diagnosis and not on time spent in hospital, as they had been before. Prices for each diagnosis are calculated for each *Land* on the basis of average costs in hospitals. This favours hospitals that work with relatively low costs per diagnosis and leads to increased cost pressure on hospitals to reduce their costs. For some companies, it raises the possibility of generating significant profits. This has made hospitals increasingly interesting for private investors and created problems for public-sector owners.

The number of hospitals has dropped by 13.4% since 1991 and the number of hospital beds has declined by 23.8% (Table 1). This has been accompanied by a 10% decline in full-time-equivalent staff. Additionally, outsourcing has become an important factor. Furthermore, the altered incentives of the DRG-System have led to a decline in the average length of stay of almost 50% (Statistisches Bundesamt, 2008a). However, the number of cases has increased by 17.1%. Thus slightly fewer employees treat more cases in a lot less time and the industrial productivity of German hospitals has risen considerably.

Over the next few years the share of private for-profit hospitals is widely expected to rise, to as much as 40% (Bähr, Fuchs et al., 2006). One reason for this shift is that many public hospitals remain inefficient. In 2008, one-third of hospitals operated in the red (Augurzky, Budde et al., 2009) and most of those are public hospitals whose deficits have to be balanced by the local budget of the municipality. From the view of many local governments, the material privatisation of hospitals is an attractive opportunity to rid themselves of these costs.

The lack of investment by the federal states in hospitals further accelerated the trend towards privatisation. Different studies quantify the backlog of needed investments between €20b (Augurzky, Budde et al., 2009), €50b (DKG, 2008) or even €100b (Simon, 2008a). From these privatisations, municipalities hope to receive the needed investment from private investors. Indeed, private hospitals receive more investment than public ones (Augurzky, Beivers et al., 2009) because their profitability makes it easier for them to receive capital from private investors. Those higher investments help private for-profit hospitals to improve their competitive position vis-a-vis public hospitals and lead to rationalisation and thus higher productivity.

Figure 2: Changes in legal form, 2002 to 2007

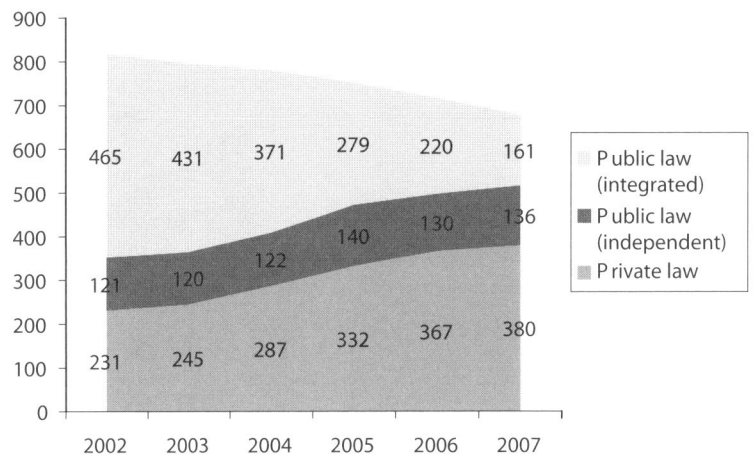

Source: Statistisches Bundesamt, 2008a

Formal privatisation of public hospitals

Intensified competition and cost pressures have led to reorganisations of many public hospitals using structural changes modelled on those of the private companies. One common approach is *formal* privatisation. This means that hospitals run directly by local government departments become fully owned subsidiaries of the states and run under private law. They are still owned by the state, but the decision-making power becomes relatively independent from the political and administrative processes of government.

As Figure 2 shows, over the last five years the number of state-owned hospitals operating under a public legal form has declined by almost two-thirds, while the share of public hospitals run under private law has almost doubled. This change has been caused by the increased competition due to the implementation of the DRG-System. The higher number of potential "veto-players" in the public authorities – i.e. actors who can obstruct rationalisation through the machinery of local government – is viewed as an obstacle under this context. The largest example of such a formal privatisation is the Vivantes Kliniken GmbH in Berlin. The company was founded in 2001 and is the result of a merger of nine city-owned hospitals.

Table 2: Outsourcing of services in German hospitals between 2004 and 2007

Sectors	% External (to an external company)	% Internal (to a subsidiary)	Total share (%)
Cleaning	19.5	33.6	53.1
Kitchen	18.4	22.0	40.4
Laboratory	24.0	3.0	27.0
Buying department	11.1	11.6	22.7
Shuttle services	8.3	11.2	19.5
Laundry	17.2	1.5	18.7
Bed preparation	9.1	8.6	17.7
Radiology	9.1	3.1	12.2
Other	10.9	10.2	21.1

Source: Blum, Offermanns et al., 2007

Functional privatisation: outsourcing

In addition to the material and formal privatisation of entire hospitals, the transfer of functions – mostly support services, rather than direct patient-care functions – into the private sector has played an important role. The outsourced work is either transferred to an external company ("external outsourcing") or into a newly established subsidiary of the hospital operator ("internal" outsourcing).

According to a survey of the German hospital association, more than 53% of all hospitals have outsourced cleaning services and more than 40% their kitchens between 2004 and 2007 (see Table 2). Increasingly, administrative and medical–technical functions are affected as well. The surprisingly low share of hospitals that have outsourced their laundry operations might be explained by the fact that these services were already widely outsourced before 2004. This has accompanied a decline in employment in these areas since 2001 that has been estimated to be as high as 41% (Jaehrling, 2007). Another form of outsourcing – involvement of private capital through public–private partnerships (PPP) – is usually used for the financing of the construction of new hospital buildings, which after completion are leased by the public authorities that run the services.

Ownership structure in international comparison

Unlike other types of privatisation, the rapid material privatisation of hospitals is unique to Germany. Currently, among major western countries only France has a higher share of private for-profit hospitals. However, France's traditionally strong private sector has declined nominally over recent years. Germany, by contrast, surpassed the US in terms of private market share by the end of 2007 (Gröschl-Bahr and Stumpfögger, 2008).

Table 3: Material ownership in comparative perspective

	Ownership	Private for-profit sector
Sweden, Denmark	Mainly public	Very few hospitals
UK (2007)	Mainly public	ca. 3% of beds
Poland (2006)	Mainly public	20.6% of hospitals 5.3% of beds
Belgium/ Netherlands (2005)	Mainly private non-profit	Very few hospitals
USA (2004)	Mainly private non-profit	17.0% of hospitals 13.9% of beds
Germany (2007)	Mixed	29.7% of hospitals 15.6% of beds
Austria (2007)	Mixed	21.5% of hospitals 9% of beds
France (2006)	Mixed	37.1% of hospitals 21% of beds

Sources: national statistics, authors' own calculations

Internationally, there are three different structures of ownership, as Table 3 shows. As in France and Austria, Germany has a mix of different owners. There are public and private for-profit hospitals as well as a large proportion of hospitals that are private, but non-profit. These hospitals are mainly run by churches and welfare associations like the Red Cross and their share is slowly declining. In other countries like the UK, Poland, Sweden and Denmark, hospitals are almost exclusively part of a public health system. The third structure can be found in Belgium, the Netherlands and the USA, where most hospitals are private and non-profit.

Private hospitals = smaller hospitals?

Although Germany has a long tradition of private hospitals, a qualitative shift in the sector occurred in the early 1990s. In the 1970s and 1980s the private hospitals were exclusively small clinics specialised on lucrative surgeries and treatments. They were not products of privatisation, but were designed and founded as small private clinics. Because of these origins, while the number of material privatisations has increased in the 1990s, private for-profit hospitals still account for a significantly lower share of beds and employees than public hospitals. While public hospitals still have more than 50% of all hospital beds, private for-profit hospitals have just 16%. Even more important is the role of public hospitals for the employees. More than 56% of all employees work in public hospitals and less than 14% in private for-profit ones (Figure 3).

Figure 3: Ownership structure in Germany by hospitals, beds and employees in 2007 (in per cent)

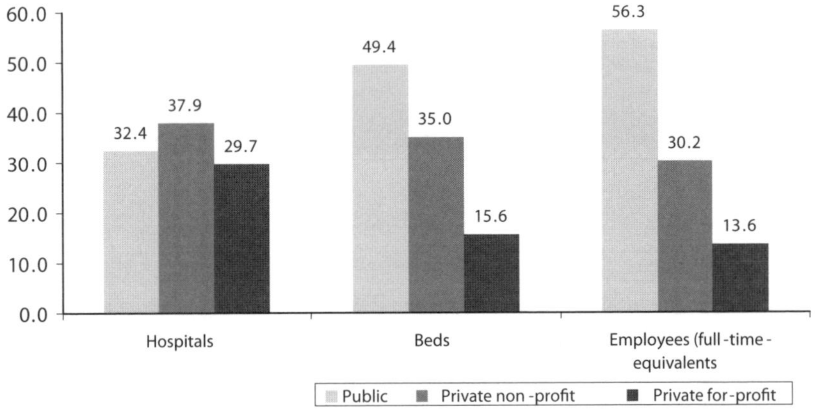

	Public	Private non-profit	Private for-profit
Hospitals	32.4	37.9	29.7
Beds	49.4	35.0	15.6
Employees (full-time-equivalents)	56.3	30.2	13.6

Sources: Statistisches Bundesamt, 2008a; authors' own calculations

For-profit hospitals, however, have been catching up rapidly in size, especially over the past five years. While the share of private for-profit hospitals has risen by more than 20%, the share of beds in those hospitals has increased by more than 60% (see Figure 4). While the first wave of privatisation predominantly hit small clinics in the area of the former GDR, this more recent wave is affecting larger hospitals in western Germany as well. Most observers assume that this wave will continue through 2010. While the effect of the crises on local government could be eased by the economic stimulus packages of the federal government in 2009, investment from the *Länder* and income from the health insurance funds (and thus income for the hospitals) is forecast to deteriorate further (Augurzky, Budde et al., 2009). Under these circumstances private hospital chains will offer to intervene as investors, and policy makers will find it difficult to reject their offers.

Figure 4: Change of the number of hospitals and beds under different ownership since 2002

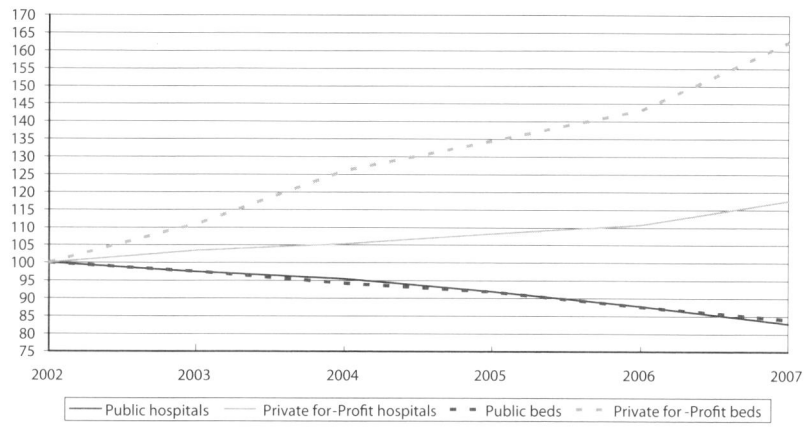

Sources: Statistisches Bundesamt, 2008a; authors' own calculations

Figure 5: Market share of private hospitals in beds in the federal states in 2007

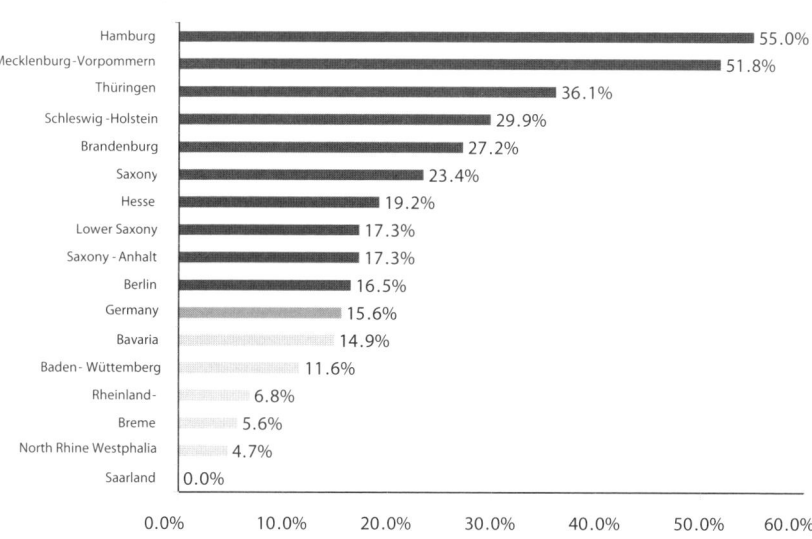

Source: Statistisches Bundesamt, 2008a

The trends described above proceeded unevenly in different *Länder*. In the "new" states in eastern Germany, the share of private for-profit hospitals is relatively high, partly due to privatisation and partly due to a weaker tradition of church-run provision. In addition, the share of private hospitals is especially high in western *Länder* where especially large privatisations have taken place. Hamburg does not have any public hospitals besides the university hospital and Hessen has privatised two of its three university hospitals. However, generally the share of private for-profit provision in large western *Länder* is significantly lower than average.

Oligopolisation of the hospital sector

The privatisation of hospitals has led to the rapid growth of a few hospital chains. The German hospital market is dominated by four major companies. Two of them are the largest hospital companies in terms of revenue and three in terms of employees. The companies are the Rhön Kliniken AG, the Helios-Kliniken-Group, the Asklepios Kliniken GmbH and the Sana Kliniken AG.

Table 4: Germany's large for-profit chains

	Hospitals	Employees	Turnover (in Mio. €)	EBIT* (in Mio. €)
Germany				
Rhön-Kliniken AG	45	26,887	2,025	157.5
Helios Kliniken Group (Fresenius SE)	56	30,043	1,841	162.2
Asklepios Kliniken GmbH (2006)	72	36,000	1,649	69
Sana Kliniken AG	33	16,338	946	49.9
Europe				
Générale de Santé (France)	196	22,900	1,651	ca.160**
Capio (Sweden)	100	14,150	1,229	no info.

* EBIT = Earnings before interests and taxes
** The numbers for Générale de Santé are projections based on data for the first half-year (81.3 Mio €) in 2007.
Sources: Stumpfögger, 2007; Handelsblatt on 10/10/2008; annual reports of the companies

The major German hospital companies are former family businesses that were founded and dominated by individual physicians. The only exception is the Sana Kliniken AG, which is run by a group of private insurance companies. The founders of Asklepios, Rhön and Helios play a major role in the management of these companies. Recently, this has changed a little due to the purchase of Helios by Fresenius SE in 2005 and the withdrawal of the founder of Asklepios in early 2008.

Overall, the basic structure of the German for-profit hospital landscape remains stable. Attempts from private equity funds to enter the market, like the British firm APAX's bid via the Swedish health-care company Capio, remain exceptional. However, the resale of private hospitals to other private companies and private equity funds will probably increase over the next years (Schmidt, 2003; Bähr, Fuchs et al., 2006). The largest private hospital owners in other countries are more closely tied to financial markets (Stumpfögger, 2007) and the need for massive investment may undermine the governance practices of these companies.

Competition on labour costs instead of quality

The competition that was created with the abolition of full-cost recovery and the implementation of the DRG-System has been further intensified due to the increasing importance of the private hospital companies. Besides paying for the operating costs and investments in their hospitals, private companies have to generate a profit for their owners. Since the DRG-system provides only limited scope for hospitals to influence their income, profit has to result from cost reductions.

Figure 6: Share of labour costs in hospitals with more than 500 beds in 2007

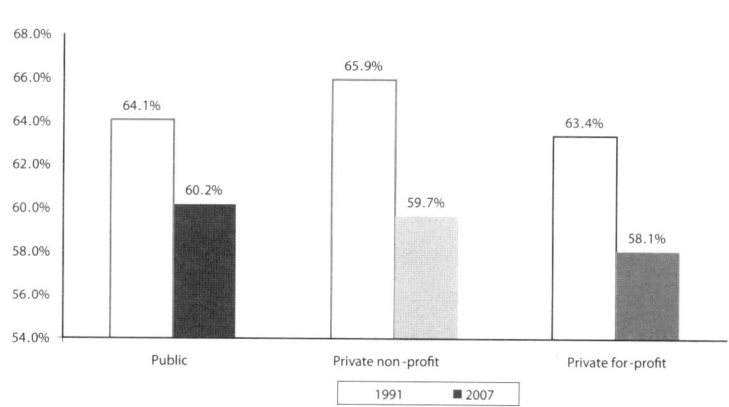

Sources: Statistisches Bundesamt, 1993; Statistisches Bundesamt, 2008b; authors' own calculations

According to the federal statistics office, the share of personnel (labour) costs in 2007 was 61.6% (2008b). For managers, labour costs are an obvious source of potential savings, and there are several possible ways to reduce them. The major hospitals (those with more than 500 beds) have reduced their share of labour costs since the early 1990s regardless of their ownership. However, the largest reduction has happened in private for-profit hospitals (see Figure 6).

Table 5: Collective bargaining coverage

	Public	Private non-profit	Private for-profit
Federal collective agreement for public services (TVÖD/TV L)	85.7%	8.1%	14.1%
Collective agreements on company level	3.1%	-	20.3%
Other collective agreements	10.7%	17.3%	41.6%*
Special regulations for church-run hospitals	-	73.6%	-
No collective agreement	0.5%	1.0%	24.0%

Includes the collective agreement with the CGB-member DHV.
Source: Blum, Offermanns et al., 2007

Table 5 shows the collective bargaining landscape in German hospitals. Private for-profit hospitals derive major cost advantages from signing collective agreements at the level of the hospital, if they sign any agreement at all (Augurzky, Beivers et al., 2009). Usually, immediately after the privatisation, private for-profit companies try to reach a new collective agreement (Gröschl-Bahr and Stumpfögger, 2008) and break away from the federal collective agreement for public services (TVöD) that is perceived as "too inflexible" (Neubauer and Beivers, 2006). Hence, 85.7% of the employees of public hospitals (excluding physicians) are getting paid according to the federal agreements, compared to just 14.1% of their colleagues in private for-profit ones. In the latter, 20.3% have a collective agreement at the hospital level and 24% do not have a collective agreement at all.

The largest group of employees in the private for-profit hospital companies have a collective agreement signed by the Bundesverband Deutscher Privatkliniken (BDPK – Federal association of German private hospitals) and the Deutschen Handels-und Industrieangestellten-Verband (DHV). The latter is a member of the Christian federation of trade unions (CGB) that opposes the German federation of trade unions (DGB) and signs agreements more closely aligned with the demands of the employers. In many other for-profit hospitals, there is a framework collective agreement that may cover certain terms and conditions of employment, but does not cover salaries. Thus the real proportion of employees in private for-profit hospitals that do not receive a wage that is secured by collective agreements is higher than the numbers in Table 6 suggest.

The erosion of collective bargaining is one trend that may be reversing itself. Over the past few years, public-sector trade union Ver.di has been quite successful in reaching collective agreements with the major hospital chains that contain wages, similar to the federal collective agreement for public services (Gröschl-Bahr and Stumpfögger, 2008). According to the Association of German Hospitals (DKG), about nine per cent of hospitals have signed so called "emergency collective agreements" that allow a temporary reduction of wages by ten per cent (Blum, Offermanns et al., 2007). The majority of those hospitals, however, are public and the purpose of these clauses is to keep them under the TVöD.

The reduction of costs is an important objective of outsourcing, and the reduction or freezing of wages is the usual result. Outsourcing usually leads to a situation where employees either have no collective agreements or significantly worse agreements than before. In particular the workers with assignments that are not directly linked to the patients often have to accept worse agreements than their colleagues (Jaehrling, 2007). According to internal union sources, cleaning personnel for example usually drop to the minimum wage for their sector, which is about 30% lower than the respective wage in the TVöD. Employees of the temporary work agencies established by some private and public hospitals are also paid significantly lower wages. This division of the workforce seems to harm the position of the core staff as well.

Table 6 shows how privatisation has affected the pay of various occupational groups. In 2007 the average cost per full-time-equivalent in private for-profit hospitals was four per cent lower than in public hospitals. Hence there is not just a lower share of the workers secured by collective agreement but a general wage drift. Wages of doctors in private for-profit hospitals are slightly higher, while those of employees in technical, functional and special services are much lower. The wages of nurses, the largest group of hospital workers, are nine per cent higher in public hospitals.

EUROPE'S HEALTH FOR SALE

Table 6: Personal costs in hospital per full-time-equivalent (2007)

	In euro			Personnel costs of the private for-profit hospitals in % of the public hospitals
	Public	Private non-profit	Private for-profit	
Physicians	89,926	91,213	91,217	101
Administrative services	48,195	47,827	48,203	100
Clinical personal	30,192	29,059	28,847	96
Med.-techn. Services	45,684	45,123	43,451	95
Supply services	35,585	35,107	33,493	94
Techn. Services	46,540	47,436	42,753	92
Functional services	47,868	47,074	43,494	91
Nursing services	47,746	46,163	43,628	91
Special services	54,481	51,998	45,951	84
Total	53,401	52,769	51,272	**96**

Sources: Statistisches Bundesamt, 2008a; Statistisches Bundesamt, 2008b; authors' own calculations

These changes have widened pay inequalities between occupational groups, with nurses and medical technical staff hit especially hard. As Figure 7 shows, the average wage of a nurse in a private hospital was just 85.1% that of all

Figure 7: Nurses' pay in relation to the average wages of all employees

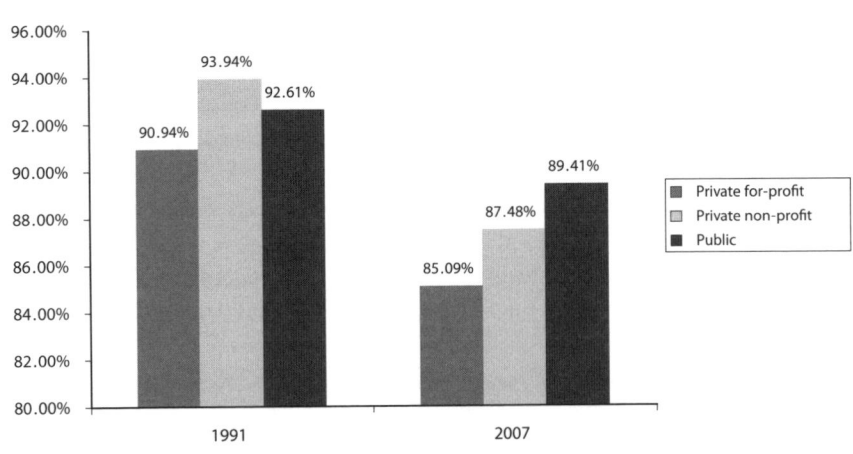

Source: Statistisches Bundesamt, 1993; Statistisches Bundesamt, 2008b; authors' own calculations

employees, down from 90% in 1991. This trend has been much slower in public hospitals, where the average wage of a nurse in relation to the overall average dropped from 92.6% to 89.4%. Generally, nurses in private for-profit hospitals earn just 91.4% of the wages earned by their colleagues in public hospitals (Statistisches Bundesamt, 2008b).

Effects on working conditions

Competition on the basis of labour costs does not only take place through downward pressures on wages. According to trade unionists and works council members, the intensification of work has also increased at private hospitals. This has negative effects on both employees and patients. One major indicator, the ratio of number of patients to the number of staff, has deteriorated sharply (Ver.di Vertrauensleute und Vorsitzende und Mitglieder von Konzernbetriebsräten und Konzern-Jugend-und Auszubildenden-Vertretungen privater Krankenhauskonzern, 2008).

Compared with the public hospitals, the staff-to-patient ratio is especially low in private for-profit hospitals. According to the federal statistics office, the number of occupied beds that one member of staff had to look after is considerably higher than in public hospitals. This applied across all professional groups (see Figure 8).

Since small hospitals cannot be compared with larger hospitals (they offer different services that require different personnel), here we compare only hospitals with more than 500 beds. In 2007, in a private for-profit hospital a

Figure 8: Occupied beds in days per full-time-equivalent in hospitals with more than 500 beds

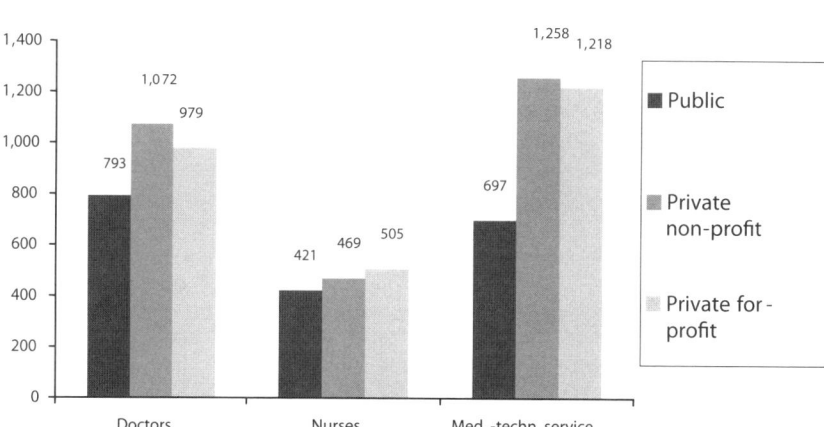

Sources: Statistisches Bundesamt, 2008a; authors' own calculations

physician had to care for almost 25% more occupied beds than his colleague in a public hospital. Each nurse in private for-profit hospitals had to care for more occupied beds as well and this discrepancy was even greater in medical–technical services (Statistisches Bundesamt, 2008a).

Effects on the quality of care

The hospital sector is facing a politically driven imperative to economise that is self-reinforcing and self-amplifying. Numerous international studies indicate that the quality of care is declining, with a decreasing number of personnel and a focus on economic success. In the USA, for example, there is a clear correlation between mortality rate and ownership. In for-profit hospitals it is higher than in non-profit hospitals (Devereaux et al., 2002). According to a recent study by the Harvard School of Public Health, patients surveyed assessed all quality criteria to be worse in private for-profit hospitals (Jha, Orav et al., 2008). These studies suggest a strong correlation between patient satisfaction and the number of nurses.

There are no German empirical studies on the effect of lower staff-to-patient ratios on the quality of care that compare private and public hospitals. However, there are surveys by the statutory insurance funds that indicate a worse quality of care for their customers in private hospitals (Braun and Müller, 2006). The major complaint was that patients were discharged home too early. Compared

Figure 9: Improvement or cure of diseases according to the patients in %

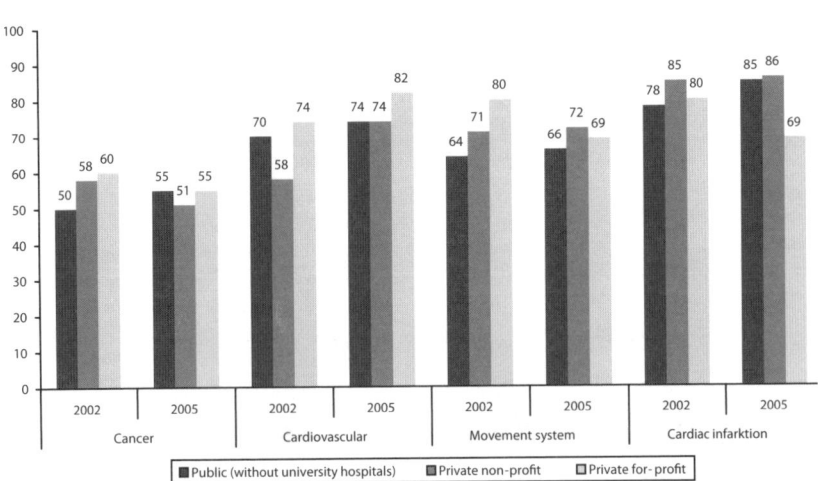

Source: Braun and Müller, 2006

to an earlier survey in 2002 this sentiment has increased in public hospitals as well, but at a lower level. Overall, the perception of the quality of treatment was worse in private for-profit hospitals than their public-sector counterparts. However, the private non-profit hospitals received the best results.

Regarding the results of treatment, patients in public hospitals have seen an improvement in their hospitals in all the main disease categories. All of these statements indicate obvious trends. Especially compared with the survey in 2002, the experiences in private for-profit hospitals show a similar tendency. However, in three out of four diagnoses, patients in private for-profit hospitals claimed lower rates of improvement and healing than in 2002. Unlike public and non-profit hospitals, private for-profit hospitals have seen a deterioration and it is probable that higher work intensity is one reason (see Figure 9).

The future of German hospitals

Against a background of financial and economic crisis, most observers expect further waves of privatisation over the next few years. The negative effect of the crisis for the hospital sector has been buffered by the federal government's economic stimulus packages. However, in 2010 the situation in most hospitals will probably become worse (Augurzky, Beivers et al., 2009). The fiscal problems of the state and local governments will make it less and less likely that they will finance deficits or increase investment in public hospitals. For the major private hospital chains, this represents a major opportunity for future acquisitions. Rhön-Kliniken AG, for example, has decided to raise €500m in capital to buy more hospitals (*Handelsblatt*, 5 July 2009).

However, there is broad public scepticism about the trend toward privatisation. In a 2008 survey, 63 per cent of the population thought that hospitals should be public and just six per cent thought all hospitals should be private (DBB, 2008). Already, there have been several cases of mass protests against hospital privatisation, some of which involved ballot initiatives for a referendum (Mittendorf, 2008). Some of these have helped to prevent the purchase; and usually when the referendum was unsuccessful it was for procedural reasons, not because a majority of the population voted in favour of the privatisation. Most of these initiatives have included a broad alliance of trade unions, physicians, social movement organisations, local politicians and local organisations (Böhlke, Greer and Schulten, 2009). There is little reason to believe that this protest will abate any time soon.

In the upcoming debate, the main question will be whether marketisation and the introduction of competition are appropriate means to organise health care. Despite the problems described above, the federal association of private hospitals (BDPK) does not hesitate to demand even more cost-cutting, since the hospital sector has become a lucrative business. They have continued to ask for more deregulation, including the abolition of hospital planning by the *Länder* (BDPK, 2007).

Because of price setting and other regulations, it is still the case that the hospital sector in Germany is not a free market (Bruckenberger, Klaue et al., 2006). It is obvious that a "hospital market" differs from classic markets in several ways that make a purely capitalistic organisation impossible. Health is existential and cannot be abandoned or boycotted. The "customer" cannot withdraw from a service that does not satisfy his or her needs or autonomously decide which service is necessary. There are thus asymmetries of power and information between patients and health-care professionals. As a collective good, health-care provision is a basic right for every person that in many countries may not be withheld from anyone; in Germany this right is grounded in article 2, section 2 of the Basic Law. For these reasons, health systems are regulated relatively strictly (Deppe, 2002).

High-quality hospital care costs money, which in Germany comes from taxes and insurance contributions. Due to the way the industry is structured, corporate hospital profits are not accumulated due to the workings of a free market but rather extracted from society using political processes of reforms. The German Association of Community Hospitals (IVKK) has argued along these lines and added that in health care profits are an extra cost with little or no benefit, and should therefore be abolished (IVKK, 2008).

Private hospital chains have two main advantages in the German healthcare industry as it is currently structured. First, they have significantly lower personnel costs and a more intense exploitation of employees. Private for-profit hospitals pay below the collective agreement and have lower staff-to-patient ratios. It is the task of trade unions to fight for equal conditions across the sector. Second, because private for-profit hospitals receive more investment, they enjoy advantages in terms of productivity. It is the responsibility of the public authorities to increase the level of investments in the public sector to counterbalance this structural disadvantage.

The advantages enjoyed by private for-profit hospitals reflect failures of public policy that have produced a shift of power to private owners. For many social and economic reasons (Weizsäcker, Orav et al., 2005), trade unions, civil society and political parties on the left should, and will, continue to resist the trend toward privatisation.

References

Augurzky, B., A. Beivers, et al. (2009) Bedeutung der Krankenhäuser in privater Trägerschaft. Essen, RWI, Institut für Gesundheitsökonomik, http://www.rwi-essen.de/pls/portal30/docs/FOLDER/PUBLIKATIONEN/RWIMAT/RWI_MAT052/M_52_PRIVATEKH.PDF

Augurzky, B., R. Budde, et al. (2009) Krankenhaus Rating Report 2009 - Im Auge des Orkans. Essen, RWI

Bähr, C., P. Fuchs, et al. (2006) Kliniken-Privatisierungswelle. Frankfurt am Main, DZ Bank AG. 29/03/2006

BDPK (2007) Mehr unternehmerische Freiheit - Krankenhäuser schrittweise entfesseln. Eckpunkte zur Gestaltung des ordnungspolitischen Rahmens für Krankenhäuser nach dem Ende der Konvergenzphase. Bundesverband Deutscher Privatkliniken, http://www.bdpk.de/media/file/50.2007-02-08_BDPK-Presseerklaerung_Ordnungspolitischer_Rahmen.pdf

Blum, K., M. Offermanns, et al. (2007) Krankenhaus Barometer. Deutsches Krankenhausinstitut (DKI), http://dki.comnetinfo.de/PDF/Bericht%20KH%20Barometer%202007.pdf, 29/04/2009

Böhlke, N., I. Greer, T. Schulten (2009) 'Deutsche Gründlichkeit: Market making and industrial relations in German hospitals', CERIC Working Paper, Leeds: Centre for Employment Relations Innovation and Change

Braun, B. and R. Müller (2006) Versorgungsqualität im Krankenhaus aus der Perspektive der Patienten. Ergebnisse einer wiederholten Patientenbefragung und einer Längsschnittanalyse von GEK-Routinedaten. Schwäbisch Gmünd, Gmünder Ersatzkasse - GEK, http://media.gek.de/downloads/magazine/GEK-Studie-Versorgungsqualitaet-Krankenhaus.pdf, Juni 2006

Bruckenberger, E., S. Klaue, et al. (2006) Krankenhausmärkte zwischen Regulierung und Wettbewerb. Berlin; Heidelberg, Springer-Verlag

Bundesärztekammer (2007) Zunehmende Privatisierung von Krankenhäusern in Deutschland. Folgen für die ärztlich Tätigkeit. Bundesärztekammer, http://bundesaerztekammer.de/downloads/Ergebnisbericht_final.pdf, 31/08/2009

DBB (2008) Bürgerbefragung öffentlicher Dienst. Berlin, Deutscher Beamtenbund

Deppe, H.-U. (2002) Kommerzialisierung oder Solidarität? Zur Grundlegenden Orientierung der Gesundheitspolitik. In: H.-U. Deppe und W. Burkhardt. Solidarische Gesundheitspolitik. Alternativen zu Privatisierung und Zwei-Klassen-Medizin. Hamburg, VSA-Verlag: 10–23

Devereaux, P.J., D. Heels-Ansdell, et al. (2004) 'Payments for Care at private for-profit and private not-for-profit hospitals: a systematic review and meta-analysis' in *Canadian Medical Association Journal*, 170(12): 1,817–24

Devereaux, P.J., et al. (2002) 'A systematic review and meta-analysis of studies comparing mortality rates of private for-profit and private not-for-profit hospitals' in *Canadian Medical Association Journal*, 166(11): 1,399–1,406

DKG (2008) Zahlen, Daten, Fakten 2007/08. Düsseldorf, Deutsche Krankenhausgesellschaft

Gröschl-Bahr, G. and N. Stumpfögger (2008) Krankenhäuser. In: T. Brandt, T. Schulten, G. Sterkel und J. Wiedemuth. Europa im Ausverkauf - Liberalisierung und Privatisierung öffentlicher Dienstleistungen und ihre Folgen für die Tarifpolitik. Hamburg, VSA-Verlag: 165–180

IVKK (2008) Gewinne in Kliniken nachhaltig reinvestieren - für gesetzliche Thesaurierungspflicht. Interessenverband kommunaler Krankenhäuser, press release, 10/10/2008

Jaehrling, K. (2007) Wo das Sparen am leichtesten fällt - Reinigungs- und Pflegehilfskräfte im Krankenhaus. In: G. Bosch und C. Weinkopf. Arbeiten für wenig Geld. Niedriglohnbeschäftigung in Deutschland. Frankfurt am Main, New York, Campus Verlag: 175–210

Jha, A.K., E.J. Orav, et al. (2008) 'Patients' Reception of Hospital Care in the United States' in *New England Journal of Medicine*, 359(18): 1,921–31

Mittendorf, V. (2008) Bürgerbegehren und Volksentscheide gegen Privatisierungen und die Rolle der Gewerkschaften. In: T. Brandt, T. Schulten, G. Sterkel and J. Wiedemuth. Europa im Ausverkauf. Hamburg, VSA-Verlag: 310–329

Neubauer, G. and A. Beivers (2006) "Privatisierung der Krankenhäuser: modischer Trend oder ökonomische Notwendigkeit?" in: Orientierungen zur Wirtschafts- und Gesellschaftspolitik 109.2006(3): 48–52

Schmidt, C. (2003) "Ein Markt im Umbruch. Kliniken im Fokus privater Ketten und Investoren" in: krankenhaus Umschau 11/2003: 1,090–1,095

Simon, M. (2008a) Das Gesundheitssystem in Deutschland. Eine Einführung in Struktur und Funtionsweise. 2., vollständig überarbeitete Auflage, Bern, Verlag Hans Huber

Simon, M. (2008b) Sechzehn Jahre Deckelung des Krankenhausbudgets: Eine kritische Bestandsaufnahme. Hannover, Studie für die vereinte Dienstleistungsgewerkschaft ver.di. https://gesundheitspolitik.verdi.de/gesundheit_von_a-z/krankenhaeuser/budgetdeckelung/data/simon_kritik_der_budgetdeckelung.pdf, 25/05/2009

Statistisches Bundesamt (1993) Kostennachweis der Krankenhäuser 1991. Wiesbaden, Statistisches Bundesamt, December 1993

Statistisches Bundesamt (2008a) Grunddaten der Krankenhäuser 2007. Wiesbaden, Statistisches Bundesamt, 10/12/2008

Statistisches Bundesamt (2008b) Kostennachweis der Krankenhäuser 2007. Wiesbaden, Statistisches Bundesamt, 15/12/2008

Stumpfögger, N. (2007) Krankenhausfusionen und Wettbewerbsrecht. Unternehmenskonzentration im deutschen Krankenhausmarkt 2003 bis 2007, http://gesundheit-soziales.verdi.de/branchen-politik/krankenhausmarkt/data/krankenhausmarkt-2007.pdf, 29/04/2009

Ver.di Vertrauensleute und Vorsitzende und Mitglieder von Konzernbetriebsräten und Konzern-Jugend- und Auszubildenden-Vertretungen privater Krankenhauskonzern (2008) Krankenhausfinanzierung: Woher die Gewinne privater Krankenhauskonzerne kommen, Berlin, Offener Brief, An Bundesgesundheitsministerin Ulla Schmidt, An die Gesundheitsministerinnen und -minister der Länder und An die Abgeordneten des Deutschen Bundestages, 02/10/2008

Weizsäcker, E.U. v., E.J. Orav, et al. (2005) *Limits to privatisation*, London: Earthscan

CHAPTER 2
Privatising the Greek health-care system
A story of corporate profits and rising health inequalities

E. Kondilis[a,b]
E. Smyrnakis[b]
S. Giannakopoulos[b]
T. Zdoukos[b]
A. Benos[a,b]
[a] *Greek Observatory on the Privatization of Health Care*
[b] *Lab of Hygiene and Social Medicine, Aristotle University of Thessaloniki*

Defining the Greek health-care system

The Greek health-care system can hardly be classified using the taxonomic criteria set by OECD in 2004[1]. In terms of the system of funding, social security (occupational sickness funds following the principles of the Bismarckian model) coexists with a tax-funded National Health System along the lines of the Beveridge model and a small but firm Private Health Insurance market, funded through individual and family contributions. Health-care provision in Greece appears equally fragmented. The Greek National Health System, which was founded in 1983, coexists with social security's polyclinics and hospitals and a constantly expanding private for-profit health-care market. This "multi-tier", "tripartite" and deeply fragmented structure defines the health system in Greece as a public–private mix[2,3,4], unclassified according to international criteria.

Contemporary features and failures of the Greek health-care system

The main contemporary features and failures of health care in Greece are, among others, the lack of a comprehensive and universal public primary health-care system, significant deficiencies in public health, the lack of quality control over services[5], especially those provided by the private sector[6], and the lack of control over the diffusion and appropriateness of biomedical technology[7].

Additionally, health financing in Greece remains regressive, due mainly to the high proportion of out-of-pocket payments and indirect taxes, as well as to the uneven social-security contributions. The Greek health-care system is also characterised by rising inequalities in access to health care[8,9] and a high privatisation rate that is reflected both in the proportionally high level of private health expenditure – one of the highest among EU and OECD countries[10] – as well as in the ongoing process of partial marketisation of public hospitals and medical centres.

A particularity of the Greek health services, if not of Greek society in general, is the widespread phenomenon, often discussed by the media, of corruption – both in public hospitals[11], in the form of under-the-table payments and pharmaceuticals kick-backs, and in private clinics (less discussed in that case by the media), in the form of multiple cases of fraud and overcharging of patients and public sickness funds. In Greece, this "hidden economy" in health care amounts to 7–25% of total health expenditure, depending on the study[12,13,14], a fact that echoes a trend in the Greek economy in general, where the "black economy" represents 25–35% of Gross Domestic Product.

The least-well-known characteristic of the Greek health-care system, especially among international observatory organisations, is its failure to meet Greek citizens' expectations. The most recent Eurobarometer survey showed that 78% of the population thought that the health system in Greece is in need of major or radical changes and only a mere 3% seemed satisfied by its function[10]. Similar survey outcomes over the years have placed Greeks as the most dissatisfied among EU citizens with their health system[10,15]. Many health-policy analysts, and most conservative and social-democrat politicians in Greece, claim that the Eurobarometer health survey results reveal Greek citizens' dissatisfaction with public health services and argue that this is undeniable evidence that suggests health-care reform towards privatisation. Empirical evidence nevertheless opposes this statement. Satisfaction surveys among users of all public health-care facilities in Greece showed surprisingly high satisfaction rates for medical and nursing services offered by public hospitals and median satisfaction rates for accommodation in public hospitals[16,17,18]. This contradiction between Eurobarometer's results and users' satisfaction surveys in Greece indicates that Greeks' dissatisfaction with their health system is a symptom of poor accessibility to health services, resulting from obstacles imposed during the process of privatisation, rather than a measure of satisfaction with public health services.

Reforming health care in Greece: from underdevelopment to deregulation and marketisation

Health policy in Greece, since the dawn of the Greek state in 1828, has always been a process of irrational, contradictory, non-evidence-based political choices. Health services, the population's health status and the socio-economic determinants of health were rarely placed high in the political agenda, and even when plans for health reform aimed at providing free universal coverage were put forward, vested groups and corporate interests seemed to block any attempt for change. Tragakes and Polyzos, two former WHO and government officers, wrote in 1998 that:

> health reform in Greece has always been an ad hoc and top down process by groups in Ministry of Health or in government planning agencies working in relative isolation, with minimal input from broader segments of the population and particularly from those actors who are the most directly and intimately affected by processes of change.[19]

Nevertheless, political unwillingness, inefficiency and local vested interests cannot alone explain the profound structural problems of the Greek health-care system. Health-care services in Greece seem to follow the "fate" of the Greek state and economic evolution[20]. Greece has always had a dependent – and still has a semi-dependent – role within the European and international economic environment. The relatively low economic growth of Greece combined with low wage rates, mainly due to massive economic emigration during the 1950s and '60s, prohibited the foundation of a welfare state in Greece. During the late '70s and '80s, when economic growth and political changes in Greece eventually allowed the implementation of a welfare state, the international oil crisis and rising neoliberal policies (Thatcherism) questioned its effectiveness, imposing economic constraints on its expansion. The history of the Greek National Health System follows the same pattern: relatively delayed foundation in 1983, half-way implementation during the '80s and marketisation during the '90s and the first decade of the twenty-first century.

From 1920 to 1980

By the beginning of the twentieth century, welfare state and social-security schemes were already established in northern and central Europe and widely expanded during the post-war reconstruction period. Greece failed to follow this European trend[21]. The catastrophic consequences of the Second World War, the civil war (1946–9) and the dictatorship (1967–74), in addition to the dependent economic development model imposed on Greece by the USA, seem to have been the key factors resulting in such a failure.

During this period the main advances that determined the future of health care in Greece were the fragmented development of social health security and the unregulated expansion of private health services.

More specifically, the first occupational sickness funds in Greece (for civil servants and sailors) were founded in the middle of the nineteenth century. The newly born trades unions, the rising labour movement, the wide spread of socialist ideas among workers, in addition to the international impact of social measures taken in the Soviet Union, forced Western governments (among them the Greek government) to endorse social protection measures in order to strengthen social coherence in advance of the coming world war[22].

In 1932, El. Venizelos' liberal government passed IKA's foundation Act (Law 5733/1932), which is recognised nowadays as the cornerstone of social security in Greece[23]. The Act was modified (Law 6398/1934) and implemented two years later in 1934 by the conservative Tsaldaris government. IKA offered coverage to urban white- and blue-collar workers. Although its foundation act foresaw the consolidation of occupational funds, this provision of the law was never implemented. This fact resulted in the fragmentation of social security in Greece and the mushroom development of even more occupational funds during the 1950s and '60s which offered a more comprehensive coverage to their beneficiaries ("privileged insurance funds"). Eventually, in 1961 the conservative Karamanlis government passed OGA's foundation Act (Law 4169/1961), offering for the first time a rudimentary coverage to the rural population, known at the time as being the silent uninsured majority of the Greek citizens[23].

During the same period, public health services remained underfinanced, unorganised and unable to offer coherent and universal health coverage. Private non-profit hospitals and a few low-quality public hospitals and rural health posts offered mainly charity care to the population. On the other hand, during the post-war period and especially during the dictatorship, private health providers expanded rapidly, without any regulatory framework, following the demand for services as expressed mainly by the upper and middle class of the Greek population[24].

From 1981 to the present

In 1981 the social democrats came to power, introducing two years later the Greek National Health System (called ESY) as a key part of a wider program of "delayed progressive modernisation"[21], attempting in other words the establishment of "social democrat welfare capitalism"[21]. This crucial attempt towards universal health coverage in Greece was facilitated by the consensus at the time among health-policy scientists on the need for an NHS[19]. It was supported by young medical doctors and health professionals who were looking to the foundation of a NHS as a means of vocational rehabilitation.[4] Nevertheless, the paradox of introducing a Greek NHS approximately 40 years later than its northern-European ancestors stumbled in the political and economical environment of the time, which was hostile towards such interventions. Cost-containment policies, managed competition and a quasi-market within health care had already begun questioning the principles of public health services in northern Europe[25], principles which the Greek ESY was now trying to imitate.

More specifically, for the first time in the history of the Greek health-care system, the ESY foundation Act (Law 1397/83) addressed health as a social right and its provision, to the entire population without any racial or socioeconomic discrimination, as a state responsibility. During the period 1983 to 1991, public hospital beds increased in number by a median 2.1% per year[26] and 200 medical centres were established in rural areas. Additionally, the ban – enforced by the law – on the establishment, merger or relocation of private clinics caused during the same period a decrease in private hospital beds by a median 4.5% rate per year[26].

Although ESY's foundation and implementation during the 1980s is considered even nowadays as a major reform in Greek health-care history[19], it suffered from severe failures that still haunt health-care services' provision and financing in Greece. For example, the unification of social-security health plans, despite the relevant provision of the ESY foundation Act, was never put forward, due to the opposition expressed by social groups that received enhanced health-care benefits from privileged funds[27], prolonging in such a way the existing inequalities among social security's beneficiaries.

Additionally, urban medical centres, 220 according to the ESY implementation plan, were never established, causing a constant flow of out-of-pocket payments for medical, dental and diagnostic services to the private health sector. This fact offers an explanation of why, contrary to expectations, private health expenditure after 1985 actually increased, with growth rates higher than those of the public sector[28]. Finally, restrictive policies during the 1980s failed to restrain private for-profit providers, causing only their "creative destruction"[29], meaning that private enterprises, taking advantage of legislative oversights, started investing in biomedical technology and diagnostic laboratories, introducing a new era of rapid expansion (Figure 1) and highly increased revenue rates[6,26].

EUROPE'S HEALTH FOR SALE

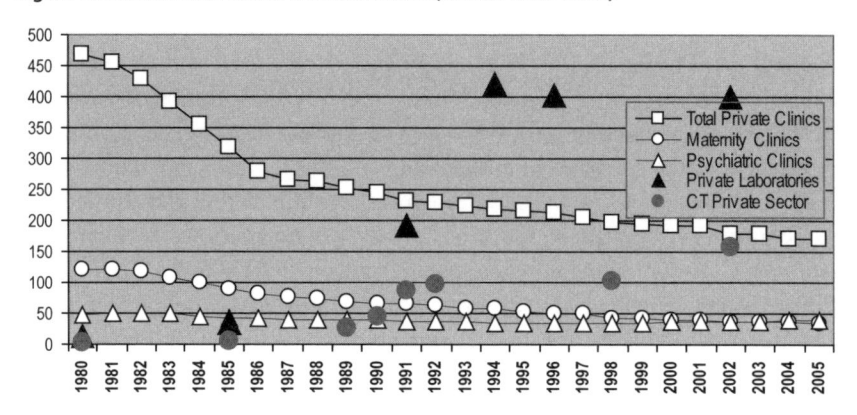

Figure 1: Private health sector's infrastructure (Greece 1980–2005)

Source: Kondilis, 2009[26]

The social democrats left office in 1989 and the conservative government, which ruled until 1993, pursued monetarist policies of retrenchment in welfare, required by the 1991 Maastricht Treaty[21]. Legislative restrictions on private hospitals were abolished[26], per diem fees for private clinics, set by the state, increased by a median annual rate of 45.7–70% per year[26], user co-payments for pharmaceuticals and user charges for outpatient visits in public hospitals were introduced[30] and tax reductions for private insurance premiums were enacted[19]. Additionally, the conservatives tried to modify the core principles of the Greek NHS. Law 2071 in 1992, which was the conservatives' reply to the 1983 ESY foundation Act, set as the state's main objective the improvement of patients' freedom of choice[31], rather than the securing of citizens' health. The new law also enabled doctors to be employed in the NHS full time or part time and abolished life tenure for the newly employed medical doctors.

Since the mid 1990s, preparations for moving to European Monetary Union (EMU) had already begun and the monetarist grip on the Greek economy intensified up to the launch of the euro in January 2002[21]. Gradually, ideological differences between social democrats and conservatives became blurred[4,19] as both of them embraced the EMU "national goal". Consequently, the conflict about public–private boundaries in health care, manifested in Greece during the 1980s and early 1990s, faded out[26]. Both the political parties that had ruled Greece since 1974 were now seeking ways of regulating a mixed (public–private) health-care market, setting the constraining of public health expenditure as their primary policy goal. Within this context, the transition to a new government in 1993 and the assumption of power once again by the social democrats brought no change of course in health policy reform. User charges and co-payments, abolition of ESY medical doctors' life tenure, and liberalisation of private health services, were policies that remained intact, despite the fact that prior to the elections the social democrat party had promised to abolish most of the legislation passed by the conservatives[6].

Nevertheless, the reference point of marketisation in public health services seems to be the "Report on Greek health services", a document published in June 1994, prepared by an international experts' committee under the chairmanship of Professor Brian Abel-Smith, assigned by the Greek Ministry of Health[5]. The report was the first effort to introduce quasi-market principles in the Greek health-care system[29]. Despite wide criticism[29,32,33], the report became the textbook for marketisation and deregulation of public health services in Greece that was used by governments throughout the 1990s and even during the first decade of the twenty-first century.[26] Policies such as outsourcing public-hospital support services (such as cleaning, security, laundry and catering), abolition of health personnel's life tenure, and private evening practice within public hospitals, are all measures implemented during the last 15 years which can trace their origin to the international experts' report.

The most recent major breakthroughs towards marketisation of health care in Greece are the adoption of public–private partnerships (PPPs) and the privatisation of primary health-care (PHC) services. From 2005 onwards, the conservative government, following guidelines set by the European Union, has enforced a new legislative framework (Law 3389/2005) under which PPPs have become the main means of capital investment for new hospital infrastructure[34]. The Greek government adopted the British model of PPPs[34], known as private finance initiatives (PFIs), according to which private consortia design, build, finance and operate new "public" hospitals[35]. Already, four new PPP/PFI hospitals in the Thessaloniki, Preveza and Katerini areas are in the design stage[34]. Additionally, the government recently presented a new Bill for the unification of the fragmented primary health-care services in Greece. Under this new legislative framework, the PHC principles of the WHO's Alma Ata Declaration have been abandoned: private enterprises now play a key role in the provision of PHC services (mainly diagnostic and curative), general practitioners are compensated through capitation (following the principles of Britain's 'fundholding GPs' in the mid 1990s) and limits are set for users' consumption of health care.

Provision of health-care services in Greece: the rise of an unregulated private for-profit market

Health-care provision in Greece is organised as a tripartite, public–private mix in primary as well as in secondary and tertiary health care. This means that the National Health System co-exists with an infrastructure of public sickness funds and private health providers.

ESY offers its services to the population through 200 medical centres and approximately 1,500 medical posts situated in rural areas and 3 medical centres in urban areas[36]. Additionally, 140 public hospitals, with a median bed capacity of 270 beds per hospital and a total occupancy rate of 85.3%, offer their services to more than 1.6 million patients per year, approximately 77.6% of total (public and private) patients discharged[26].

In parallel, many sickness funds in Greece run their own facilities, offering mainly ambulatory care to their beneficiaries. For example, IKA owns 42 polyclinics and 5 small hospitals where specialist services are provided by salaried, part-time medical doctors[36].

On the other hand, private for-profit companies seem to play an ongoing role in the provision of health-care services in Greece. For example, in primary care 25,000 physicians and 12,000 dentists run their offices[36], absorbing, along with the at-least-400 operating private laboratories[6], 65% of total private health expenditure in Greece – which means more than 4 billion euros per year[26].

Despite the restrictive policies in place through the 1980s, private clinics in Greece still remain a dynamic profit-making machine for their investors. In 2005, 170 private clinics, with a median bed capacity of 85 beds per clinic and a total occupancy rate of 79.7%, offered their services to 4,022,000 patients[26]. According to market estimates, during the period 1993–2006, the median rate of increase of revenues in the private health sector reached as much as 13% per year[37]. In 2006, total private-health-sector revenues (excluding medical doctors payments) amounted to up to 1.54 billion euros[37], with a total net profit before taxes of 169 million euros (Figure 2)[26]. In the private health sector in Greece, a

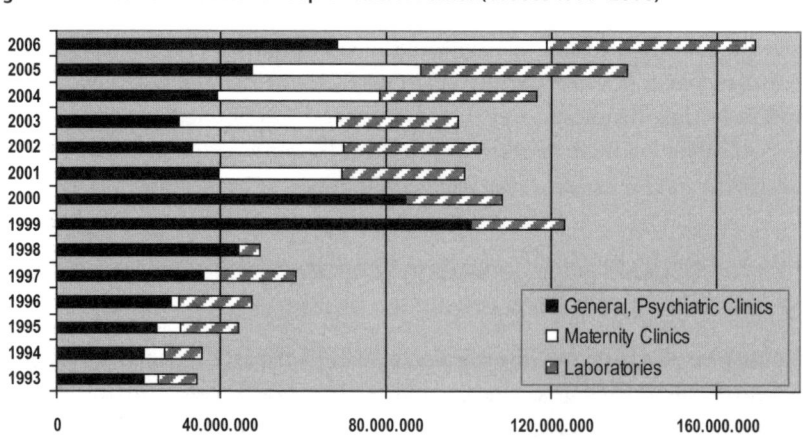

Figure 2: Private health sector's net profit before taxes (Greece 1993–2006)

Source: Kondilis, 2009[26]

process of mergers and acquisitions, originally initiated in 1996 and concluded five years later in 2001, led to an oligopoly market with high concentration rates. Recently, three multinational corporations acquired shares in the three largest Greek health-care enterprises, using Greece as their operational centre for aggressive merger policies throughout south-east Europe and especially Cyprus, Turkey and the Balkans.

Financing of health-care services in Greece: the rising health-care inequalities

The financing of health-care services in Greece is characterised by the paradoxical coexistence of all four known sources of financing: public health insurance, state budgets, private health insurance and out-of-pocket payments. Under this fragmented financing structure, the Greek population's contributions to total health spending consist simultaneously of: income-based contributions to social security funds; risk-rated contributions to private health-insurance schemes; direct and indirect tax contributions; out-of-pocket payments for services not covered by social or private insurance programs; and formal co-payments and under-the-table payments in public hospitals and private laboratories and clinics. In other words, the Greek population contributes to the country's health spending in at least three – and up to seven – different ways.

Taxation – state budget

The state budget became a main source of financing in Greece only in the late 1970s, when the central administration adopted fixed per diem payments for reimbursement of public hospitals. The state then became responsible for subsiding public hospital deficits, which occurred due to the divergence between actual per diem costs and fixed per diem payments, by which sickness funds were now compensating public providers for the services used by their beneficiaries. Nowadays, state budgets are also used for NHS payroll costs, public health interventions, and the public procurement program for new hospital infrastructure and medical equipment.

Actual data concerning the relative contribution of the state budget to total health expenditure (THE) do not exist in Greece, due to methodological problems related to the calculation of health spending in the country. Nevertheless, according to WHO estimates in 2005, the state budget's share of THE amounted to 21%, equal to 2.1% of the country's Gross Domestic Product[38]. Taxation in Greece has always been over-dependent on indirect taxes. According to the National Bank of Greece, indirect taxes in 2005 amounted to up to 56.4% of total state tax income[39]. This over-reliance of the state's health budget on indirect taxes makes it a regressive form of financing, as the less-privileged fragments of the population remain the most vulnerable to such forms of taxation.

Social health security – public sickness funds

Social security in Greece consists of 36 occupational and social-security sickness funds, financed through proportional employers'/employees' contributions and state subsidies, offering mandatory coverage to 95% of the population. Social security in Greece is deeply fragmented due to the historical factors already discussed. This institutional fragmentation would not by itself give much cause for concern, if it were only a formalistic survival of the past[29]. On the contrary, in Greece such fragmentation extends very deep into divergent contribution and entitlement micro-regimes.[29] Depending on the membership of the sickness fund, different population groups face different contribution schedules and are entitled to different benefit packages. For example in 2007, according to the Greek General Secretary for Social Security, employee contributions ranged between 0% and 6% of salary and employers' contributions ranged between 2% and 12.5% of the employee's salary.[40] Strong inequalities also exist in coverage for ambulatory and dental care, in the access beneficiaries have to private clinics and laboratories, and in the levels of sickness funds' maternal benefits. As a result, the per capita health spending by sickness funds in 2002 ranged from €150 per year in the case of TEVE and TAE (merchants and self-employed sickness funds) up to €700 per year in the case of the so-called "privileged funds", such as those of civil servants and bank employees (Figure 3)[26].

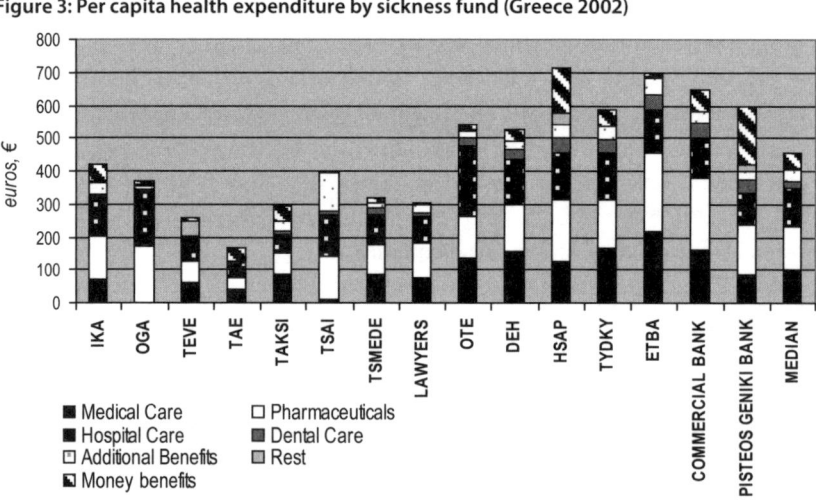

Figure 3: Per capita health expenditure by sickness fund (Greece 2002)

Source: General Secretary of Social Security; social budgets, adopted from Kondilis, 2009[26]

Private health insurance

Actual data about the number of private health insurance beneficiaries are not available in Greece[26,41]. Several studies nevertheless estimate that private health insurance (PHI) programs offer duplicate or supplementary coverage to 8–15.6% of the Greek population[10,42,43]. PHI in Greece offers coverage mainly to the most wealthy Greek citizens, voluntarily, on a family basis, through risk-rated contributions, providing them with better access to private clinics and laboratories as a way of by-passing queuing problems in public hospitals. Indeed in 2005, according to the Household Budget Survey, the highest income classes in Greece spent a percentage of their total household expenditure on PHI that was seven-times higher than that of the lowest income classes (0.43% compared with 0.06% of total household expenditure)[26,44].

Despite the preference for it among the wealthiest, the private health insurance market in Greece remains one of the most underdeveloped among the EU countries. It is estimated that less than 2% of the country's THE comes from this source of financing[3,19,38,42]. Many researchers have tried to explain this peculiarity as an outcome of Greeks' reluctance to pay a third party, meaning that Greek patients are accustomed to paying their doctor or hospital directly, as an assurance for quality of care[3]. A second and most important reason is the fact that private health insurance in Greece has barely adopted the principle of managed care, such as integration with providers or selective contracting[26]. On the contrary, according to the OECD's recent taxonomy, PHI schemes in Greece fit the category of indemnity insurance[43]. This means that very few contractual arrangements exist between private insurers and providers, and indemnity health insurance plans pay their share of the costs after receiving the bill. This fact, in addition to the inflated prices of private hospitals in Greece, has resulted in low rates of profit (and, in some cases, even bankruptcies) for insurance enterprises, making them reluctant to invest in health insurance programs[26,45].

Private health expenditure – out-of-pocket payments

Private health expenditure (PHE) in Greece in 2006, according to revised data from the Ministry of Economics, amounted to up to €7.6 billion, equal to 3.5% of the country's GDP, and representing 38.4% of the country's THE[10]. This is recognised as one of the highest among European Union and OECD countries[10]. PHE in Greece consists of PHI premiums, official private payments for services not covered by sickness funds (such as private physicians' fees, payments for nursing care at home or therapeutic devices), user co-payments for services covered by social security programs (such as patients' payments equal to 10–25% of the cost of pharmaceuticals, payments for evening out-patient consultations in public hospitals) and unofficial or under-the-table payments, especially in hospital sector[30,46].

Private health expenditure shows a continuously rising trend, absorbing a gradually larger share of Greek household budgets. Indeed, PHE rose from 4.8% of total households' expenditure in 1982 to 7.15% in 2005 (Table 1)[26]. This means that in 2005 Greek households spent an average of €1,538 per year on health[44], in addition to their social security and tax contributions.

Table 1: Private health expenditure by household income class, % household's expenditure (Greece 1981/82–2004/5)

Households by income class	1981/2	1987/8	1993/4	1998/9	2004/5
1st (low)	5.1%	4.4%	7.60%	9.36%	12.45%
2nd	5.1%	4.3%	6.14%	6.80%	9.64%
3d	4.1%	4.2%	4.80%	5.61%	7.80%
4th	3.9%	4.2%	4.30%	5.55%	7.66%
5th	4.5%	5.0%	4.87%	5.64%	7.19%
6th	4.1%	5.1%	5.15%	5.89%	6.46%
7th	5.2%	6.2%	5.50%	6.85%	6.30%
8th (high)	6.2%	5.9%	6.07%	8.66%	6.84%
Total households	4.83%	5.13%	5.66%	6.82%	7.15%

Source: Greek National Statistical Service; Household budgets' surveys, adopted from Kondilis, 2009[26]

The people most vulnerable to private expenditure on health seem to be the low income classes of the Greek population, which means that they devote to health a significantly larger share of their total household budget compared to the highest income classes (twice as much in 2005) (Table 1)[26,44]. It is also worth noticing that marketisation policies which followed the ESY foundation and implementation period (1981–9) have widened the divergence between low and high income classes in Greece (Table1), in other words increasing health-care financing inequalities in the country.

Conclusion

Our analysis indicates that the health-care system in Greece shows many symptoms of crisis, such as:

(a) Poor satisfaction rates with the overall performance of health-care services in the country, due mainly to access and accommodation problems affecting public services

(b) Rising health-care inequalities, due to high rates of indirect taxes, out-of-pocket payments and uneven social security contributions and benefits; and

(c) A flourishing private for-profit health-care market with high profit rates.

Surprisingly, many of these symptoms fit the "mixed health systems syndrome" recently identified in the case of developing countries. This denotes a situation where health systems involving a public–private mix show poor performance, as indicated by their poor responsiveness, failure to achieve fairness in financing, and inability to achieve equity in outcomes[47].

The Greek experience shows that, at least in the case of a developed country with a semi-dependent role within the international economic environment, the symptoms of severe malfunction which compose the "mixed health system syndrome" can and will occur when an underdeveloped public health sector is pushed towards privatisation and marketisation, while at the same time private for-profit providers are left unregulated.

Notes

1 OECD, *Proposal for a taxonomy of health insurance*, Paris: Organization for Economic Co-operation and Development, 2004
2 Mossialos, E., Dixon, A., Figueras, J. and Kutzin, J., *Funding health care: options for Europe. Policy Brief*, UK: European Observatory on health care systems, 2002
3 Mossialos, E., Allin, S. and Davaki, K., 'Analysing the Greek health system: a tale of fragmentation and inertia', *Health Econ*, 2005, 14: S151–S168
4 Kyriopoulos, J.E. and Tsalikis, G., 'Public and private imperatives of Greek health policies', *Health Policy*, 1993, 26: 105–17
5 Abel-Smith, B., Calltorp, J., Dixon, A. et al., *Report on the Greek health services*, Athens: Pharmetrica, 1994
6 Kondilis, E., Giannakopoulos, E., Zdoukos, T., Gavana, M. and Benos, A., 'Privatisation of health care in Greece: the development of private for-profit health care providers (1980–2002)', in Benos, A., Deppe, H.U. and Lister, J., eds, *Health Policy in Europe: contemporary dilemmas and challenges*, Britain: International Association of Health Policy Europe, 2007: 145–57
7 Liaropoulos, L. and Kaitelidou, D., 'Health technology assessment in Greece', *Int J Technol Assess Health Care*, 2000, 16: 429–48
8 Van Doorslaer, E., Koolman, X. and Puffer, F., *Equity in the use of physician visits in OECD countries: has equal treatment for equal need been achieved?* Rotterdam: Equity II Project Working Paper No. 3, 2001
9 Pappa, E. and Niakas, D., 'Assessment of health care needs and utilization in a mixed public–private system: the case of the Athens area', *BMC Health Serv Res*, 2006, 6: 146
10 OECD, *Heath Data 2008: Statistics and indicators for 30 countries, CD Rom*, 1st ed. Paris: Organization for Economic Co-operation and Development, 2008
11 Liaropoulos, L., Siskou, O., Kaitelidou, D., Theodorou, M. and Katostaras, T., 'Informal payments in public hospitals in Greece', *Health Policy*, 2008, 87: 72–81
12 Niakas, D., Skoutelis, G. and Kyriopoylos, J., 'Investigation of hidden economy in health care: a preliminary quantitative approach', *Health Review*, 1990, 1: 42–5 [in Greek]

13. Kyriopoulos, J. and Karalis, G., 'Recent trends of hidden economy in health care in Greece', *Health Review*, 1997, November–December: 46–7 [in Greek]
14. Kyriopoulos, J., 'Economy and hidden economy in health care system', *Society Economy and Health*, 1992, 1: 3–10 [in Greek]
15. European Commission, *Health statistics. Key data on health 2002*, France: European Communities, 2003
16. Niakas, D. and Gnardellis, C., 'In patient satisfaction in a regional general hospital of Athens', *Iatriki*, 2000, 77: 464–70 [in Greek]
17. Niakas, D., Gnardellis, C. and Theodorou, M., 'Is there a problem with quality in the Greek hospital sector? Preliminary results from a patient satisfaction survey', *Health Serv Manage Res*, 2004, 17: 62–9
18. Polyzos, N., Bartsokas, D., Pierrakos, G. et al., 'Comparative surveys for patient satisfaction between hospitals in Athens', *Archives of Hellenic Medicine*, 2005, 22: 286–97 [in Greek]
19. Tragakes, E. and Polyzos, N., 'The evolution of health care reforms in Greece: charting a course of change', *Int J Health Plann Manage*, 1998, 13: 107–30
20. Antonopoulou, L., 'Regulation and reforms of the Greek National Health System: comparisons with the European experience', *Social Coherence and Development*, 2008, 3: 109–20 [in Greek]
21. Carpenter, M., 'On the edge: the fate of progressive modernization in Greek health policy', *International Political Science Review*, 2003, 24: 257–72
22. Tsalikis, G., 'Foundation of (anti)social insurance in Greece (1840–1940)' in: Kyriopoulos, G., Liaropoulos, L., Boursanidis, C. and Economou, C., *Health insurance in Greece*, Athens: Themelio, 2001: 19–47 [in Greek]
23. Venieris, D., 'Health policy in Greece: the history of reform' in: Kyriopoulos, G. and Sissouras, A., *Unified Sickness Fund: necessity and illusion*, Athens: Themelio, 1997: 151–72 [in Greek]
24. Antonopoulou, L., 'Le système de santé en Grèce et son intégration dans l'environnement économique et social', Thèse pour le doctorat, France: Université de Dijon, 1979
25. Woolhandler, S. and Himmelstein, D.U., 'Competition in a publicly funded healthcare system', *BMJ*, 2007, 335: 1,126–9
26. Kondilis, E., *Private health sector in Greece: development features, comparative quality evaluation, recent trends and perspectives (Ph.D. thesis)*, Thessaloniki: Aristotles University of Thessaloniki, 2009 [in Greek]
27. Mossialos, E. and Allin, S., 'Interest groups and health system reform in Greece', *West European Politics*, 2005, 28: 420–44
28. Liaropoulos, L. and Tragakes, E., 'Public/private financing in the Greek health care system: implications for equity, *Health Policy*, 1998, 43: 153–69
29. Matsaganis, M., 'From the North Sea to the Mediterranean? Constraints to health reform in Greece', *Int J Health Serv*, 1998, 28: 333–48
30. WHO, *Heath Care Systems in Transition, Greece*, Copenhagen: World Health Organization, Regional Office for Europe, 1996
31. Mossialos, E. and Karokis, A., 'Greece: health care reforms', *Lancet*, 1992, 41–2
32. Benos, A., 'Competition or solidarity? The proposal of primary health care' in: Kyriopoulos, J., ed., *Health policy in Greece*, Athens: Themelio 1995: 137–47 [in Greek]
33. Tsalikis, G., 'Neoliberalism, visions and misprints for health' in: Kyriopoulos, J., ed., *Health policy in Greece*, Athens: Themelio, 1995: 39–54 [in Greek]
34. Kondilis, E., Antonopoulou, L. and Benos, A., 'Public–private hospital partnerships: ideological preference or evidence based choice in health policy?', *Archives of Hellenic Medicine*, 2008, 25: 496–508 [in Greek]
35. NHS Executive, *Public private partnerships in the national health service: The private finance initiative. Good practice overview*. UK: Treasury Taskforce Publications, 1999
36. Tountas, J., *Health care services in Greece 1996–2006*, Athens: Center for Health Services Research, 2008 [in Greek]
37. ICAP, *Private health services. Sectoral study*, Athens: ICAP AE, 2007 [in Greek]

38 World Health Organization, *National Health Accounts, Greece*, 2008: www.who.int/nha/country/grc/en
39 Bank of Greece Economic Research Department, *Bulletin of conjunctural indicators*, Athens: Bank of Greece printing works, June 2008: 119–20
40 General Secretary of Social Security, *Social Budget of year 2007*, Athens: Ministry of Labor and Social Protection, 2007 [in Greek]
41 Liaropoulos, L., 'Health services financing in Greece: a role for private health insurance', *Health Policy*, 1995, 34: 53–62
42 Mossialos, E. and Thomson, S.M., 'Voluntary health insurance in the European Union: a critical assessment', *Int J Health Serv*, 2002, 32: 19–88
43 OECD, *Private health insurance in OECD countries*, France: Organization for Economic Co-operation and Development, 2004
44 National Statistical Service of Greece, *Household Budget Survey 2004/5*, 2008: www.statistics.gr
45 ICAP, *Private insurance. Sectoral study*, Athens: ICAP AE, 2007 [in Greek]
46 Siskou, O., Kaitelidou, D., Papakonstantinou, V. and Liaropoulos, L., 'Private health expenditure in the Greek health care system: where truth ends and the myth begins', *Health Policy*, 2008, 88: 282–93
47 Nishtar, S., 'The mixed health systems syndrome', *Bull World Health Organ*, 2010, 88: 74–5

CHAPTER 3
In between Basaglia and Einthoven
The chronicle of a predictable failure of mental-health reform in Greece

George Nikolaidis
Psychiatrist, MD, PhD,
gnikolaidis@ich-mhsw.gr
geornikolaidis@hotmail.com
Director of Department of Mental Health and Social Welfare,
Centre for the Study and Prevention of Child Abuse and Neglect,
Institute of Child Health

Introduction

During the last 20 years an entire paradigm shift has taken place in research and practice on health service management (Mohs, 1991; Lincon, 1992). A whole bunch of new methodologies has been introduced and, subsequently, applied especially in north America (Iglehart, 1993), such as: cost-benefit, cost-utilisation and cost-effectiveness analyses; evidence-based medicine – DRGs; Root Cause Analysis, Failure Mode and Effect Analysis; Managed Competition, Managed Care, Outsourcing, Health Maintenance Organisations, Public Private Initiatives and Partnerships, Global Budgeting, Personal Accounting and so on. The generalised implementation of such methodologies has not been a straightforward process. More particularly, health services reform has raised a number of controversies (Twinn, 1991) in relation to cost containment and quality. At the end of the day, despite some decades of enacting and implementing managerial reforms, the problem in more or less all developed countries remains equally pressing: how to ensure quality health services to wider populations at lower cost.

Moreover, the development of a new series of evaluation tools for practically anything has created an intellectual "space" in which it is sensible to question the reliability, effectiveness and efficiency of any novel intervention in health services. This critical "meta-analytical" public discussion about policies applied and management techniques corresponds directly with the scientific approaches developed concerning the assessment or evaluation of quality in health services. The very dominance of the term "assessment" in relevant scientific literature (after previous decades' usage of terms like "control" or "surveillance" regarding monitoring of managerial procedures and policy implementation) is quite indicative.

Additionally, it should be noted that as this discourse on the assessment of the quality of health services was developed, it was mainly approached from two distinct perspectives, namely the "output" versus the "process" type of evaluation/assessment, the former mostly predominant in US-produced literature, the latter mostly common in European. Nowadays it seems almost impossible even to make reference to any intervention either specifically into health care or into wider public health without attaching an evaluation component that apparently seems to vindicate the usefulness of the respectful intervention. However, the same principle does not appear in the discussion of *managerial* policies proposed or applied. With one voice, policy makers along with public health scientists subscribing to a certain tradition seem to advocate reform of health services (which is almost identically neoliberal across the globe): yet these reforms face no equivalent demand for legitimisation or evaluation and après-coup measurement of their impact. In fact, a "double standard" rule often seems to apply in the various international fora: each individual health-care intervention is required to provide documentation to show its effectiveness and efficiency, while health services' reform plans are immune to such commitment. This inconsistency seems to legitimise the question: why not evaluate health reform as well?

Overall theoretical framework and resources

Given the considerations above, this essay is an attempt to evaluate the outcome of the recent reform of mental-health services in Greece. Furthermore, three theoretical resources of analysis will be evoked, namely:
- The differentiation between entrepreneurial legal rights (ownership) and the managerial role in capital's relation and bourgeois class function (Poulantzas, 1973)
- Radical criticism of the dominant "managed competition" model (Waitzkin, 1994)
- And critical critique of the mainstream model of psychiatry (Foucault, 1964).

These resources are going to be utilised in order to enlighten the divergence between public rhetoric and expressed objectives of the whole enterprise on one hand and its actual overt or hidden outcomes on the other.

Some preliminary remarks should be made on the nature of mental-health services in developed capitalist societies. At first, it should be noted that in the case of mental-health services the traditional critical account of the "medico-industrial complex", originally introduced by Vicente Navarro (Navarro, 1974), bears certain peculiarities, viz. that, for a big portion of severe mental-health illnesses, the function of repair (thus, reproduction) of the impaired working class' ability to labour is doubtful. Consequently, the historical focus of capital investment in technologies and resources of mental-health services is not necessarily targeting the entire population, as was the case for acute physical illnesses during the golden era of "welfare states" in European societies. That is to say that the overall bourgeois interest in repairing working-class capacities to be exploited is limited by the chronic character of severe mental illness and thus relativised in respect to financial capacity of the patients and their families.

Furthermore, due to the inability of many chronic psychiatric patients to pay for commercialised health services, invested capital in mental-health services tends to manifest an overt "dualism": it addresses needs of either very rich or very poor parts of the population. As a result, the neoliberal reforms of the last two decades have either focused on "clients" with less chronic and severe types of mental illness, or have utilised public funds in some form to tackle the treatment and rehabilitation of severe chronic mental illnesses.

Mental illness and its management also reflect the dominant ideology, especially on aspects like social control and deviation management. As a matter of fact, it seems that in the case of mental-health services in modern developed capitalist societies this has been the predominant driving force and rationale of the state's intervention (expressed in the expansion of the public sector) rather than any consideration of wider bourgeois interest in maintenance of working-class capacity to be exploited (which dominated the development of public physical health services for the poor). Of course, all the above were modified in relation to the class struggle and the level of its development in each particular society.

In addition, the widespread utilisation of the managed competition models in health services during the last 20 years in OECD countries, as part of the dominance of a neoliberal approach, has created an entire new series of troubles. One should bear in mind that managed care and competition models had their origins mainly in Einthoven's "old wine in a new barrel" (White, 1993). Einthoven's theoretical work and practical application were originally to be implemented in the defence sector in the US (Einthoven, 1978; Einthoven and Kronick, 1989). Despite the original enthusiasm for Einthoven's "magical recipes", the truth gradually became known, namely that during Einthoven's duty in the US Ministry of Defence the managed competition model showed remarkable inefficiency, failing to meet its original targets of cost reduction and improvement of services' quality (Waitzkin, 1994). As a matter of fact, it seems that the US defence sector's expenditure rose substantially, without any resulting gain in quality, during the years of the "planning, programming, budgeting system" (PPBS) which had been applied by Einthoven and his colleagues.

Contemporary situation of health sector in Greece

Despite all the aforementioned controversial features of these new managerial tools and techniques, the academic and political apparatus in Greece attempted with a remarkable eagerness to import and implement them in the health sector. This is especially evident in the public health sector in Greece, despite its documented peculiarities and its radical difference from the Hellenic private health sector. More particularly, the public health sector in Greece has a unique structure including a public health service for hospital treatment (only developed in the 1980s) without any sort of primary care service, in which black market and corruption (in the form of out-of-pocket illegal payments of public-sector doctors and nursing personnel, but also implemented through the direct control and payments of high-level medical staff by health corporate industries) undermine its public status, function and social apprehension, along with chronic under-budgeting and under-costing of services, especially those which include manpower (Zdoukos, 2005). Also, it is staffed by personnel who are tired and demoralised (Kyriopoulos et al., 2003) and who have to deal with a constantly increasing workload (due to the increasing shortage of income available for the purchase of private health services). Its management is dominated by favouritism, including a controversial and largely unreliable procedure for personnel employment and professional development along with bureaucratic stagnation, a hostile stance towards the user, and a lack of demarcation in authorities and duties between services, specialties, even between professionals within a single department (Dolgeras and Kyriopoulos, 2000).

By contrast, the private health sector has a chronic division between, on the one hand, a number of small, often low-price, low-quality units closely linked with one single professional (usually a doctor) and on the other a big oligopoly of high-price corporate businesses which is gradually taking over the biggest proportion of health market. Simultaneously, it also has a growing dependence on direct and indirect state funding, for example via publicly owned and run social security funds (Kondilis, 2005). The private health sector in Greece also has a persistent focus on high technology investments (Souliotis, 2002) as well as a limited engagement in addressing the largest of the population's health-care needs. It has an almost unbroken record of extended over-costing of its services, and practices of induced demand in addition to lower indicators of personnel employment and larger inequalities in staff pay than the Hellenic public health sector (Souliotis, 2000). To sum up, the main difference between the public and private health sectors in Greece is the relative orientation of the latter in technology-driven labour distribution and organisation and its relatively lower percentage of wages in the overall health services' product (see Table 1).

Table 1

	Public Sector	Private Sector
Doctors per 100 beds	56.7	22.8
Nursing personnel per 100 beds	100	37.5
Percentage of wages	63%	54%
Percentage of laboratory tests and hygiene materials (technology %)	14%	24%

Source: Souliotis, 2000

Preliminary problems of mental-health reform in Greece

Within this overall background, the enterprise of mental-health reform was initiated in Greece during the 1980s. Prior to that there had been a limited discussion regarding asylumisation and its implications in Greece, mainly focused on outliners and radical professionals. Public interest on this issue was boosted as a result of international reportage on the inhumane conditions of care in the mental-health institution on Leros, an island on which several thousand psychiatric patients were kept – often described as the "living dead". Publication of images and stories from this institution created some international pressure on the Hellenic government to promote alternative models of mental health care (Bairaktaris, 1994). As a result, the motivation for the reform of the overall mental health care "system" in Greece was more external than internal. In any case, once this reform enterprise was initiated, it inevitably embraced all aspects of mental-health services in Greece, and was therefore presented as an overall mental-health-reform project (Gionakis and Hondros, 2005). Once again, externality overpowered internal demands, since the main source of funding for the consequent mental-health-reform initiatives was the EU's Supportive Framework (SF) and especially the third SF for Greece, in which the "Health and Welfare" Operational Program was particularly focused on funding mental-health reform (see Table 2).

Table 2

	Million euros	%
Health	217.6	42.4
Mental Health	218.6	42.6
Social Welfare	25.6	5
Human Resources	41.1	8
Technical Assistance	10.3	2

Source: M.O.D. [Unit of Financial Management], 2005

In addition to this sudden increase in the flow of money, it should be noted that mental-health services in Greece were (and, by and large, still are) relatively underdeveloped as a specific sector within health services; that is to say that, as opposed to high-technology-oriented medical specialties, psychiatry has never been much of a priority for governments, professional associations or the general public (as has been the case in some European countries). Psychological and social services for mental patients are still in an embryonic stage of development; merely biological treatments aiming at sedation rather than cure are still the dominant instruments of Hellenic society towards mental disorder, along with confinement of mental patients. Mental-health reform in Greece began in this "atmosphere", initiated by unexpected EU funds, motivated by international disavowal and with practically no tradition in alternative mental-health services experiments. On top of all that, EU-funded projects, especially as implemented in Greece, exhibit some particular complexities, including a high degree of administrative and scrap costs, a strong emphasis on paperwork and visibility rather than actual service provision, and high levels of "window-dressing" and "virtual reality" activities.

Despite this, a first period of anticipation from the public-sector mental-health services wanting to respond to the goal of mental-health reform in Greece had proved fruitless (explained on the grounds of its weaknesses discussed above, and reluctance towards change, as well as resistance by local communities – which were quite hostile towards the whole enterprise – and the overall features of a public health sector in Greece characterised by bureaucracy and waste of public funds, micro-political conflicts and limited overall interest by professionals and administrators). So it was decided that the funds available would be directed according to the methodology of outsourcing global management. Moreover, to keep up the appearances of a social character to the program, its structure prioritised NGOs and non-profit civil corporations (some of which were originally set up for this purpose). This led to a two-fold outcome: on one hand, there were no recorded profits out of this business while on the other actual profits were maximised via illegal means, like over-costing, over-pricing and the exaggeration of virtual costs. In turn, this led to a rapid increase in the funds absorbed, but with an increasing uncertainty about the reliability and effectiveness of the utilisation of the funds.

It should be added that more or less all these NGOs were based on a manpower model that did not require trained mental-health professionals. This was justified by reference to anti-Psychiatric and radical theories (mainly the Trieste model of de-asylumisation). In other words, references to anti-Psychiatry were used in order to vindicate the employment of laymen in these mental-health rehabilitation units instead of the more expensive professionals (psychiatrists, nursing personnel, psychologists, social workers and so on). This approach was actually incorporated in the Program's text itself, in operational requirements for these rehab units, in which the minimum required level of scientific personnel were very limited. Furthermore, to secure the "profits" of these "non-profit" organisations, the Hellenic government enacted a legal mandatory regulation of personnel costs in those organisations, enforcing fees and salaries lower even than the private sector's average in each specialty. All these measures were indicative of the pressure to ensure EU funds were absorbed by giving the NGOs greater incentives to participate in the program.

However, even if the issues of profitability and the exploitation of employees are set aside, the actual performance of this "third" sector was rather discouraging in terms of "cost-efficiency", as can be seen even in the official program's Interim Report, despite optimistic efforts to exaggerate the "last-minute" compliance with its anticipated outcomes (see Table 3).

Table 3

	Operational (2002–2005)	Estimated (2006)
Shelters	10	10
Hostels	63	48
Protected Apartments	72	32
Beneficiaries	1293	927

Source: M.O.D. [Unit of Financial Management], 2005

Among other things, one can obviously note the overrepresentation of relatively "heavier" types of units like hostels, explained by the relatively higher funding they attract. That is just another instance of how external factors and mainly funding over-determine the whole process, in place of scientific or social motives and rationale.

De-asylumisation "alla Greca": administrative failure

This peculiar mental-health reform, based on both the Basaglia and Einthoven doctrines, has faced a series of intrinsic, not circumstantial shortcomings, despite support from and promotion by various governmental and international organisations (including WHO) and their experts. These shortcomings characterised the totality of the enterprise. More particularly, on the level of planning and design of this reform a number of deficiencies arose, including:

- The lack of any concrete reference to any alternative theoretical or applied robust designing model for mental-health services. This created a chaotic, nominally "a-theoretical" but practically "a-scientific", approach to mental disorder and its complexities. The absence of any scientific approach, rather than pluralism or eclecticism, characterised the majority of NGOs and units.
- There was no plan for any constant surveillance mechanism for these rehabilitation units. Regular supervision was assigned to already understaffed governmental mental-health organisations (which declined such a role) and finally was reduced to administrative checking by governmental financial services of the legality of procedures and the costs incurred. This was performed by professionals totally lacking any skills to evaluate the actual service provided.
- The original underestimate of the necessity for permanent and authoritative monitoring of these units (which was defended by the widespread reference to a blurred mixture of fragments of "anti-Psychiatric" discourse). The only plan for any evaluative process was actually external (outsourced to individual "experts" by the outsourcing NGOs). Even this assessment was relinquished after a couple of reports and a survey conducted by the end of the program. The management of this program on governmental level by irrelevant and unskilled individuals led to the application of the very same quality-assessment methods as in EU-funded training programs. In the case of training programs the rationale is that a bad performance in assessment will later be a future disadvantage for a single beneficiary; but when it comes to services that care for living people (and in practice hospitalise them), when any beneficiary obviously fails to meet a minimum of quality standards (i.e. is constraining or even torturing mental health patients) some authority to intervene at an earlier stage seems more than reasonable.
- It seems fair to say that in this particular reform there was a lack of any awareness of the necessity for monitoring and surveillance of health interventions, especially front-line ones dealing with living people. This is shown by the fact that even the limited requirements for the employment

of scientific and technical personnel were in the course of implementation of the program interpreted as "indicative" not "mandatory". There was therefore a total lack of any clearly defined quality assessment variables, and this enabled all kinds of malpractice (see below).
- There was no prediction at all of potential failures of the beneficiaries (NGOs) and no plan for any kind of buffering system for unexpected events or failures. For instance, if one of these civil non-profit corporations terminated its operation, there was no plan at all for patients' futures. It was argued that everything would go just fine without any underperformance and no ill behaviour on behalf of even one of the participants. Unfortunately, as will become clear below, reality ended up very differently.

During the implementation phase, things got even worse. Dominant practices in the way this program was run left room for:

- A combination of favouritism and lack of clearly described credentials leading to outsourcing of mental-health rehabilitation units to various businessmen that obviously had no previous involvement or knowledge of the field area, and clearly no concern or interest in the patients but only in the funds available.
- A combination of micro-political interests with the lack of any regulatory framework thus allowing room for all kinds of excuses for any type of practices within these units. Any kind of consideration was instantly dismissed as slowing down the process of the entire reform; any demand for transparency on procedures was ignored.
- The lack of legal harmonisation with existing legislation regarding mental disorder and patients' rights (or, even worse, lack of awareness of its necessity), thus leading to daily insoluble problems in the treatment of patients. For instance, there is still a gap concerning the legal procedure of admission and discharge of any particular patient to one of these units. The very same omission of legal regulation also applied in the legal and administrative features of the procedures to be followed after the end of the first 18-month phase of EU funding, after which regular funding was supposed to be provided by social insurance funds and the regular budget of Ministry of Health and Social Solidarity.
- Ironically, the combination of references to "radical" models (e.g. the Trieste model) on the one hand with oppressive mental-health approaches on the other resulted in a much greater confinement of patients in the majority of these units, which had the nominal objective of reintroducing patients into local communities. More particularly, with a superficial pseudo-radicalism as a banner, all kinds of unscientific and obsolete

techniques and practices were called in. "Laymen's criteria" and "common sense" were referred to in order to legitimise various violations of patients' civil rights, along with subjecting them to practices such as indirectly forced labour, the imposition of rigid tight schedules, forbidding sexual activities, compulsory cold showers, and compulsory attendance at religious ceremonies and the like. The irony was that all these were vindicated in the name of Basaglia and other advocates of anti-Psychiatric doctrines.

The immediate results of such grave shortcomings in design included a widespread selection bias in terms of "patient selection" by NGOs: rehab units preferred patients who were young, physically healthy, preferably working, and with strong family ties to people that cared for them. This left the rest in big mental-health public institutions (in some instances, it was actually the case that an NGO was set up by a relative of a director in one of these mental-health institutions, who chose patients according to internal "inside" information from the psychiatrist). Additionally, soon the "revolving door phenomenon" appeared: "bad" patients were easily sent back by the NGOs to the public mental-health hospitals.

Moreover, a new phenomenon described as "neo-asylumisation" appeared: new mental-health rehab units more or less resembled traditional asylums, but on a smaller scale (which from some aspects is even worse than larger ones, since it allowed only limited socialisation by patients); the only difference being in tidiness and order, and a rather more depressive overall atmosphere. Legal issues (the generalised violation of patients' rights) and in some cases even systematic patient abuse were overlooked, and actual performance was replaced by "virtual reality" dissemination with the "window-dressing" of indicators and evaluative reports. At the same time the over-exploitation of personnel and volunteers led to an endemic "burn-out" syndrome, while accounting based on over-costing, over-pricing and forged invoices was widespread as a means of profit-making in those "non-profit" organisations: the result was a cost increase instead of a decrease, and for fewer services.

The later impact of this program's design and administrative failure was that after the end of the first 18-month phase of EU funding, troubles became gigantic. Since the regular Ministry of Health budget could not support the same level of grants as in EU funding, and given that no actual rehabilitation or social reincorporation of the patients had been done, a generalised crisis spread throughout these units.

Units were merged, requiring many more patients to share the limited space; employees were forced to work unpaid for months; operational costs of these units were downsized in every possible way, including not providing for heating during the winter, decreasing food portions and minimising any recreational activities; some of the NGOs were also merged, sold or bought out. In this entirely new situation the NGOs and their owners created a pressing dilemma for politicians in the Hellenic Ministry of Health as well as society in general: you either keep up the increased funding, or units will shut down, leaving patients and employees on the street. Of course, nationalising those structures and units and incorporating them in the Hellenic public-health-services sector (after all, these "philanthropists" owning those NGOs had not actually paid a single euro out of their own pockets) was not even considered.

De-asylumisation "alla Greca": financial failure

According to official reports of the program and the public rhetoric of the ministers and administrators, one of the original targets set by this program had been a financial one, viz. to reduce costs and implement the reform of mental-health services towards a more "social" and "community-oriented" model. More particularly, it was officially calculated that the annual cost per mental health patient within the big traditional mental-health institutions lay somewhere between 52–54,000 euros. Of course, anyone can object reasonably about such estimates, since there are obvious and severe methodological considerations concerning such rough and ready calculations. For instance, the overall cost seems to be calculated by including the costs of out-patient services and administrative costs in addition to the original in-patient costs that are the only ones comparable with costs for services provided by this reform program. In any case, the official original target set was actually to reduce the annual cost almost to half of the aforementioned figure.

However, during the first 18-month phase of EU funding the annual cost per patient was predicted to be a bit more than half the previously estimated institutional cost of care. More precisely, according to the program, the annual cost per patient in this first phase was to be as much as 41,000 euros (924,000 euros for any 15-member unit). Nevertheless, only a portion of the actual costs were included in this. For instance, medication costs, which were included in global budgets of big traditional mental-health hospitals, in the case of these newly created rehab units were mostly covered by social insurance. Given the rising cost of mental-health medication, such a cost can be roughly calculated per person on an annual basis as up to 5–6,000 euros. Additionally, provision of physical health care and the costs of long-term general medical treatment were also included in institutional expenses, but were paid independently by social insurance accounts for patients in rehab units. Given that many of the mental-health patients were old enough to face various and chronic medical conditions, the extra cost to be reimbursed by social insurance could be calculated as up to 600 euros for regular laboratory tests plus 150 euros for medical examinations per year. These rough calculations indicate a total of approximately 750 euros in addition to the cost of any actual medication for chronic treatment (which again after transferring a patient from a hospital to a rehab unit is paid from the social insurance accounts and not as before by the caring institution). All these figures add up roughly to an annual cost of 50,000 euros per patient. In other words, the newly introduced reform clearly failed in the financial targets that had been set, given that the annual costs per patient eare comparable with the previous cost in a big traditional mental-health institution.

Moreover, at this instance, another significant issue emerges. That is the apparently inexplicable fact that in the middle of a neoliberal ideological domination in health economics in more or less all OECD countries, overt overspending for health services appears in a particular case. If, on top of the calculations above, one bears in mind that in many of these units the pensions and benefits of the patients were also used to cover their personal expenses (in practice patients were forced to use their own financial means for personal expenses) as well as the fact that in some cases patients' families were also asked to contribute, the overall cost of living of those poor patients rises substantially. So under this new reformed mental-health policy it seems that the full annual cost of caring for each individual patient is around 60,000 euros if all funding sources (direct cost + medical expenses + pensions + out-of-pocket payments) are included.

To look at it another way, if the overall EU payments for the entire time of the program were to be divided by the number of beneficiaries per time, again, the outcome is 65,650 euros annually – or 5,470 euros per month per patient, plus the other resources mentioned above. In other words it costs around 5,000 euros per month per patient to deliver rather limited services for these people compared to average social standards (they are living in residencies along with other 14 people, their living expenses are collectively met, etc.), in a country like Greece, in which average monthly salaries of the working class hardly exceeds 1,200 euros.

This apparent "paradox" needs an urgent explanation: why in a country like Greece, given the dominance of a neoliberal political agenda during the last 20 years or so, are workers denied any reasonable increase in salary when "sane", but apparently entitled to four times as much when "insane"? Unfortunately, the only reasonable answer to that is that most of these funds are ultimately benefiting other people than their apparent and nominal beneficiaries. Thus, current pseudo-dilemmas, requiring the government to keep up with elevated levels of funding for fear that otherwise employees and patients will end up on the street, appear even more suspicious and cynical than just the craving for power of some NGO officials.

De-asylumisation "alla Greca": scientific failure

To begin with, some of the dominant fundamental provisos of the process of de-asylumisation in Greece as applied in practice should be mentioned. That is to say that despite some commonalities (or even grandiose references and exemplary cases) mentioned in official reports, implementing the reform entailed certain codes of conduct widespread throughout the vast majority of units and structures that were supposed to enable reincorporation of mental-health patients in local communities. Of course, one can trace the origins of such behaviour and practices back to the lack of robust methodology, the inadequacies in implementation or in the hypocritical reference to radicalism used to vindicate baseless and anti-scientific approaches. Whatever the reason, the following practices are the founding principles of the daily function of most of the mental-health reform units in Greece, irrespective of the type of unit or structure or its nominal approach or reference:

- Using fear of return to the asylum as a means to ensure patients' behavioural compliance. This is used even in minor incidents as a daily reminder of the comparatively upgraded situation in order to secure obedience from the patients. However, the threat is sometimes carried out, hence the "revolving door phenomenon" in any case where patients do not stick to the regulatory patterns introduced by NGO officials.
- The vision of reason towards insanity as a means of mental-health intervention, as a "golden rule" of logic over insanity. This milestone of mental-health reform in Greece entails seeing, evaluating, measuring and criticising behaviours and practices of "insane" patients by the "sane" (though unskilled) personnel.
- Apathy towards insanity, expressed as indifference to the meaningfulness of deviant behaviours. Consequently, deviant behaviours by patients acquire meaningfulness only to the personnel (thus, becoming "symptoms", "signs", "phases" and the like), while they lack any significant meaning for the subjects per se.
- Work as an antidote to insanity is more and more used to serve simultaneously as a means of complementary funding and as a therapeutic tool. It is not accidental that one of the main focuses of the entire reform was the foundation of non-profit cooperatives aiming at re-entry of mental-health patients to the labour market. Moreover, it is not accidental that in practice personnel and officials of the new rehab units are day after day repeating trivial phrases like "the curative function of work" and "the malevolent dangers of laziness and restfulness" to the patients hosted in these units. This early mercantilist–capitalist morality is called upon, despite the fact that the results of the application of working therapy to severe mental-health illnesses are generally rather disappointing.

- The model of traditional family roles and the ascription of a role of permanent immaturity to patients is the constant and repetitive motto of more or less all units of mental-health reform. In some of the units this perspective is covered by reference to various psychotherapeutic doctrines, while in others it is carried through in the most material ways: for example, in one instance, in one of the oldest NGOs for mental-health rehabilitation in Greece, a regulation was introduced requiring every patient to be forced to declare one of the units' personnel as a co-beneficiary in every bank account or other piece of property they were currently holding.
- Tidiness and quiet-ness are used as substitutes for mental-health rehabilitation and social incorporation or inclusion of patients to local communities. With a slight twist in discourse, a successful rehab outcome was identified as "being quiet", "living humanely" or otherwise projecting the values, ideals, preferences and decisions of the personnel or NGO officials for patients. Since the whole enterprise was run (and evaluated) by people who had never had any previous involvement with mental-health services and their complexities, it became the ultimate proof of vindication to present patients living quietly in clean environments, like "dead" volcanoes (although, often, the patients' entire previous life overtly indicates that their subjective will was exactly the opposite).

The means used within de-asylumisation structures to secure and enact those fundamental principles mentioned above are varied. Nevertheless, one can easily indentify that in more or less all such units these means include a common ground, which mainly consists of:

- Silence (erecting tranquillity and lack of disturbance as an ultimate value and rule in units' daily function)
- Internalisation of guilt (systematically implanted in patients, who are regularly expected to feel responsible for their actions, even if totally harmless, if those "deeds" threaten the overall atmosphere of tidiness and tranquillity envisaged by NGO officials and their employees)
- Mirror recognition of the patients (who are constantly asked not only to check themselves and become self-disciplined and self-controlled, but also to present proof of this self-monitoring either in terms of verbal or actual reconsideration and regret)
- The Permanent Jury for the patients (constituted by the personnel continually judging patients about their positive or negative image as well as their performance against criteria set by the Jury itself) and
- Mystification and upgrading of the role of officials or, in general, "people in charge" (where in virtue of an upstream high hierarchical structure of roles and responsibilities, various steps of potential report of patients' misbehaviour have been created).

Briefly then, contemporary mental-health reform in Greece has entailed every one of the features that Michel Foucault (in his legendary work *History of Madness in the Classical Era*, of 1964) criticised about Samuel Tuke's mental-health reform in the UK – back in 1798! Additionally, these issues have been widely highlighted and discussed in subsequent scientific literature, along with the experiences of alternative mental-health services that attempted to overcome such criticism while tackling the complexities of mental disorder. Probably the most peculiar thing about this reform in Greece is that it actually was able to evoke all this 40-year-old criticism (originally directed towards a 200-year-old pattern of mental-health services) while consuming almost 212 million euros in the name of "mental-health reform", "community-oriented mental-health services" and, at some instances, "anti-Psychiatry" and radical criticism of dominant mental-health services doctrines.

De-asylumisation "alla Greca": legal and human rights issues

Apart from being an administrative, financial and scientific failure, mental-health reform in Greece had also to inflict some other discrepancies intrinsic to the nature of its design and implementation. The most significant of these discrepancies was that it evoked a systematic violation of the existing legal framework for the protection of the rights of mental-health patients (L.2071/1992). More specifically, currently legislation about mental patients in Greece is quite explicit about circumstances and preconditions of any restriction imposed on any patients, relying entirely on jurisdictional orders for any such act to be implemented. Nevertheless, by the time these rehab units began functioning, personnel and officials had to face a practical but very crucial dilemma: if a patient asks to go outside, should we act against his or her will on the grounds of our own consideration of his or her mental-health condition?

In the vast majority of cases, this dilemma was resolved by introducing regulations (or, even worse, unspoken rules) that clearly contradicted existing legislation (i.e. giving personnel the right to suppress the individual rights of patients "for their own good"). In turn, this implied the growth of a gradual authoritarianism towards patients as well as of contempt for existing legislation for the protection of mental patients' rights. On some occasions, even extreme measures have been recorded such as physical restraint, hitting or abusing patients, neglecting patients' fundamental needs (such as for example heating during the winter), locking them in a room or outdoors, outside of the residence: these practices are, in general, highly incompatible with any kind of rehabilitation process. As a matter of fact, such extreme events tended to appear the more the personnel involved were unskilled, and decreasing in numbers (due to financial issues after the first 18-month phase), and the more staff became demoralised and frustrated due to the gradual decay of the whole reform enterprise.

Quite recently, some images of inhumane, brutal treatment of mental-health patients were "smuggled" out of one of these "rehab" units and publicised in electronic independent media, depicting partially naked patients restrained by hand and foot on beds (Athens Indymedia, 2009). These disgraceful images are probably the best witness of all the considerations described throughout this paper.

Aside from such extremes, milder forms of violation of patients' rights are much more widespread, including forcing patients to comply with tight daily schedules, forcing them to follow the choices of NGO personnel and officials concerning their lifestyle, habits, even sexual behaviour and the like. Such violations of civil rights might look relatively "innocent". Nevertheless, the issue at stake here is the central question in any de-asylumisation process: projecting the "sane" values onto the "insane" is what led patients to asylums in the first place. It should also be added that another type of rights violation is a tacit or overt financial exploitation (for example patients being forced to declare NGO officials or personnel as co-beneficiaries in their bank accounts), which, of course, if it occurred with any other than mental-health patients would certainly constitute criminal behaviour and evoke some legal intervention.

De-asylumisation "alla Greca": après-coup NGOs "window-dressing" evaluation

The most recent phase in this so-called "reform" was its official evaluation. It should be noted that this evaluation was mainly a "process" (as opposed to "output") type of evaluation, focusing on the procedures of the organisations involved – and not on the mental-health condition of patients. This alone is quite indicative of the severe shortcomings of the procedure. However, this was not the only shortcoming: it was performed through the "self-administration" of questionnaires by all participant units, irrespective of their legal status. Consequently, that meant that the ones which chose to fabricate a nice image of the conditions in their units were rewarded, while others that reported problems were downgraded. Moreover, it is well known that self-evaluation can be meaningful only in a series of assessments over a period of time: in this case, it was performed only once. This did not prevent the Hellenic Ministry of Health and the program's executives from drawing conclusions from these – obviously untruthful – reports, viz. that NGOs did much better than the core public mental-health sector.

Nevertheless, it is still worth trying to see whether this evaluative procedure was only meant to legitimise predefined conclusions, or whether it actually aimed at specifying potential flaws and deficits in mental-health reform's enterprise. One preliminary answer to this can be provided by the very content of the questionnaire delivered by the Ministry's executives to rehab unit officials (see Table 4).

Table 4

Entries' number	68
Space availability	15
Written availability of organisations' policies/procedures	13
Personnel issues	12
Functional issues	9
Relations with relatives and local communities	6
In-taking and medical coverage of beneficiaries	5
Beneficiaries' mental health	8

Source: data processed by YYKA, 2005

One cannot help noticing that actual services provided and the condition of patients seem to be significantly under-represented, probably as not requiring much attention. On the contrary, technical and administrative concerns are rather dominant (i.e. more attention is paid to units' square meters than to patients' mental health). Furthermore, the nature of the entries (questions) included led to similar considerations (see Table 5).

Table 5

Quality Assessment for mental-health rehab units – Entries (questions)
Are special needs of beneficiaries showing signs of institutionalisation being met?
Do personnel address beneficiaries always in a friendly, positive and kind way?
Are regulations regarding beneficiaries limited to the minimum necessary?
Is there an informed consent process in any beneficiary's treatment?
Are daily positive activities provided?
Are beneficiaries encouraged to maintain their autonomy within the unit?
Are physical restrictions and containment not being used?
Has no beneficiary been locked up in an isolated room?

Source: data processed by YYKA, 2005

The vagueness of the first six questions is striking, especially given that the questionnaire was self-delivered: it is unclear who is expected to reply negatively to such general and unspecified questions. In addition, since this questionnaire's replies were marked and ranked in a quantitative manner, one particular unit (by trusting the truthfulness of its official) was able to reply positively in the last couple of questions (and admit that in that unit patients were physically restrained and locked in) and still achieve a better grade than if its facilities had been more spacious (which was assessed in 15 consecutive questions). Whether this can be called a mental-health "rehabilitation" and "social inclusion and incorporation" reform seems rather irrelevant. On the grounds of all the above, this après-coup self-administered process of evaluation can be expected to increase rather than minimise the bureaucratic and demonstrative character of the whole reform instead of reinforcing focus on patients' needs and their fulfilment.

The contemporary situation and its perplexities

Despite the subsidies for the "third" sector, even within the mental-health rehabilitation domain, current figures reveal a situation very different from predictions (Table 6). The public health sector, even if undermined in various ways, still delivers most of the services.

Table 6

	Public sector	NGOs sector
Rehab units	269 (70%)	114 (30%)
Personnel	1,525	1,536
Patients	N/A	≈ 3,000

Source: Bilanakis, 2009

However, as already mentioned, this reform had a series of severe implications other than its declared one of NGOs taking over from the public mental-health sector (which, clearly, they did not). After the conclusion of the first 18-month EU funding period and the sharp reduction in reimbursement by the Hellenic Health Ministry, the results included cuts in staffing, reduction of costs and activities, and the expansion of various forms of forced financial contribution by patients' families. Some of the NGOs left personnel unpaid for six months or more, many others cut vital living expenses for patients, and a big wave of mergers, buyouts and closures is still spreading throughout these "mental-health reform" NGOs. Moreover, the current situation for the last couple of years is characterised by pressing pseudo-dilemmas (i.e. whether to keep up with previous reimbursement rates even though waste and fraud were common knowledge, or shut down structures, leaving personnel unemployed and patients in the streets), and a general shuffling of the cards in the mental-health business sector. And a new emerging entrepreneur class of businessmen has been created, hiding behind the mask of NGOs in mental health – some of which insist on claiming that their work is "socially beneficial" or even "radical" – along with a widespread theoretical and ideological confusion (the vast majority of NGOs and their affiliated academics and activists are claimed to be for "civil society" and against the oppressive state, anti-Psychiatric agents against traditional medicalised mental-health services and so forth).

Conclusions

Nevertheless, if one single conclusion can really be drawn out of this painful experience, it is that not each and every innovation serves functionality and efficiency. Every trendy managerial scheme that is promoted by the state's executives (like outsourcing global budgeting) cannot be trusted as necessarily making things better – it can equally make things much worse.

Even in tragic situations (like the one in Greek mental-health asylums prior to this reform) poorly designed, bureaucratically implemented, and neoliberal-oriented interventions can result in severe negative developments. Furthermore, if this case can be used as an exemplary case study in health economics, one should agree that it implies that a global budgeting model of outsourcing brings certain implications, and threatens to undermine the quality of services.

Another conclusion is that professional "ideologies" and social attitudes – although "immaterial" – can play a leading role in determining final outcome (thus, success or failure) of a given intervention, despite its supposed benefits.

In his well-known À *la Recherche du Temps Perdu*, Marcel Proust claimed that "three quarters of clever people's diseases are due to their cleverness" (Proust, 1919). On the basis of the recent experience of Hellenic mental-health reform, one can similarly argue that the vast majority of dysfunctions of contemporary "clever" health-management methodologies and models are due to that very "cleverness".

References

Athens Indymedia (2009) http://athens.indymedia.org/search-process.php3?lang=el&keyword=%F8%F5%F7%E9%E1%F4%F1%E9%EA%DE+%E2%E1%F1%E2%E1%F1%FC%F4%E7%F4%E1&medium=all

Bairaktaris, K. (1994) *Mental Health and Social Intervention – Experiences, Systems, Policies,* Enallaktikes Ekdoseis publ., Athens [in Greek]

Bilanakis, N. (2009) "Civil non-profit corporations in mental health sector: at last, let speak frankly", http://www.psych.gr/anakoinwseis_temp.aspx?id=121, 26/04/2009 [in Greek]

Dolgeras, A. and Kyriopoulos, J. (eds) (2000) *"Equity, Effectiveness and Efficiency in Health Services"*, Themelio publ. [in Greek]

Einthoven, A.C. (1978) "Consumer-choice health plan", *New England Journal of Medicine*, 298, pp.650–8

Einthoven, A.C. and Kronick, R. (1989) "A consumer-choice health plan for the 1990s", *New England Journal of Medicine*, 320, 29–37, pp.94–101

Foucault, M. (1964) *Histoire de la folie á l'âge classique*, Galimard/Plon, Paris, translation in Greek: P. Bourlakis, Kalentis publ., Athens, 2007

Gionakis, N. and Hondros, D. (2005) "Psychiatric Reform in Greece and its recent development (Psychoargos Program)" in Zisi, A., Polemikos, N. and Kaila, M. (eds), *Mental Health*, Atrapos publ., Athens, pp.35–70 [in Greek]

Iglehart, J.K. (1993) "Managed competition", *New England Journal of Medicine*, 328, pp.1,208–12

Kondilis, E. (2005) "Private for profit health sector in Greece. Development characteristics (1980–2002)", Oral Presentation in XIVth International Association for Health Policy Conference: "Health Policy in Europe: Contemporary dilemmas and challenges", Thessalonica

Kyriopoulos, J., Gregory, S., Georgoussi, E. and Dolgeras, A. (2003) "Professional Profile of National Health Service Physicians in Greece and Their Self-Expressed Training Needs", *Journal of Continuing Education in the Health Professions*, 23: pp.1–8

Lincon, Y.S. (1992) "Fourth generation evaluation, the paradigm revolution and health promotion", *Canadian Journal of Public Health*, 83 (suppl. 1), S6–10, Mar.–Apr.

M.O.D. [Unit of Financial Management] (2005) Interim Evaluation Report, Operational Program "Health – Welfare", E.U.'s 3rd Support Frame Program, 2000–2006, Athens [in Greek]

Mohs, E. (1991) "General theory of paradigms in health", *Pediatr. Infect. Dis. J.*, 10 (6), pp.428–33, Jun.

Navarro, V. (1974) "Medicine under Capitalism", Prodist, New York

Poulantzas, N. (1973) "Les classes sociales dans le capitalisme aujourd", Seuil, Paris, translation in Greek: Miliopoulos, N., Themelio publ., Athens, 1984

Proust, M. (1919) *À la Recherche du Temps Perdu, Vol. II: A l' ombre des jeunes filles en fleurs*, Grasset, Paris, reprinted by Bibliotheque de la Pleiade/Gallimard, Paris, 1954, translation in Greek: P. Zannas, Athena's French Institute, 1988, reprinted by Estia publ., 2001, Athens

Souliotis, K. (2000) *The role of private sector in the Hellenic Health System*, Papazisis publ., Athens [in Greek]

Souliotis, K. (2002) *"Health Expenditure in Greece"*, Papazisi publ., Athens [in Greek]

Twinn, S.F. (1991) "Conflicting paradigms of health visiting: a continuing debate for professional practice", *Journal of Advanced Nursing*, 16 (8), pp.966–973, Aug.

Waitzkin, H. (1994) "The strange career of managed competition: from military failure to medical success?", *American Journal of Public Health*, 84 (3), pp.482–9, Mar.

White, K.L. (1993) "Health care research: old wine in new bottles", *Pharos*, 56 (3), pp.12–6, Summer

YYKA [Hellenic Ministry of Health and Social Solidarity] (2005) "Guide of Quality Assessment and Assurance in Psycho-Social rehabilitation Units", Athens, YYKA publ. [in Greek]

Zdoukos, T. (2005) "Aspects of deregulation and privatization in the Greek National Health System", Oral Presentation in XIVth International Association for Health Policy Conference: "Health Policy in Europe: Contemporary dilemmas and challenges", Thessalonica

CHAPTER 4
The effect of health reforms in Turkey:
Out-of-pocket payments are increasing

Kayıhan Pala
Harika Gerçek
Alpaslan Türkkan
Hamdi Aytekin
Uludag University Faculty of Medicine Department of Public Health, Bursa/TURKEY

Introduction

From the foundation of the Republic in 1923 to 1982, health services in Turkey were considered as a required service that the government should provide. At first, the state provision of health services was regulated by law. Afterwards, it was included as a provision in the 1961 constitution. The most important step towards the practice of modern medicine in Turkey was taken by the "Law on the Socialisation of Health Services" which was adopted in 1961. The law was regulated through an egalitarian approach, stipulating that health services in Turkey are a duty of the state. This law ensures everyone benefits from health services, by spreading primary services to the rural areas. Furthermore, the law aims to carry out both preventive and rehabilitative health services in an integrated way. Finally, the law introduces the central administration of health services in the public sector, and the principle of community integration and full-time working for doctors in the public sector.

The socialisation law succeeded, especially in terms of health indicators. During the 1960–2000 period, life expectancy in the OECD countries increased by approximately nine years, whereas in Turkey, the increase was 20 years. Thus, in terms of increased life expectancy, Turkey ranks second among the OECD countries (1).

A new ideology was introduced to the world in the 1970s. Neoliberalism is the dominant ideology permeating the public policies of many governments in developed and developing countries and of international agencies such as the World Bank, International Monetary Fund, World Trade Organization, and many technical agencies of the United Nations, including the World Health Organization. This ideology postulates that the reduction of state intervention in economic and social activities and the deregulation of labour and financial markets, as well as of commerce and investments, have liberated the enormous potential of capitalism to create an unprecedented era of social well-being in the world's population (2).

Both developed and developing countries were prompted to make reforms in their health systems in the light of this new ideology. Neoliberal reforms have promoted privatisation and decentralisation as strategies to improve equity, efficiency, and the quality of health services. After 10 years of privatisation in Colombia and 20 years of decentralisation in Mexico the reforms have had the opposite of the desired effect: in each case they have not improved equity or efficiency, but have increased health expenditures, and have not shown a positive impact on quality (3). The neoliberal reforms have improved neither the efficiency nor quality of health systems in Latin America despite the resources that have been invested (4). The Chilean health reform has lessons for other countries in Latin America and elsewhere: privatisation of health insurance services may not have the results that might be expected according to neoliberal doctrine. On the contrary, it may increase unfairness in financing and make access to quality care even more inequitable (5).

The attempts to change the health system in Turkey under the name of "reform" were revived with the amended constitution, especially following the 1980 military coup. Health services in Turkey, as an obligatory service of the state, were excluded from the new constitution with regard to Article 56. According to the new constitution, the state was charged to organise health institutions centrally, and to make them provide services accordingly. According to the constitution, the state would fulfil its duty by procuring services from health and social institutions in the public and private sectors, and monitoring them. The primary transformation in the provision of health services in Turkey after 1980 has been the precedence of the private sector in supply of services. The neoliberal transformation in health initiated by global capitalism during the 1970s first made itself felt in the 1982 constitution. This approach called "health reform" foreshadowed a privatisation in health; the state has been withdrawing from health services for the past thirty years (6).

At first, health policies in Turkey after 1980 focused on the non-enforcement of the Law on Socialising Health Services adopted in 1961. As a result the public health services collapsed. Since the collapse of health services resulted in dissatisfaction among society, the "reform in health" was revived as a solution. The reform was initially based on three basic components:

- The separation of finance from presentation in health care and provision of finance via general health insurance
- The withdrawal of the state from health service provision
- And finally, employment of the health care labour force as contracted staff rather than civil servants.

"The Basic Health Services Law", adopted in 1987, is the first attempt to adapt the health-care sector in Turkey to the open market economy. The law defined the first steps for establishing a general health insurance, and included the regulations required for public hospitals to introduce their own business and staff policies. Since critical parts of the law were abrogated by the Supreme Court, this law failed to be implemented, although it is still in effect (7). The 1990s marked a distinctive increase in the number of health institutions providing a private service in Turkey, and pointed to a development of health care as a "market" for private health insurance (8).

The health sector in Turkey has grown almost three-fold in numbers over the last 20 years. The role played by the public sector has been a determinant factor in this growth. Furthermore, the health expenditures of the social security institutions have become the engine of the public sector; however, public health finance has benefited from the extra-budgetary resources (especially from the revolving funds).

However, the determinant feature of the health sector in this period has been the transfer of resources from public to private sector and from the private sector to abroad. The health sector in Turkey has preferred a way of growth and "modernisation" that transfers resources abroad regularly. The role of the state is to guarantee the infrastructure of resource transfer, to pay salaries of public health staff, and to assist in the period of discharging of the public sector. The Ministry of Health, the authorised institution on this matter, has become totally dysfunctional. At the end of the period that began in 1980, public health services and public health institutions have collapsed whereas public health expenditures have increased (9).

The share of total health expenditures of Turkey in the gross domestic product was 4.9% in 2000 and 4.8% in 2001. While the share of the general government expenditure was 62.9% in 2001, this rate increased to 72.5% in 2006. When 2001 and 2006 are compared, although the rate of the private health expenditures in general health expenditures diminished from 37.1% to 27.5%, out-of-pocket expenditures within private health expenditures increased from 74.6% to 84.2%. Per capita government expenditure on health was $272 US in 2000, and rose to $423 in 2006 (10).

On the one hand, the general health expenditures have increased in Turkey (especially following 2002); but on the other, the private health sector has also been supported, by ensuring that the social security institutions purchase health service from the private sector. The share of private hospitals in the expenditures of social security institutions almost tripled to 17.3% from 6.2% (2008) (11).

Recent years have witnessed the rapid growth of the private sector in the country. The expectations of society, especially demands from people with high-income levels, are increasingly prompting the private sector to make investments in health care. On one hand, these developments result in improvement in the infrastructure and increase in patient satisfaction; on the other, they raise inequalities among many income groups in the health-care field. Moreover, this improvement, maintained in an uncontrolled manner, increases doubts on the quality of the services provided and the state of health outputs. In this sense, it is generally expected that deficiencies of the public health systems should be compensated, and Turkey should continue its progress on this matter, instead of privatising further in health-care (7).

The neoliberal health policies, called "Reform in Health" by the governments after 1980, were introduced as "Transformation in Health", with a name change in 2003, and had not been widely implemented until the Justice and Development Party came to power alone in 2002. It can be said that the slow process of change had been due to the administration of the country by coalition governments, and to the power of social opposition by trade bodies/unions.

The Ministry of Health explains the main principles of the program called "Transformation in Health" as follows: anthropocentrism, sustainability, continuous quality development, participation, reconciliation, volunteerism, checks and balances, decentralisation and competency in service (12).

When the principles stated by the Ministry of Health are considered, the main approach of the "Transformation in Health" is to maintain health finance through an insurance system, and to provide health services generally by private health sector. The encouragement for private-sector investment in health care is clearly expressed in the Ninth Development Plan, to run between 2007 and 2013 (13).

The Ministry also argues that the out-of-pocket health expenditures would be reduced by the Transformation in Health program. This study was carried out in order to analyse the differences in out-of-pocket health expenditures which people make after the health reforms went into effect in Turkey.

Materials and methods

Research area

The study was carried out in the district of Bursa which is in the west of Turkey. Bursa is the fourth-largest city of Turkey. It is situated in the north-west part of Turkey and has 17 districts. Gemlik is a district affiliated to the province of Bursa. Its population was 88,690 in 2000. This study is a repeat of the cross-sectional research conducted via the same method and in the same place in 2001. The study of 2001 was published before (14).

Subjects

In the scope of the research, there are 43 streets at the district centre and 3 villages in the rural area. The streets and villages are determined via a cluster sampling method. Every related street and village is visited, and every individual in the house is involved in the research. In 2001, 10,290 people living in 3,011 houses were included in the study, and in 2006 7,016 people living in 2,215 houses.

In both studies, the data were collected in April–July. The data were collected by teachers at the Department of Public Health of the UUSM (Uludag University School of Medicine) as well as the senior students who were interns at this department. The teachers and students were given training on how to fill in the questionnaire before the data-collection phase.

At first, the participants were given information on the study, and the questionnaire composed of 8 questions was filled via a face-to-face method. The questionnaire questions were asked to one of the spouses. If the spouses were absent, the questions were directed to the family members who were present, and to the oldest person aged over 15. If there was not any person matching these requirements, this household was excluded from the scope of the study for the first visit. A second visit was planned for the houses in this situation.

In the research, the number of people living in house, their ages, genders, social health securities, the occurrence of illness within the last month, out-of-pocket health expenditures within the last month and type of the expenditure (diagnosis/treatment, medication etc.) and cost were recorded.

In Turkey, health insurance is obtained from six sources. The sources in the questionnaire are as follows:

1. General government budget (for active civil servants)
2. GERF (Government Employees Retirement Fund, a scheme for retired civil servants)
3. SSK (Social Insurance Organisation, a scheme for active/retired workers)
4. Bag-Kur (The Social Insurance Agency of Merchants, Artisans and the Self-Employed, a scheme for self-employed people)

5. Green Card (A scheme for poor people)
6. Private health insurance.

The out-of-pocket health expenditure is considered as the money that the individuals spend from out-of-pocket for the diagnosis/treatment when they apply to any health institution, and as the money that they spend on medication (from any health institution). In order to consider this money as an out-of-pocket expenditure, it should not be refunded in any way (from the employed institution or insurance).

The people who do not have any social health insurance, or who have an insurance which did not give them adequate cover, should pay for their health expenditures out of their own pockets. In some cases people who depend on any social-security system should contribute to health expenditures. For instance, they contribute to 10–20% of ambulatory treatments, and to expenditure on orthesis-prosthesis, etc. at specific rates. The people in this group have to pay any expenditure out of their pockets for health services from other than the provided health institutions. In the present study, out-of-pocket health expenditures were calculated as stated by the people who had made the expenditures related to diagnosis/treatment and medication within the previous month. The total expenditure cost per capita was calculated later, based on this data.

At the end of study, while calculating the out-of-pocket expenditures, annual expenditures were found by multiplying the monthly expenditure cost by 12 and dividing it by the total number of people within the group of social insurance. Health expenditures were calculated in US dollars.

People who did not make any health expenditure within a month or who said that they made expenditure but did not remember its amount were excluded.

Constraints of the Study:
1. Details about the out-of-pocket expenditures (the place of expenditure and the reason for it, the relationship between the illness and out-of-pocket expenditure) were not questioned during the study.
2. Since only expenditures in the March–July period were questioned in the research, possible seasonal changes in out-of-pocket expenditures could not be analysed. However, this situation was valid for both researches.
3. The one-month period was questioned during the questionnaire. This period may be too long for some people to remember their expenditures.
4. In accordance with a protocol signed with the Ministry of Health between 1980 and 2001, Gemlik became the application area of the Uludağ University Public Health. During these years, the Department of Public Health gave training at the campus of Gemlik, provided public health services and performed field research. Afterwards, the University decided to leave Gemlik, arguing that the Ministry of Health did not abide by the protocol

provisions. Because of this decision, houses could not be visited for the second time in the 2006 research, which restricted the number of participants in the 2006 research.

Results

In research, 3,011 houses were visited in 2001 and 2,130 houses in 2006. The number of individuals per house was 3.4 in 2001 and 3.3 in 2006. There were 5,229 women (50.8%) and 5,061 men (49.2%) included in the research in 2001. The number of women was 3,511 (50.0%), and the number of men was 3,505 (50.0%) in 2006.

It was noted that 27.9% of the participants in 2001 and 13.5% of the participants in 2006 were out of the social security system. The people most likely not to be able to benefit from health services via insurance even though they are covered by social insurance are self-employed and others in the Bag-Kur scheme, who have not been able to pay their health insurance premiums. As a result the number of people without health insurance increases. Due to the premium debts, 959 people in 2001 and 198 people in 2006 could not benefit from the health services even though they were under Bag-Kur. In this case, the rate of people without health insurance was calculated as 37.2% in 2001 and 16.4% in 2006. The rate of people without health insurance in the research field decreased in 2006, when compared to 2001 ($P<0.05$). There is a significant increase observed in the proportion of individuals who are insured under the SSK (see Table 1).

It was reported that 17.6% of the participants (1,808/10,290) in 2001 and 28.5% (1,999/7,016) of them in 2006 made out-of-pocket expenditure within the last month. The rate of people who made out-of-pocket expenditure was found to be higher in 2006 than in 2001 ($p<0.05$). While the rate of the people who paid for diagnosis/treatment within the last month in 2001 was 7.3%, this rate increased to 9.1% in 2006. The people who paid for medication increased from 15.4% to 25.3%. The distribution of the out-of-pocket expenditure in terms of expenditure types is given in Table 2.

The total amount of the out-of-pocket health expenditure of the participants within the last month was $71,284 in 2001. 39.5% of this amount was spent on medication expenditures and the rest was spent on diagnosis/treatment. In 2006, the total amount of the out-of-pocket health expenditure of the participants within the last month was $145,231. 22.5% of this amount was spent on medication expenditures, and the rest was spent on diagnosis/treatment.

The total out-of-pocket health expenditure per capita in the research field was $83.1 USD in 2001, whereas it was $248.4 USD in 2006, an increase of 198.9 %. The out-of-pocket expenditure of the people who own Green Cards as the health insurance of the poor increased from $4.7 to $52.8 USD, an increase of 1,023.4%. The out-of-pocket medication expenditure of the members of GERF decreased by 39.2%, the other out-of-pocket expenditure increased. The distribution of the annual out-of-pocket expenditure in terms of expenditure type is given in Table 3.

Discussion

The reduction in the number of people without any health insurance in the research field is a significant finding, which is actually applicable throughout Turkey. According to the official data in Turkey, the number of people with social security increased from 79.0% (2001) to 91.7% (2005) (15). One of the most important reasons for this increase is the rise in the numbers of people who should have insurance under SSK. While the rate of those insured under SSK (active + passive) was 45.2% in 2001, this rate increased to 56.8% in 2005 (15). The increase in the number of insured persons under SSK is not related to the decrease in the unemployment rate (associated with the increase in employment rate) because it is a known fact that unemployment is a structural problem in Turkey and did not decrease between the years 2001 and 2005. According to the official data, the unemployment rate was 8.4% in 2001 and it rose to 10.3% in 2005 (16). The increase in the number of persons with obligatory insurance is mainly related to the premium exemption and to the decrease in the number of unregistered workers. The rate of unregistered workers was 52.9% in 2001 and this rate decreased to 50.1% in 2005 (16).

According to the research findings, the proportion of people who made out-of-pocket expenditure within the last month in 2006 was higher than 2001. It is not possible to explain this situation with the increase in seasonal illnesses because both researches were carried out in the same season – and there was no report of any extraordinary situation like epidemics which would make people use health services during the period when the study was conducted in 2006. Although no data were collected on doctor consultations, the increase in the number of the people who made out-of-pocket expenditure might be related to the increase in the number of applications to the health institutions. It is known that the applications to health institutions increased thanks to the implementation of the health reform in Turkey. According to the official data of the Ministry of Health, the number of applications to health-care centres increased by 85% from 65 million in 2002 to 120 million in 2006. Similarly, the number of patient examinations in public hospitals increased from 110 million to 191 million, with a rise by approximately 75% (17). When the public training hospitals are evaluated together with university hospitals, health-care centres and public hospitals, the number of medical examinations increased by

73.6% between 2002 and 2006 (18). When applications to the private sector are also taken into account, it is observed that the applications to the health institutions have recently increased thanks to the health reforms.

Furthermore, there are some situations like making out-of-pocket expenditures for reasons like getting medication without any application to doctor and just getting it from the pharmacy. However, the main driver of out-of-pocket expenditure is the making of an application to a health institution.

Having health insurance does not mean having direct access to the health service which is always a necessity. Depending on the level of cover, there can be differences for the individuals with insurance in accessing health services. When Turkey's health finance is considered, for instance, it can be thought that most hospital expenditure is met by the public. However, in Turkey, the patients who stay in hospitals are obliged to buy 30% of their medications out of hospital.

Health insurance alone cannot be enough for the diseases with high treatment costs (e.g. HIV/AIDS). In USA, having health coverage, whether through federal, state, or private policies, does not guarantee receiving appropriate treatment for HIV/AIDS (20). Barriers to health care can be insurmountable for low-income families, even those with insurance coverage (21). Low economic status and the absence of supplementary health insurance act as financial barriers to accessing optimal care (22).

Evidence showing that the extension of health insurance does not decrease out-of-pocket expenditures can be found in the researches in various countries. China is one of the countries that can be taken as an example. Since the middle of the 1990s, China has undertaken a significant reform in urban employee health-insurance programs. Using data from the pilot experiment conducted in Zhenjiang, a study examines changes in the pre- and post-reform distributions of out-of-pocket expenditures across four representative groups by chronic disease, income, education, and job status. Major findings suggested increased out-of-pocket expenditures for all groups after the reform (23).

Thus, increase in health insurance in the present study did not result in any decrease in the out-of-pocket expenditures; on the contrary, it increased them. According to the findings of the research, when the years 2001 and 2006 are compared, there is an increase in out-of-pocket expenditures for both diagnosis/treatment and medication within the last month (see Table 2).

At this point, an analysis is required of the increase in the number of the applications of people to the health service in terms of the current health system of that country. The increase in the provision of curative services especially can be considered as the result of a kind of "supply creates demand" attempt in health systems that support the private sector. Here, the private sector should not be considered as institutions which provide only health services. As a component of neoliberal health reforms, particularly medication and medical technology, the private sector manifests itself in almost every institution, public or private, within the health-care field. In public hospitals, provision of advanced medical technologies, such as CT and MR, rented from the private sector is one of the striking examples. The main problem is that people with health insurance should not be obliged to pay out of their pockets to benefit from health services.

In Turkey, obtaining finance via general health insurance, including shares, institutionalises the term of "user fee". User fees have been introduced with the aim of preventing unnecessary service use, developing a graded system which requires patients to pay different levels of fees for different levels of health care, increasing the quality of service and satisfaction of users and developing awareness of expenditure in service producers and users. However, user fees also cause significant problems as well, bringing increasing inequalities for the poor who are prevented from accessing health care, and making it more likely that patients will choose curative services, and thus decreasing effectiveness and raising administrative expenditures. Furthermore, it was determined that the poor spent proportionally more than the rich on the use of the service (24, 25). On the one hand, the general health insurance means an additional health tax with obligatory premium payment; on the other, with the concept of "user fee", it denotes a significant obstacle limiting access by the poor or the people on low incomes to health services.

Another study carried out in India showed that out-of-pocket expenditures have an increasing effect on the poverty rate in the country. As a result of out-of-pocket health expenditure, over 32 million persons fell below the poverty line in a single reference year in India (26).

In the past two decades, powerful international trends in market-oriented health-sector reforms have been sweeping around the world, generally spreading from the northern to southern, and from the western to the eastern hemispheres. Global blueprints have been advocated by agencies such as the World Bank to promote privatisation of health-service providers, and to increase private financing – via user fees – of public providers. Furthermore, commercial interests are increasingly promoted by the World Trade Organization, which has striven to open up public services to foreign investors and markets. This policy could pave the way for public funding of private operators in the health and education sectors, especially in wealthy, industrial countries in the northern hemisphere. Although such attempts to undermine public services pose an obvious threat to equity in the well-established social-welfare systems of Europe and Canada, other developments pose more immediate threats to the fragile systems in middle-income and low-income countries. Two of these trends – the introduction of user fees for public services and the growth of out-of-pocket expenses for private services – can, if combined, constitute a major poverty trap (27).

The increase in out-of-pocket expenditures from $83.1 to $248.4 in the last five years requires us to be sceptical of the claim that out-of-pocket expenditures would be reduced by the health reforms.

In fact, the results of household research conducted by the State Institute of Statistics indicate that the share of health service expenditures in consumption expenditure has not decreased. The rate of health expenditures in the household consumption expenditures was unchanged at 2.3% in 2002 and 2007 (28).

More evidence showing that out-of-pocket expenditures do not decrease emerges in the data of World Health Organization. When the years 2001 and 2006 are compared, out-of-pocket expenditure increased from $75.3 to $98.0, with a rise of 30% (calculation based on the data of World Health Statistics in 2009) (10).

The out-of-pocket expenditure calculated according to WHO data shows similarities to the amount found in 2001; however, there is a major difference with the amount found in 2006. It is thought that this difference depends on the increase in the share of the private sector within the provision of health service and on the difficulties experienced in registering private-sector expenditures. It is predicted that general health expenditures are higher than the official data due to unregistered (informal) expenditures in Turkey (29). Thus, according to the results of the household research carried out by the Ministry of Health, out-of-pocket expenditure per capita was $178 in 2001 (19).

The amount of out-of-pocket expenditure varies according to the insurance status and the affiliated insurance institution. When out-of-pocket expenditures of in-patient and ambulatory diagnosis/treatment are analysed, the lowest increase rate was monitored among the private-sector members within five years (19.1%). The highest increase was observed among the members of green card, which is the health insurance of the poor (1,023.4 %). This rate is even higher than the increase rate of the uninsured persons. It is considered there are two main reasons for this. Firstly, the out-of-pocket expenditures among green-card members were very low, amounting to $4.7 in the 2001 study. Since the medication expenditures were not covered in those years, the number of applications by green-card members was low. When the significant part of the medication expenditures was covered by a legal regulation adopted in the February of 2005, the number of applications by green-card members increased, and the scale of the out-of-pocket expenditures increased accordingly. After the government covered 80% of medication expenditures for green-card members, green-card expenditures increased to 11.4 % of the public health expenditure in 2007 from just 4.6 % in 1999 (18). Secondly, although they are poor, the uninsured people are not within the poorest section of society (only the poorest people without any property and income can get a green card), so they might be deprived of the support that might increase the number of applications to the health institutions. In accordance with the Ministry of Health data, the annual average number of applications (physician contact) of insured people for ambulatory treatment was 5.1, whereas this number amounted to 2.3 for the uninsured (19). Furthermore, although the out-of-pocket expenditures by green-card members increased further in proportional terms, it is still at the level of $52.8. In fact, the spending on diagnosis/treatment expenditures per capita among the uninsured persons is $418.6, which is very high. It is possible to say that this amount is an out-of-pocket expenditure that might lead a family in Turkey into medical poverty.

In out-of-pocket expenditures, the situation differs in two aspects in terms of diagnosis/treatment expenditures. Firstly, out-of-pocket medication expenditures of the members of GERF decreased in 2006, when compared to 2001. Secondly, the increase in out-of-pocket medication expenditures is lower, when compared to the diagnosis/treatment expenditures.

It is thought that the decrease in medication expenditures of the members of GERF is related to the covering of some expensive medications which were not covered before, with the change in medication policy. Since the private health insurances do not make any policy regulation about medication in favour of the insured persons, out-of-pocket medication expenditures increased by 137.8% between 2001 and 2006.

For members of GERF, out-of-pocket expenditures for diagnosis/treatment increased sharply while spending on medication decreased. The members of GERF (since they are civil servants) are relatively old and middle-income people. It is known that the members of GERF benefit from health services more than the other classes in society. It was found in another study carried out in Gemlik in previous years that on average the members of GERF seek medical treatment 6.6 times a year. In the same study, this number was 3.3 for SSK members, and 1.9 for the uninsured people (30). The tendencies of these people to get services from a private health institution at a higher level, with the effect of health reform, might increase their out-of-pocket expenditures for diagnosis/treatment. More detailed studies are required on this matter.

The share of medication expenditures decreased in 2006, when compared to 2001. The government changed its medication policy along with the health reform, and facilitated access to medication for insured persons, especially for green-card holders and the members of SSK. According to the official data, 693-million items of medication were consumed in 2001, and this number increased to 1,272 million in 2006 (an increase of 83.5%) (17). Although there was an increase in the number of medications consumed, the decrease in the out-of-pocket medication expenditures within the general out-of-pocket expenditures mostly depends on the covering of the medication expenditures mainly by the public budget and social security institutions. The increase in the green-card expenditures in the public health budget was mentioned before. Similarly, an increase was noted in the medication expenditures of the social security institution. The expenditure for the medication increased about 3.4 times (from 2,434 million TL in 2001 to 8,372 million in 2006) (11). Facilitating access to medication is an appropriate policy. However, the government should analyse the change in the medication policy along with rational medication use and increase in medication expenditures.

Conclusions

As a conclusion, the claim that the neoliberal health reforms implemented by the government would reduce out-of-pocket health expenditures could not be proven. On the contrary, out-of-pocket expenditures increased through the reform. The social security of health also increased in the research area; however, this increase did not cause any decrease in the out-of-pocket health expenditures.

The health system in Turkey is directed to an approach in which the state almost completely withdraws from the provision of services, and also focuses on the curative health services. The private sector is dominant in the "market" which is created in this way, and therefore access for the low-income and disadvantaged part of the society, especially the poor, to health services might gradually become limited. It is possible to estimate that this structure would increase the inequalities experienced in health sector.

Acknowledgements

We would like to thank the senior students of Uludag University Faculty of Medicine and our assistants who worked in the field during this study.

References

1. OECD, *Towards High-Performing Health Systems Summary Report, The OECD Health Project*, Paris, 2004, http://www.oecd.org/dataoecd/7/58/31785551.pdf (August, 21, 2009)
2. Navarro, V., 'Neoliberalism as a class ideology; or, the political causes of the growth of inequalities', *International Journal of Health Services*, 37(1): 47–62, 2007
3. Homedes, N. and Ugalde, A., 'Neoliberal reforms in health services in Latin America: a critical view from two case studies', *Pan American Journal of Public Health*, 17(3): 210–20, 2005
4. Ugalde, A. and Homedes, N., 'Neoliberal health sector reforms in Latin America: unprepared managers and unhappy workers', *Pan American Journal of Public Health*, 17(3): 202–9, 2005
5. Unger, J-P., De Paepe, P., Cantuarias, G.S. and Herrera, O.A., 'Chile's neoliberal health reform: An assessment and a critique', *PLoS Med*, 5(4): e79. doi:10.137/journal.pmed.0050079, 2008
6. Pala, K., Türkiye İçin Nasıl Bir Sağlık Reformu? Milliyet Gazetesi Örsan Öymen Anısına Yılın

İnceleme Ödülü, 2006, http://halk-sagligi.uludag.edu.tr/turkiye_icin_nasil_bir_saglik_reformu.pdf (21 August 2009)
7. Savas, B., Serdar et al. in Thomson, S. and Mossialos, E., eds, *Health care systems in transition: Turkey*, Copenhagen, European Observatory on Health Care Systems, 4(4), 2002
8. WHO, *Health Care Systems in Transition HiT summary, Turkey*, European Observatory on Health Systems and Policies, 2004
9. TTB, Sağlıkta Dönüşüm Programı 2003 Türkiye'sinde Halka Hekimlere Sağlık Personeline Ne Getiriyor? Türk Tabipleri Birliği, Ankara, 2003
10. WHO. World Health Statistics 2009 http://www.who.int/whosis/whostat/EN_WHS09_Full.pdf (12 August 2009)
11. SGK. Sosyal Güvenlik Kurumu 2009 http://www.sgk.gov.tr/wps/wcm/connect/bd8860804f1899e1abe6bf22801f22d5/2009_06_mali.xls?MOD=AJPERES (12 August 2009)
12. Ministry of Health, *Transformation in Health*, Ministry of Health of the Republic of Turkey, Ankara, 2003
13. DPT, *Ninth Development Plan, 2007–2013*, T.R. Prime Ministry State Planning Organization, http://ekutup.dpt.gov.tr/plan/ix/9developmentplan.pdf (12 August 2009)
14. Pala, K., Aytekin, H., Aytekin, N. and Aydın, N., Gemlik'te Cepten Sağlık Harcamaları. *Toplum ve Hekim*, 18(4): 279–87, 2003
15. DPT, *Economic and Social Indicators, The Population Covered By Social Insurance Programs (1950–2006)*, T.R. Prime Ministry State Planning Organization, http://www.dpt.gov.tr/PortalDesign/PortalControls/WeblcerikGosterim.aspx?IcerikRef=1678&WorkArea=ctl39 (12 August 2009)
16. TUİK, *Labour Force Status by Non-Institutional Population*, Turkish Statistical Institute, http://www.tuik.gov.tr/PreIstatistikTablo.do?istab_id=569 (12 August 2009)
17. Akdağ, R. (Ministry of Health), Nereden Nereye Türkiye Sağlıkta Dönüşüm Programı Kasım 2002 – Haziran 2007, Ankara, 2007
18. TEPAV, Türkiye Ekonomi Politikaları Araştırma Vakfı İstikrar Enstitüsü Mali İzleme Raporu 2008 Yılı Şubat Ayı Bütçe Sonuçları, Sağlık Harcamaları Sağlıklı mı?: Sağlık Politikaları ve Ülkemizde Kamu Sağlık Harcamaları Sorunu, 2008
19. Liu, Y., Çelik, Y. and Şahin, B., Türkiyede Sağlık ve İlaç Harcamaları. Sağlıkta Umut Vakfı, 2005
20. Stevens, P.E. and Keigher, S.M., 'Systemic Barriers to Health Care Access for U.S. Women with HIV: The Role of Cost and Insurance', *International Journal of Health Services*, 39(2): 225–43, 2009
21. Devoe, J.E., Baez, A., Angier, H., Krois, L., Adlund, C. and Carney, P.A., 'Insurance+Access not equal health care: typology of barriers to health care access for low-income families', *Annals of Family Medicine*, 5(6): 511–18, 2007
22. Kwan, J., Razzaq, A., Leiter, L.A., Lillie, D. and Hux, J.E., 'Low Socioeconomic Status and Absence of Supplemental Health Insurance as Barriers to Diabetes Care Access and Utilization', *Canadian Journal of Diabetes*, 32(3): 174–81, 2008
23. Liu, G.G. and Zhao, Z., 'Urban employee health insurance reform and the impact on out-of-pocket payment in China', *International Journal of Health Planning and Management*, 21: 211–28, 2006
24. Creese, A., 'User fees: They don't reduce costs, and they increase inequity', *BMJ*, 315: 202–3, 1997
25. Kutzin, J., *Health insurance for the formal sector in Africa: "yes, but..."*, World Health Organization, WHO/ARA/CC/97.4, ARA Paper Number 14, 1997
26. Garg, C.C. and Karan, A.K., 'Reducing out-of-pocket expenditures to reduce poverty: a disaggregated analysis at rural-urban and state level in India', *Health Policy and Planning*, 24: 116–28, 2009
27. Whitehead, M., Dahlgren, G. and Evans, T., 'Equity and health sector reforms: can low-income countries escape the medical poverty trap?', *Lancet*, 358: 833–6, 2001
28. TUİK, *Household consumption expenditure by types of expenditure*, Turkish Statistical Institute, http://www.tuik.gov.tr/PreIstatistikTablo.do?istab_id=330 (12 August 2009)
29. Tatar, M., Özgen, H., Sahin, B., Belli, P. and Berman, P., 'Informal Payments in The Health Sector: A Case Study From Turkey', *Health Affairs*, 26(4): 1,029–39, 2007
30. Pala, K., Gemlik İlçe Merkezinde Kişilerin Hastalanma Sıklıkları ve Hekime Başvuruları. Yayınlanmamış Doktora Tezi. Uludağ Üniversitesi Sağlık Bilimleri Enstitüsü, Bursa, 1997

THE EFFECT OF HEALTH REFORMS IN TURKEY

Table 1 – Health insurance status of participants (2001–6)

health insurance	2001 n	2001 %	2006 n	2006 %	Difference (%)
General government budget	971	9.4	314	4.5	-4.9
GERF	550	5.3	353	5.0	-0.3
SSK	3405	33.1	3771	53.7	20.6
Bag-Kur	2084	20.3	1176	16.8	-3.5
Green Card	333	3.2	400	5.7	2.5
Private health insurance	76	0.7	52	0.7	0
No insurance	2871	27.9	950	13.5	-14.4
Total	10290	100.0	7016	100.0	

Table 2 – Out-of-pocket health expenditures within last month (USD)

health insurance	2001 N (%)	2001 Mean (95% CI)	2006 N (%)	2006 Mean (95% CI)
General government budget				
Total	131 (13.5)	21.9 (13.2–30.5)	77 (24.5)	35.2 (21.7–48.7)
Diagnosis/treatment	44 (4.5)	39.4 (15.4–63.4)	31 (9.9)	44.3 (26.9–61.6)
Medicine	118 (12.2)	9.7 (7.7–11.6)	64 (20.4)	20.9 (11.7–30.1)
GERF				
Total	136 (24.7)	41.0 (21.7–60.2)	109 (30.9)	103.8 (46.4–253.9)
Diagnosis/treatment	41 (7.5)	59.7 (26.4–92.9)	31 (8.8)	325.5 (215.9–866.9)
Medicine	124 (22.5)	25.2 (9.2–41.2)	93 (26.3)	13.1 (10.1–16.1)
SSK				
Total	649 (19.1)	33.5 (27.4–39.6)	1094 (29.0)	37.1 (30.2–43.9)
Diagnosis/treatment	281 (8.3)	47.5 (35.3–59.7)	251 (6.7)	132.8 (64.5–201.0)
Medicine	550 (16.2)	15.2 (13.1–17.4)	1003 (26.6)	14.6 (11.9–17.4)

health insurance	OUT-OF-POCKET HEALTH EXPENDITURES (USD)			
	2001		2006	
	N (%)	Mean (95% CI)	N (%)	Mean (95% CI)
Bag-Kur				
Total	244 (21.7)	37.0 (16.3–57.7)	277 (28.3)	130.2 (4.0–256.5)
Diagnosis/treatment	81 (7.2)	79.5 (19.3–139.6)	162 (16.6)	204.7 (-10.8–420.3)
Medicine	220 (19.6)	11.7 (9.7–13.9)	209 (21.4)	13.9 (10.6–17.3)
Green Card				
Total	61 (18.3)	26.5 (17.2–35.8)	138 (34.5)	29.5 (17.7–41.2)
Diagnosis/treatment	10 (3.0)	13.1 (6.4–19.8)	19 (4.8)	92.6 (32.8–152.5)
Medicine	58 (17.4)	25.7 (15.8–35.4)	133 (33.3)	17.3 (11.3–23.4)
Private health insurance				
Total	13 (17.1)	40.9 (2.3–84.0)	10 (19.2)	57.2 (19.0–95.5)
Diagnosis/treatment	7 (9.2)	51.4 (35.7–138.5)	5 (9.6)	58.6 (-25.5–142.7)
Medicine	10 (13.2)	17.1 (3.7–30.7)	8 (15.4)	34.9 (3.3–66.5)
No insurance				
Total	574 (15.0)	52.2 (37.3–67.1)	294 (25.6)	169.9 (56.6–283.2)
Diagnosis/treatment	285 (7.4)	65.6 (38.2–93.0)	136 (11.9)	294.5 (58.3–530.6)
Medicine	505 (13.2)	22.3 (17.9–26.8)	262 (22.8)	37.8 (25.0–50.6)
Total				
Total	1808 (17.6)	39.5 (33.3–45.6)	1999 (28.5)	72.7 (46.9–98.4)
Diagnosis/treatment	749 (7.3)	57.6 (44.3–70.8)	635 (9.1)	189.1 (106.2–271.9)
Medicine	1585 (15.4)	17.7 (15.7–19.9)	1772 (25.3)	18.4 (15.8–21.0)

Table 3 – Per capita annual out-of-pocket health expenditures, USD (2001–6)

| health insurance | PER CAPITA ANNUAL OUT-OF-POCKET HEALTH EXPENDITURES (USD) |||||||||
| | Diagnosis/Treatment ||| Medicine ||| Total |||
	2001	2006	Difference (%)	2001	2006	Difference (%)	2001	2006	Difference (%)
General government budget	21.4	52.4	145.1	14	51.2	265.9	35.4	103.6	192.8
GERF	53.3	343.0	543.6	68.2	41.5	-39.2	121.4	384.5	216.7
SSK	47.0	82.3	75.1	29.6	46.6	57.5	76.5	129.0	68.6
Bag-Kur	68.6	406.9	493.2	27.6	35.7	29.4	96.3	442.7	359.7
Green Card	4.7	52.8	1023.4	53.5	69.2	29.3	58.3	121.9	109.2
Private health insurance	56.8	67.6	19.1	27.1	64.5	137.8	83.9	132.1	57.4
No insurance	58.5	418.6	615.6	35.3	103.6	193.4	93.9	522.2	456.1
Total	50.3	192.6	282.9	32.8	55.8	70.0	83.1	248.4	198.9

CHAPTER 5
Working conditions of physicians employed in public institutions in Turkey

Nilay Etiler
Assoc. Prof., Kocaeli University, Faculty of Medicine,
Public Health Department, Turkey
nilayetiler@gmail.com

Betul Urhan
PhD, Kocaeli University, Faculty of Economics and
Business Administration, School of Labour Economy, Turkey
beturhan@gmail.com

1. Conceptual framework

The capitalist regime of accumulation which realised fast growth between the end of World War II and the mid 1970s entered a crisis with falling growth rates and dwindling profit ratios. During this period, Keynesian economic policies, the welfare-state approach and state policies aiming at national development were regarded as rigid policies that needed to be overcome in front of the new capital-accumulation regime. Through IMF and World Bank structural harmonisation programmes there was an effort to have all countries of the world adopt a market-based development model rather than state-induced development strategies.

The impact of global instability and economic downturn was also felt in Turkey. It has been observed that approaches aiming at a restructuring of the state have been adopted in line with the standard austerity packages the IMF has imposed on many underdeveloped countries and the structural reform programmes more often developed by the World Bank. Health-care reform, aiming for a restructuring of the health services system, was also an important aspect of neoliberal policies.

In fact, the absolute zero point was the September 1980 military coup. Policies aiming for a restructuring of health services and institutions continued throughout the 1980s. This tendency gained a new impetus with the new government coming to power in November 2002, after the victory of the Justice and Development Party in national elections. The Health Transformation Program (HTP) was announced by this government early in July 2003. It envisaged reform in three areas (Ministry of Health, 2003), namely:

1. A General Health Insurance (GHI) would be established, to be financed by a model called 'public insurance system'.
2. Privatisation of primary health care: primary health services would be provided through a family medicine model. Primary health-care units would be closed down and preventive health care would be provided through so-called "community health units", to be set up. Some individual preventive care and outpatient treatment would be provided by family practitioners who would have contracts with the Social Security Organisation. These would be remunerated out of the GHI fund annually, based on the number of patients for whom they are responsible for providing medical and health services.
3. Hospitals would be transformed into public enterprises with administrative and financial autonomy.

In the words of the Ministry of Health, 2002 to 2007 was a period in which "many stones have been turned over" (Ministry of Health, 2007a).

When HTP is realised, the Ministry of Health will no longer be the service provider, but will merely assume a planning and supervisory role. In the words of the Health Minister Recep Akdağ, "the Health Ministry will not row the boat any more, but will be at the helm of the ship." In fact, this is a succinct expression of a new understanding of public enterprise whereby the "regulating state" is envisaged as a construct which merely carries out a function of coordination, supervision and control, acting according to market rules.

Public-sector reforms put in place in developing countries led by the World Bank and the IMF foresee a flexible approach vis-à-vis the regime of public personnel. The basic tenets of this approach take shape in four areas: reducing the number of public employees; extension of contract public employees; implementing flexible employment; and putting in place a performance-based wage structure.

Following the example of the private-sector operational approach, flexible public personnel regimes were progressively put into practice, spread out over a long period. In fact, a flexible approach in the public personnel system means flexibility in the traditional personnel regime and the issue of gradually placing on the agenda arrangements seeking to do away with the public employee system completely (ILO, 1998; Erdoğdu, 2005).

Contract personnel in the public sector were introduced after the healthcare reform. What was sarcastically referred to as the "Law of the Permanently Crucifying Posts" was passed as an alternative to compulsory public service. With other legislation, instead of employing health personnel as staff with job security, their services were to be purchased through a subcontractor. In this way, the service cost was to be met from the revolving fund. Following these arrangements, tenders whereby physicians provided services in public health institutions not as public employees but as subcontracted workers became rapidly widespread. Under another arrangement, the wages of health personnel were to be paid out of the revolving fund, and non-continuous work personnel could be employed on a contract basis per article 4B of the Public Employees Law (No. 657). Personnel employed in this status do not have job security either. Contract work is more widespread among health-care personnel who are not physicians.

In 2006, 247 specialist physicians, 2,080 practitioners and 13,524 other health services personnel were employed on a contract basis (Ministry of Health, 2008).

Another leg of the transformation in health services was the pressure applied on the basic salaries of physicians and the implementation of a remuneration system that would increase the intensity of labour. The wages of health-service employees declined starting in the 1980s and this decline became a clear policy after the 1990s. In Turkey, while the salary of physicians has declined year by year, additional payments such as the revolving fund are increasing (Belek, 2001).

The main additional payments resource is the revolving fund, which consists of out-of-pocket payments from users and reimbursement to hospitals from the Social Security Organisation. The performance-based supplementary remuneration scheme started in all Ministry of Health facilities in 2004. In fact, the government, rather than increasing the salaries of physicians, which have been falling in real terms and are extremely unsatisfactory, has extended the use of non-appropriated funds. Thus, part of their salaries has been linked to their performance, making salaries variable and providing for wage flexibility. At the outset, physicians have taken on additional employment to compensate for the real losses in their wages which constitute the basis for pension and other personnel rights (Turkish Medical Association, 2005).

2. Research on working conditions of physicians employed in the state health sector in the province of Kocaeli

The arrangements accompanying health reform have brought about dramatic changes for physicians, as has been the case in other countries where such reforms have been put in place (McKinlay and Marceu, 2002; Ostry and

Spiegel, 2004). In particular the working modes, conditions and remuneration systems of physicians, who have a special place among health workers, have undergone significant change through these reforms. The second part of this study will look at professional issues for physicians working in the public institutions in the Kocaeli province in light of these changes in Turkey, such as their working conditions, part-time work and economic and social situations, as well as the results of a study aimed at eliciting their views on the recently topical health reforms.

Method of the study

This is a cross-sectional study aiming to determine the working conditions, economic and social status, and job satisfaction of the physicians in public institutions in Kocaeli Province, Turkey.

Kocaeli is an industrial city in north-west Anatolia, to the east of neighbouring Istanbul, with a population of approximately 1.4 million. In Kocaeli Province, there are almost 1,700 physicians. Of these, approximately 1,000 work in the public sector, especially in primary health care units and hospitals. At the time of this study, the population of the study was 961 physicians who were employed in public institutions such as the Ministry of Health, municipalities and other institutions in Kocaeli. Physicians working in university hospital were excluded, as they are working in many different academic positions. As public physicians have the right to work as freelance, some of them work part-time in the public sector. According to arrangements within the medical profession, freelance physicians, even if they work in the public sector at the same time, are obliged to notify and to get permission from the Turkish Medical Association (TMA). The comparisons were also made with freelance physicians on the TMA's registers.

The sample size was determined as 200 after calculations. Sampling was made after stratification by districts and whether practitioner or specialist. In the second step, a random number table was used to select the physicians from the list.

It was planned to invite two hundred physicians to participate in the study; however, six physicians were excluded from the study for various reasons. A total of 194 physicians were thus included in the study and they received the questionnaire.

Data was collected using a self-reported questionnaire which did not identify the respondents. The questions are divided into groups: demographic features, socioeconomic origins, professional history, working modes and hours, job satisfaction, professional problems, membership of the union, and opinions on the health reforms.

The participation rate of the study was 71.2% (n:138) in total, 67.5% among specialists and 73.9% among practitioners. The data were analysed using SPSS software.

Results

The median age of the physicians was 40 and 56% of them were male. The participants of the study were younger and included more women than the freelance physicians in Kocaeli when compared to the TMA's registers. This is consistent with the private health sector, which mainly consists of older and male physicians.

According to class origins, most physicians' parents were either white- or blue-collar workers. Although 42.7% of GPs' parents were blue-collar workers, the same result for the specialists was 17.9% ($p<0.05$).

- Professional characteristics

According to the Kocaeli Medical Association office, 32% of all physicians are GPs, while in this study, 57% are GPs. Most specialists (63%) are either employed in the private sector or self-employed (Kocaeli Medical Association, 2008). While public-sector physicians are frequently GPs, in the private health sector most physicians are specialists. This may be related to the fact that preventive health care occupies a more significant position in the public health sector than clinical care in the private sector.

Half of the public physicians were employed in hospitals (Figure 1). As the public sector includes both preventive and clinical health care, GPs are more frequent than in the private health sector.

Figure 1: Distribution of the public institutes of the physicians

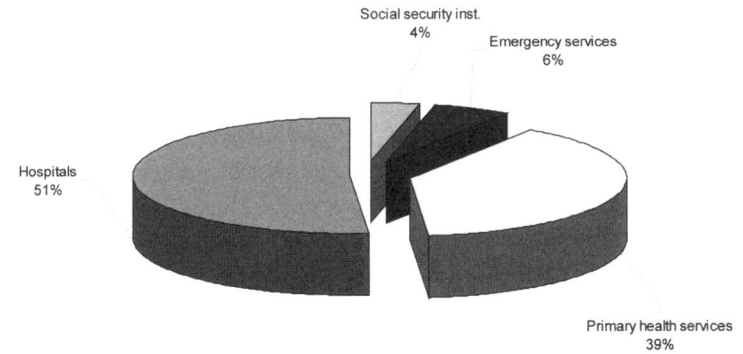

- Working Mode

Three out of every four (75%) of all participants were full time. 70.1% of GPs were working full time, compared with 80.4% of specialists. As an additional job, working in occupational health care units is most frequent among GPs, while working in private hospitals and clinics is more common among specialists.

The Ministry of Health reported that only 11% were working full time in 2002 (Ministry of Health, 2007b). Five years ago in the same study, 62.3% of the physicians reported themselves as part time. However, the introduction of a performance-based supplemental payment system, the increase in the supplemental payment ratio for the maximum wage level for full-time physicians, and a deduction in pay of part-time physicians led to an increase in the number of full-time physicians. In other words, the physicians were given the following clear message by the government: "by working more, you can earn what you would earn in private health institutions by working in your own public health institution". In fact, this intention was repeatedly announced by the top officials of the Health Ministry. Between 2003, when the process of turning public health institutions into enterprises was launched, and 2007, it was observed that the ratio of full-time physicians went up to 62% while that of part-time employed dropped to 36% (Ministry of Health, 2007b).

- Working hours

Mean working hours were 46.9±7.8 hours; and 12.3% were found to be working more than 50 hours. While there was no difference between specialists and GPs, part-time physicians worked more than full-time ones (see Table 1).

According to the available information, Turkey has the longest working hours in health services, with an official 45-hour working week in the health service, while the ILO reported in 1998 that in most European countries weekly working hours were below 40 (ILO, 1998, Part 5). Weekly working hours are often extended due to the mode of working, particularly for specialists. If any emergency case appears, specialists are called in to the hospital for consultation. In our study, 16% physicians work within this "on-call" framework (see Figure 2).

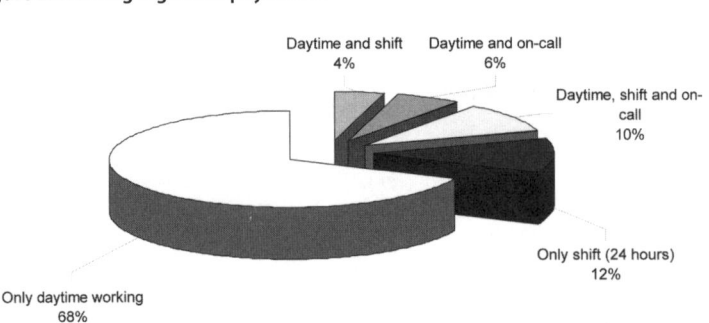

Figure 2: Working regime of physicians

- Daytime and shift 4%
- Daytime and on-call 6%
- Daytime, shift and on-call 10%
- Only shift (24 hours) 12%
- Only daytime working 68%

Table 1: Comparison of the working hours according to speciality and working modes

Working hours	Mean ± SD
Speciality†	
GPs	46.4 ± 9.1
Specialists	47.6 ± 5.5
Working modes‡	
Full time	45.7 ± 4.7
Part time	50.6± 12.8
Overall	46.9 ± 7.8

† $p>0.05$ ‡ $p<0.05$

- Physician income

The mean monthly income of physicians was $3,029 US (median: $2,977, min.–max. $1,143–$7,809) (see Table 2). As expected, specialists earn significantly more than GPs. There is no difference between levels of income of full-time and part-time workers. These results indicate that part-time physicians work longer but have similar income when compared with the full-time workers in general. The part-time physicians explained that they did not want to lose their second job opportunity because they did not trust the frequently changing employment policy of the government.

Table 2: Income of the physicians by specialities and working modes

Monthly income (USD)	Mean ± SD	Median
Speciality†		
GPs	2,518 ±591	2,546
Specialists	3,775 ± 1,167	3,607
Working mode ‡		
Full time	2,973 ± 949	2,980
Part time	3,197 ± 1,363	2,867
Overall	3,029 ± 1,067	2,977

† $p<0.000$ ‡ $p>0.05$

Half of participants' income is from revolving funds (see Figure 3). The proportion of additional payments such as performance-based additional payments from the revolving fund, shift wages, and wages from private practice, is lower in GPs according to their salaries. Thus, the proportion of GPs' salary is higher within their income (see Figure 4). Most GPs are employed in primary health units which deliver preventive health measures that have lower performance points for Ministry of Health's criteria (Ministry of Health, 2007c). According to working modes, part-time physicians have lower additional payments from the revolving fund budget.

Figure 3: Remuneration of physicians

- other 11%
- salary 41%
- revolving fund 48%

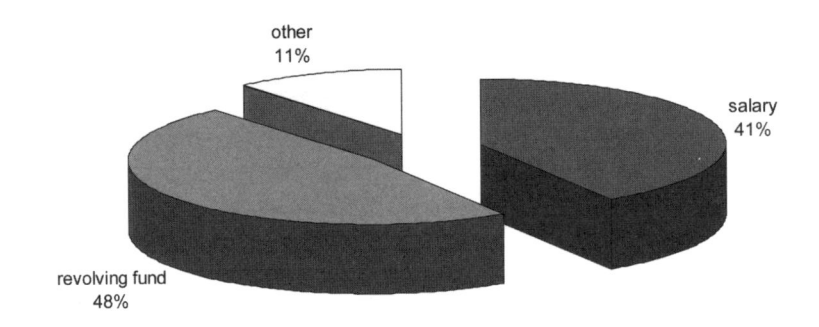

Figure 4: Salary as a proportion of total income (%)

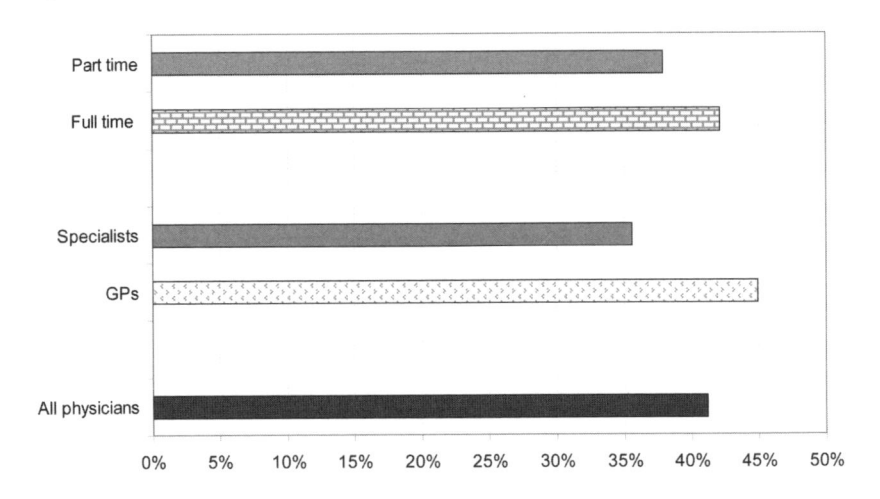

- Job satisfaction

One-third of participants declared that they had job satisfaction. Almost half of them (45%) mentioned that if they had an opportunity to choose any job again, they would choose a different profession rather than be a physician (see Table 3). Although only 24% were satisfied with their working conditions, 60% participants said that they didn't intend to leave their current job. For satisfaction in working conditions, there was no significant difference between GPs and specialists (p>0.05) while more specialists than GPs intended to leave their job (50% versus 30%) (p=0.02) (not shown).

It has been reported that the part-time physicians had a higher burn-out level in Turkey (TMA, 2005), but we didn't find a significant difference in job satisfaction among those with additional jobs.

Table 3: Job satisfaction of the participants

Questions	%
Are you satisfied with your current job?	
Absolutely not	8.7
No	37.7
Undecided	21.7
Yes	26.1
Absolutely yes	4.3
If you have a chance, would you choose to be a physician again?	
Absolutely not	8.7
No	21.7
Undecided	23.9
Yes	34.1
Absolutely yes	10.9

3. Conclusion

The last wave of health reforms caused radical changes in the employment characteristics of the employees in public services. Under privatisation, physicians as well as all health workers are governed under general private-sector labour laws and their employment offers no public protections, especially against insecurity. This situation is not new for ancillary staff, for example for cleaning, catering and laundry (ILO, 1998).

Within the AKP government's neoliberal integration period, the most re-structured sphere is Turkey's health system. These reforms were usually embedded in a set of government reforms intended to improve the quality of public services in general and to reduce the government's operating costs (Rigoli and Dussault, 2003). Thus, dramatic changes have been observed at employment in not only health but also in all public services. Flexible employment laws which have existed in the private sector were immediately transferred to the public arena. Physicians, too, have been considered a part of flexible manpower with some new arrangements such as contracting-out removing the job security special to the traditional civil-servant regime, performance-tied wages, purchasing from private sector.

Despite the historical transformation, physicians always have a privileged position amongst health workers (McKinlay and Marceu, 2002). Physicians retained the opportunity to earn income above their salary: indeed, some of these privileges are the opportunity of part-time working, which allows physicians a share of the revolving fund budgets, and additional performance payments which focus the physicians' labour. This privileged position is therefore a guarantee of higher income. Furthermore, it is claimed that as a result of these privileges most physicians try to connect as volunteer to that political project of capitalism (Uçkuyu, 2004). Similarly, it is claimed that governments give a special status to public physicians so that their special status derives from governments (Soyer, 2005).

In Turkey, with the 1980 arrangements after the military coup, physicians lost the privileges of higher income they had acquired under the Full-Time Act of 1978. Instead of increasing basic wages, the governments have introduced income from additional local budgets. Now, the proportion of additional payments in total income is so high that additional payments are sometimes twice the basic salary including a performance-based payment. Performance-based payment is one of strategies to reduce the central budget of government, and the reforms have tried to limit central-government expenditure by decentralising social and health services at the local level (Rigoli and Dussault, 2003).

Since additional payments are not reflected in retirement wages, this means serious personnel rights are being lost. Furthermore, in the long run, basic wages have been relatively decreasing in terms of real values. In our study, it was observed that physicians tended to full-time status because of higher coefficents of full-time working. Interestingly, part-time workers had higher working hours per week, but get approximately the same level of income compared to full-time workers.

Performance-based payments caused the income inequalities to deepen – by speciality, profit level of hospital, working modes, etc. This means that the principle of "equal payment for equal work" has been damaged by the neoliberal transition.

As the state is the largest single employer, it has an enormous impact on the labour market, and one which is carried over into the private and even the informal sectors (ILO, 1998, section 3). The Ministry of Health often emphasises that increasing wages is the basic strategy to motivate physicians. We argue that this claim is being used by the Ministry of Health to integrate the physician to the new health system and to prevent any resistance by physicians and their professional association.

References

Belek, I. (2001) 'Türkiye sağlık reformları' [Health Reforms in Turkey], *Toplum ve Hekim [Community and Physician]*, 16(6): 438–47 [in Turkish]

Erdoğdu, S. (2005) 'Yeni Liberal Küreselleşme Sürecinde Esnek Kamu Personel Rejimi' [Flexible public employee management in new liberal globalisation], *Toplum ve Hekim [Community and Physician]*, 20(1): 53–64 [in Turkish]

ILO (1998) *Terms of employement and working conditions in health sector reforms*, International Labour Office, Geneva

Kocaeli Medical Association (TMA's local office) (2008) 'Characteristics of Registered Members to Kocaeli Medical Associaiton' [in Turkish]

McKinlay, J.B. and Marceu, L.D. (2002) 'End of the Golden Age of Doctoring', *Int J Health Serv*, 32(2), 379–416

Ministry of Health of Turkey (2003) *Health Transformation Programme*, Ministry of Health of Turkey, December 2003, Ankara

Ministry of Health of Turkey (2007a) *The Progress So Far: Turkey Health Transformation Programme, November 2002 – June 2007*, chief editor: R. Akdağ, editors: S. Aydın and H. Demirel, Ministry of Health Publication No.713, Ankara

Ministry of Health of Turkey (2007b) *Sağlıkta Performans Yönetimi: Performansa Dayalı Ek Ödeme Sistemi [Performance Management in Health Services: Performance Based Supplementary Remuneration System]*, S. Aydın and M. Demir, eds, 2nd edition, Ankara [in Turkish]

Ministry of Health of Turkey (2007c) 'Human Resources in Health and Policy Dialogue Workshop', Ministry of Health & Refik Saydam Hygiene Center, School of Public Health, Ministry of Health Publication No: 718, SPH Publication No: SB-HM-2007/16, Ankara

Ministry of Health of Turkey (2008) *Health At a Glance, Turkey 2007*, Ministry of Health & Refik Saydam Hygiene Center, School of Public Health, Ankara, p.217

Ostry, A. and Spiegel, J.M. (2004) 'Labor Markets and Employment Insecurity Impacts of Globalization on Service and Healthcare-Sector Workforce', *Int J Occup Environ Health*, 10, 368–74

Rigoli, F. and Dussault, G. (2003) 'The interface between health sector reform and human resources in health', *Human Resources for Health*, 1: 9

Soyer, A. (2005) 'Hekimlerin Toplumsal ve Sınıfsal Konumu Tartışmalarına Zoraki Bir Girizgah Denemesi' [An Introductory Treatise on the Debate of Doctors' Social and Class Status] in: *Hekimlerin Sınıfsal Kökeni [Class Origin of Doctors]*, Sorun Publication [in Turkish]

Turkish Medical Association (TMA) (2005) *Türkiye'de Tabip odalarına Kayıtlı Olan Bir Grup Hekimde Tükenmişlik Sendromu ve Etkileyen Faktörler [The Burn-out Syndrome and Factors Influencing it Among a Group of Doctors Registered with the Turkish Medical Association]*, Turkish Medical Association Publication, Ankara [in Turkish]

Uçkuyu, Y. (2004) 'Hekim ücretleri nasıl belirleniyor? Hekimlerin ücret mücadelesinin ekonomi-politik zemini üzerine düşünceler' [How are Doctors' Fees Determined? Thoughts on the Economical-Political Basis of Doctors' Struggle for Fees], *Toplum ve Hekim [Community and Physician]*, 19(3): 203–9 [in Turkish]

CHAPTER 6
The struggle for the right to health in Turkey:
2003 to 2009

Öztürk Osman, MD
*General Practitioner, Istanbul Medical Association,
Turkish Medical Association, Former Executive Committee Member*

Çerkezoglu Ali, MD
*Forensic Medicine Specialist, Turkish Medical Association,
Turkish Medical Association Executive Committee Member*

Ağkoç Süheyla, MD
*General Practitioner, Istanbul Medical Association,
Turkish Medical Association, Committee for Health Policies*

Neoliberal restructuring in health

The pro-Islamic Justice and Development Party (Adalet ve Kalkınma Partisi-AKP) came to power on 3 November 2002, gaining 66% of the parliamentary seats with 36% electoral support. In June 2003, they declared a "reform" program called the "Health Transition Program". Basic elements of this program were:

1. Separation of delivery from the finance of health-care services; health-care financing through General Health Insurance (GHI)
2. Abolition of public "health centres" as primary-health-care providers, and establishment of a "family doctor" model based on private office setup
3. Commercialisation of public hospitals as "health-care enterprises", functioning within a market

4. Withdrawal of Ministry of Health from health-care provision; transfer of public health institutions to local governments – and consequently privatisation
5. Incentives directed to support the private sector publicly.

Struggle for the right to health

The Health Transition Program did not have any authority, as almost identical programs had already been proposed by various governments over the preceding twenty years. Especially during 1991–3, centre-right and centre-left coalitions proposed an almost identical program under the name of "health reform". These previous attempts could not be implemented due to political instability, short-lived multi-party coalitions, lack of necessary legislation – and mostly due to opposition from health organisations. These attempts have helped create a deep awareness and consciousness among health organisations, employees and the Turkish Medical Association (Türk Tabipleri Birliği-TTB) as to the purpose and content of these "reforms".

For decades TTB had assumed a radical stance, defending public provision of health care and equal access, and also had a significant experience of mobilisation. Owing to these strengths, TTB had a leading role in analysing the real intentions behind the Health Transition Program, constructing the arguments of the opposition and gathering unions and professional organisations into a joint opposition. TTB claimed that the program aimed to destroy public provision of health, commercialise and privatise it. The union of public health employees, Union of Public Employees in Health and Social Services (Sağlık ve Sosyal Hizmet Emekçileri Sendikası-SES), also had a parallel stance and became an active component of the opposition. TTB, SES and other organisations closely scrutinised every step of the government on health care, and when necessary reacted massively.

Hundreds of diverse forms of activities were organised during these six years: forums, symposiums, press conferences, press declarations, massive street marches, meetings, strikes, collective night duties at the hospitals, marches beginning from different cities to the capital city Ankara, and referendums of health workers and the public. During these years, posters, banners, leaflets, bulletins, brochures, books, magazines and reports were widely used to explain to the public and to health workers the damage of a neoliberal transition in health.

We won't try to make a detailed chronicle of this struggle here, merely describe its prominent phases.

One of the most prominent actions of the health employees had been de facto strikes called "*G(ö)rev*" (The similarity in pronunciation between *grev* (strike) and *görev* (duty) was used as a facilitator). Although public employees have won the right to unionise as a result of years of struggles, legislation doesn't allow health employees to strike or bargain collectively. For this reason, TTB and SES called for a one-day strike (*G(ö)rev*) on 5 November 2003. The basic demands of the action were; "wage increase, employment security and right to health". Other professional health organisations, public employees and workers unions declared their support.

The participation in the de facto one-day strike led by TTB and SES was much broader than expected. Outpatient examinations, laboratory and elective surgeries stopped as a whole, except for emergency departments and for the patients already in the hospital, paediatrics, obstetrics and oncology. The action was the most significant news of the day, and the mainstream media reported the action in live programmes. The strike found a wide coverage in the next day's newspapers.

The Minister of Health preferred to ignore the strike at first, although he had threatened health workers with punishment for participation in the illegal action. However, the participation was so high and the media coverage was so extensive that the Prime Minister criticised the action on the same day at a ceremony.

Similar strike "*G(ö)rev*" actions were repeated on 24 December 2003, 10–11 March 2004, 21 April 2005 and 14 March 2007. Participation in later strikes and their influence on public opinion were not as strong as the first time. Nevertheless, they could mobilise broad sections of the physicians and health employees, and were strongly supported by the public. Thus they provided persistence for the struggle against the neoliberal program in health.

The first significant structural change attributable to the Health Transition Program was the transfer of the health institutions of the Social Security Institution (Sosyal Sigortalar Kurumu-SSK) to the Ministry of Health.

SSK, founded in 1946 as the social security organisation of the workers affiliated to the Ministry of Labour, started to establish its own health institutions from 1948 on. Thus, SSK formed a model for health services where finance and provision were unified under the same umbrella, and eventually it had the broadest health organisation after the Ministry of Health. SSK had a total of 573 health institutions with 148 hospitals and 54,000 employees in 2004.

The government presented the so-called transfer of the SSK health institutions to the Ministry of Health as gathering health services provision under a single umbrella. However, the opponents argued that the hidden agenda was to separate the financing and provision functions in the health services, and to establish a general health insurance. The SSK health institutions with their current structure constituted an obstacle to this program and thus ministers desired their liquidation.

Other labour organisations also supported the objections of the health organisations and organised a series of actions from September 2004, when the Draft Law about the issue first appeared, to January 2005 when it was approved in the Turkish Grand National Assembly (TGNA). Certainly the most significant of these actions was the demonstration in Ankara of 20 November 2004. The demonstration was called by the Labour Platform which was constituted by nearly all labour and professional organisations and the organisation of the retired workers. 100,000 workers participated in the demonstration and there were also protests against the closure of the Rural Services General Directorate, another public institution.

An important component of the Health Transition Program is the establishment of family medicine in primary care health services instead of health centres. The establishment of family medicine was started in the end of 2004 in Düzce, a relatively small city in Turkey, then afterwards gradually extended to the other cities. TTB considered the process to be the privatisation of primary care health services. In particular, the general practitioners organised under TTB fiercely objected to the process, and organised mass demonstrations not restricted to physicians.

The largest demonstrations against the neoliberal transformation in health were performed during the legislation process of the general health insurance.

The AKP prepared four draft laws at the end of 2004 called "Social Security Reform". One of the drafts about retirement pensions and another about general health security were combined later on and presented to the TGNA under the title of "Draft Law on Social Security and General Health Security (SSGHS)". The Draft Law was a toughening of the conditions for retirement and a reduction of pensions. It also stipulated regular premium payments for access to health and imposed a series of limitations and extra payments for health services.

Seventeen organisations which constituted the Labour Platform reacted strongly against this with leaflets, posters and rallies when the Draft Law was presented to the Turkish Grand National Assembly in January 2006. However, this protest campaign did not last long in the ensuing months. Hence the struggle against the SSGHS Draft Law was led by the left-wing members of the Labour Platform: the Confederation of Progressive Workers' Trade Unions (Devrimci İçi Sendikaları Konfederasyonu-DİSK), the Confederation of Public Employees' Trade Unions (Kamu Emekçileri Sendikaları Konfederasyonu-KESK) of whom SES is an affiliate, the Union of the Chambers of Turkish Architects and Engineers (Türk Mimar ve Mühendis Odaları Birliği-TMMOB) and TTB organisations. These organisations made an appeal to the government and demanded the Draft Law be put to a referendum. When the government did not respond, they organised an extensive civilian referendum. More than two million people participated in the referendum in hospitals, workplaces, neighbourhoods and main squares throughout the country, and an overwhelming majority said "No" to the Draft Law.

In spite of these protests the government, under pressure from the International Monetary Fund (IMF), passed the Draft from TGNA. But some articles of the SSGHS Law were annulled by the Constitutional Court just fifteen days before the Law came into force (1 January 2007). The political atmosphere had been very tense both due to the presidential and general elections. Therefore, the government had to delay the implementation of the SSGHS Law several times.

The AKP government prepared a new modified Draft Law in November 2007. This new Draft not only answered the grounds for the annulment by the Constitutional Court, but also proposed new restrictions to the rights to retirement and health. This again caused the labour and professional organisations, left-wing and socialist parties and groups, and the Labour Platform to make massive protests.

The government declared that the new Draft Law would be brought to the TGNA in March 2008. Consequently on 13 March 2008 street demonstrations were held in many parts of Turkey called by the Labour Platform. On 14 March, "Medicine Day" in Turkey, a two-hour general strike took place with broad participation in the whole country. The strikers not only stopped work in their workplaces but also held massive rallies and demonstrations in the hospitals, streets and squares. Some demonstrators occupied intercity roads and blocked the traffic. Demonstrators also gained strong support from the public.

The AKP government had a great majority in the TGNA and passed the draft laws without paying any attention to the opposition. However, the two-hour general strike on 14 March 2008 was so influential that even the AKP government had to take a step backward. Prime Minister Recep Tayyip Erdogan had declared that the debate on the Draft Law in TGNA would be delayed and that it would be reviewed – together with the trade unions and the professional organisations, which he had previously accused of being "dishonest" and "liars".

Discussion

The struggle against neoliberal transformation in health since 2003 in Turkey has accumulated a rich experience.

We should state that the attitude of TTB and SES was not a partial opposition to the neoliberal program in health care, but a total confrontation. They considered the Health Transition Program as an assault against the health employees and people's right to health. TTB and SES tried not only to protect the rights of the health employees, but were also strongly committed throughout the struggle to the right to health for all sections of society.

The aim of the struggle was not restricted to explanations and protests. The strategic aim was to stop the neoliberal assault as a whole. The struggle was so active, interventionist, audacious and courageous beyond its force that it attracted the attention of the entire society. Thus, the most powerful opposition to the social policies of AKP power came from the sphere of health.

Although the struggle for the right to health was run under the leadership of TTB and SES, these organisations succeeded in mobilising health employees who were not their members, and who held different political opinions – including supporters of the party in power. At the same time, they also achieved the active participation of the other professional health organisations, trade unions representing public employees and other workers, and left wing-socialist parties and structures, in different stages of the struggle. In this way, from time to time all labour and professional organisations of the country acted together.

Above all, the organising body which appeared during this struggle against the SSGHS Law named "Platform for Health/Secure Future for All" was a genuine and a new organisational experience. The platform played an active role in the country-wide two-hour general strike on 14 March 2008, and organised various actions throughout Turkey.

The contributions of DISK, KESK, TMMOB and especially of Dev Sağlık-İş, which is organising the subcontracted workers in the public health institutions in the struggle, must be specifically emphasised.

The opposition movement, which addressed not only the consciousness and conscience of the health employees but also society as a whole, developed a rich, creative and colourful style. The ideological hegemony of TTB for long years in the field of health especially made a significant contribution to the creation of such a style.

TTB and SES did not attribute the neoliberal transformation in health to AKP policies; rather they insistently emphasised the role of neoliberal globalisation, the IMF, the World Bank and international and domestic capital as the underlying dynamics of this process.

As a result, the struggle for the right to health was highly respected not only in the eyes of the health employees but also of the politicians and broad sections of society. This dynamic had been a focus that everyone had to take into consideration, whether in opposition or in power.

It is also essential to reflect on the constraints and inadequacies of the struggle for the right to health in addition to the positive aspects.

Since 2002 when AKP came into power, the political atmosphere in Turkey has experienced great tensions. This is mainly shaped around the anti-secular opinions and activities of AKP and the reactions of the secular sections. Therefore, the reactions against the social policies of AKP did not attract enough attention from society.

The period of AKP power up to 2008 overlapped with the growth period of the world capitalist system and Turkey also took her share of this growth. During the whole period, large amounts of foreign capital came in to Turkey. Thanks to this, while the national income was rising on the one hand, the share of the national income allocated to health increased on the other, and the lack of resources which has been a chronic problem of the Turkish health sector was less of an issue in this period. This also caused society to pay less attention to the reactions of the health organisations against privatisations and marketisation in health.

Although TTB and SES accomplished the participation of the other labour and professional organisations, and left-wing and socialist parties and groups, in the struggle for the right to health, they could not show the same success in gaining the attention and support of the greater forces.

Similarly, they did not show the same success that they accomplished in explaining the damages caused by the Health Transition Program, in developing simple, applicable and convincing alternative proposals to the broader sections of society.

Conclusion

For six years the AKP government has made a series of regulations in order to implement the Health Transition Program. However, in the summer of 2009 the program is not completed.

The general health insurance which was to be enacted on 1 October 2008 is not fully implemented; only 33 of the 81 cities in Turkey could pass to family medicine; the draft law which requires public hospitals to be run according to market conditions and to be privatised if found necessary, is not yet in force; the implementation of the obligatory chain of referral between the health service providers is also repeatedly being delayed.

The most significant point is that no steps are being taken by the Ministry of Health to withdraw from service provision, which is one of the strategic targets of the program. The private health sector, which is constantly fed by public funds, now has a significance which hitherto it never enjoyed – but despite this, health service provision in Turkey is still delivered mainly by the public health system.

Also, although total health expenditures which were $11 billion in 2006 rose to an estimated $36 billion in 2008, popular complaints about the health system continue to a great extent. As a result, the Health Transition Program could not still pass the critical threshold, despite the large majority of AKP in the parliament, the favourable economic conditions and international support.

Moreover the deepening crisis in the capitalist system since 2008 constitutes a big threat against the Turkish economy. After 19 previous stand-by agreements with the IMF, Turkey has again for months been negotiating for a new agreement. Information leaked out that the IMF has made insistent demands for reductions especially in public health expenditures. It will not be a surprise if such a restriction increases the discontent and reaction against the Health Transition Program. This might initiate developments that can put an end to the neoliberal transformation in health.

Of course, it would not be correct to attribute the fact the neoliberal transformation in health could not be completed in six years, and the possibility that it will not be completed, only to the struggles led under the leadership of TTB and SES. However, it would be a similar injustice to discount the impact of this campaign, and to look elsewhere for the dynamic which delayed/prevented this program aiming to marketise and to privatise health services – and which still sustains the hope for a pro-public and egalitarian health system.

References

Universal Health Insurance and the changing role of the Ministry of Health, Ministry of Health, Ankara, 2007

Restructuring of Public Administration: 9/Social Security Reform: problems and Solutions, Ankara, Prime Ministry of Turkey, April 2005

Öztürk, O., *What does health transition program solves and does not solve? Another Equitable, Free and Qualified Health System is Possible*, pp.91–100, Ankara, Union of Health and Social Security Employees

Öztürk, O., 'Notes on the struggle against neo-liberal transition of health in Turkey, 2003–2008' in: *Social Dimensions of Health Transition Program*, pp.88–121, Ankara, Revolutionary Solidarity of Health and Social Security Employees

Transformation in Health, Ministry of Health, June 2003

What does Health Transition Program promise to people and physicians/health workers in Turkey?, Ankara, Turkish Medical Association, October 2003, 1. Ed.

Health Agenda: Equal opportunity for all or domination of free market?, Ankara, Turkish Medical Association, October 1992

The last link of the pro-market destruction of health: AKP (Justice and Development Party), Ankara, Turkish Medical Association, June 2007, 1. Ed.

Epoch of decline of the right to social security, Ankara, Turkish Medical Association, November 2008, 1. Ed.

'Our view about draft law on Social Security and General Health Insurance', DİSK, KESK, TMMOB, TTB, *Voice of DİSK*, Special Supplement, May 2006

World of Medicine, Ankara, Turkish Medical Association, Special Issue, November 2005

World of Medicine, Ankara, Turkish Medical Association, Special Issue, April 2006

Community Health Conference, 10–11 November 2007, Coordination of Istanbul Professional Health Associations, Istanbul, August 2008

CHAPTER 7
Fighting privatisation in Madrid

Delia Alvarez

Anton Saiz
CAS Madrid

The CAS Madrid organisation (Anti-Health-care Privatisation Coordinating Platform of Madrid) was created in 2004, following the confirmation of the first signs of the Popular Party (PP) government's plans to start, quietly and without asking the public, an unprecedented neoliberal reform of our public health system.

We were aware of the fact that, as has been proved in other countries, the imposition of a market in health services can only lead to the increase in inequalities in access to services, and the use of patients and workers of this sector as mere instruments to generate financial profits. So we decided it was necessary to create a Coordinating Committee aimed at joining efforts and organising ourselves to defend our public health system; and as a group of professionals from the public health service (doctors, health workers and non-health personnel), joined with associations of users and neighbours, organisations such as CNT, CGT – MSE, Workers' Solidarity, the EMT trade union platform and the Health Trade Union Assembly to form CAS Madrid.

CAS is a completely independent organisation, which does not accept any kind of financial aid from any political party, business or the government. We survive thanks to volunteer work and donations, because we consider it absolutely necessary to keep our autonomy and to keep denouncing the process of privatisation of the health system, whichever party may be in power.

For years, the health policy in the Autonomous Region of Madrid has been designed to cause the continuous worsening of the public service and, by so doing, to justify its privatisation. For that reason, instead of increasing the budget for health care according to the increasing needs of an increasing population, our health authorities have been assigning to health care a clearly insufficient budget, which has ended up sending our region down to the second-to-last place among the Spanish regions in public spending per person. At the same time, contracting out to the private sector of those services considered unprofitable has increased. This has allowed the appearance of many companies which are ready to feed off the public sector. The spending deficit, together with the increase in the population and the actual freeze on the numbers of personnel, has caused an important worsening of care in all hospitals and health centres in our region. Alongside the introduction of each and every privatising measure taken, the government of Madrid employs an intense advertising campaign to disguise the reality and convince people these are important and unavoidable improvement plans.

The problem is that none of the actions taken by the right wing in Madrid go against any law: the passing back in 1997 of the State Law 15/97 "of New Forms of Management in Health Care" – approved thanks to the votes from PSOE (theoretically, a social-democratic party) as well as the PP (conservative) – opened the way to the transformation of the health-care public sector into an open market, and naturally, yet another opening for private businesses. Although the regional level Law for the Health-care Management in the Madrid Region (LOSCAM) was passed in December 2001, this Madrid decision was just the consequence of what the Law 15/97 had already legitimised four-years earlier.

Since 2005, the government of the Region of Madrid has accelerated the privatisation process, passing on to private companies the management and financial administration of eight new hospitals through a concession model, with contracts lasting at least 30 years; this model is the same as the Private Finance Initiative (PFI) which has been applied in Great Britain with the negative results we all know about, and which have even been admitted by the World Health Organization (WHO).

Taking advantage of the 2007 Budget Law, the PP (Popular Party) took another step forward in its strategy and passed the legal mechanisms which allow the conversion of the current health-care centres into "businesses of private law", together with the creation of six businesses of private law to manage "the health-care side" of the new centres (the side which, so it was claimed, would never be privatised). This system, which has been applied by the Socialist Party (PSOE) in Andalusia over the last years, tries to avoid the normal controls of public law, and to increase the working flexibility and insecurity of the workforce.

As a consequence, our health-care system has moved from being one of the best in quality tests to have the second-lowest budget for health care in Spain – the one with least doctors and nurses, and the most crowded primary-health-care surgeries. If we add the half-a-million-people increase of the population between 2003 and 2008 to the tiny current level of financing, we can easily understand the terrible situation in which we find ourselves now.

The privatisation of health care in Madrid started with the (partial) opening last year of seven new hospitals following the PFI model and another one – Valdemoro – whose management was directly given to a private firm (Capio/Apax Partners). The health-care personnel in these new hospitals come from the public system and receive their salary from the public centre they come from; the rest of the services are placed in the hands of the private business.

Alongside this, public health and mental health centres have been dismantled; the clinic analysis processing service is being outsourced; so are the most profitable radiological tests; and a privately owned macro-laboratory has been created. Also, at this time, a so-called Liberty of Choice Law is about to be passed, a law with the sole aim of fragmenting the continuity of care, and the creation of a primary-health-care system which should work as a barrier to reduce the access of the patients to the hospitals; to make this sieve work, medical personnel will receive extra incentives if they reach the perverse economic goals marked by the private sector.

The opening of the new PFI hospitals has been carried out, with 5,000 doctors and nurses who were previously employed in traditional hospitals and with a much lower than average number of beds per thousand people. Despite the information blackout practised by our authorities over the last years, the numbers do not lie: the numbers of medical personnel – doctors and nurses – are, respectively, 55% and 71% lower than in other hospitals of the same kind; for non-medical staff, the cut of personnel runs as high as 50%, and their salary conditions are much worse after contracting out.

Although the government of Madrid justifies the measures taken as being spending cuts, the cost of the PFI model has proved to be six-times more expensive than traditional funding, and the Health Care Department has to face a huge debt, with the private firms to be paid by all the tax-payers over the next 30 years. This debt places that department on the verge of bankruptcy, which is why it had to ask for loans to pay the salaries of the employees during the first months of this year.

The consequences of this privatising process are evident to most of the population:

- Worsening quality of medical care: crowded surgeries, shortages of staff, lack of organisation and care increasing deficiencies, urgent care services overloaded with work in hospitals and medical centres

- Increase in waiting lists for surgery and closed lists for first medical appointment and specialised-attention follow ups
- The transfer of patients to private centres for simple surgical interventions with no hospitalisation required
- Cuts in investment and search for economic profits as priority goals, regardless of the population's health-care needs; instability of employment for employees, which affects their freedom of diagnosis and therapy
- Lack of coordination among the levels of care; management focused on achieving economic goals and policies designed according to political affinities and not the quality of knowledge or efficiency
- Breakdown in access to and equity of the public system
- Unmotivated professionals and dissatisfaction among the population; the increase of social pressure, with frustrated expectations, the feeling of ill-treatment and abandonment by the government, low salaries and the accusations from public opinion generate an increasing lack of motivation in all workers, many of whom are quickly burnt-out; which leads to a dramatic loss of resources and achievements and an increase of absenteeism
- Increase of medical errors, and litigation caused by the lack of personnel.

What is more, a report made by the Provincial Work Inspectorate of Social Welfare, published only a few months ago, shows many irregularities in the new hospitals connected with issues such as security problems, inadequate storage and garbage disposal, general lack of personnel, construction mistakes, and a lack of the necessary instruments. This institutional report shows the new health centres have been built without the necessary conditions to offer adequate health-care assistance, without following the regulations on security at work, while the lack of staff causes a decrease in the quality of the service.

Consequently, given the fact that the privatisation model which is being installed in our country is championed and developed both by the right wing and the socialist parties, we the members of CAS Madrid will keep our independence, carrying out our work without accepting any funds from any external source.

We are sure of the fact that with the support of the communities, we must fight this battle for the abolition of the 15/97 Law, against setting economic goals on health care, and against the privatisation of the health-care services.

CHAPTER 8
Global Neoliberalism and the consequences for health-care policy in the English NHS

Clive Peedell
Consultant Clinical Oncologist, James Cook University Hospital, Middlesbrough and Member of the National Council of the British Medical Association and of its Political Board

> *Services are coming to dominate the economic activities of countries at virtually every stage of development, making services trade liberalisation a necessity for the integration of the World economy.*
> International Chamber of Commerce[1]

> *The commodification of public space has now become an aggressive Blairite objective.*
> Roy Hattersley, Labour MP (quoted in the *Guardian*, 7 November 2005)

> *All public services have to be based on a diversity of independent providers who compete for business in a market governed by Consumer choice. All across Whitehall, any policy option now has to be dressed up as "choice", "diversity", and "contestability". These are the hallmarks of the "new model public service".*
> John Denham MP, former Health Minister quoted in 2006

Introduction

According to former Health Secretary, Frank Dobson, the creation of the NHS was "Labour's greatest achievement. It is a working example of the best interests of the people in this country. It is the most popular institution in Britain"[2].

Neglect of the NHS was a principal cause of the Conservative government's downfall and a major issue that helped New Labour mobilise mass political support for a landslide election victory in 1997. Labour's election manifesto in 1997 warned that only Labour could "save the NHS" and a decade of New Labour in government has resulted in the largest-ever sustained increase in health-care spending in the history of the NHS. The King's Fund has since reported that significant improvements have been made in quality of care, with "huge progress" in the reduction of waiting times and "more and better services"[3].

However, the reform of the NHS has been described as "Labour's greatest domestic political challenge over two terms in power"[4], with NHS reforms proving to be highly unpopular both within and outside the mainstream Labour party. In 2001, David Hinchcliffe, the Labour Chair of the Health Select Committee warned that, if pushed to their logical limits, the reforms could amount to "a complete betrayal of everything that the Labour party stood for" and "would cause outrage within the mainstream Labour party circles"[5]. At the 2005 Labour party conference a resolution was passed that attacked the government's move "towards fragmenting the NHS and embedding a marketised system of providing public services with a substantial and growing role for the private sector"[6]; and in April 2005 more than two-thirds of signatories to a 1997 statement in *The Times* backing Labour's policies on health announced that they would not do so again.[7]

The government continues to deny systematic piecemeal privatisation of the NHS and are always quick to point out that health care remains "free at the point of delivery". However, despite the rhetoric, it is clear that a market-based approach has become central to health-care delivery and the role of the private sector is expanding. Labour MP, Michael Meacher summed this up well recently:

> Equity, equal rights according to need, public accountability, a professional standard of care and integrity are being replaced by targets, cost cutting, PFI top slicing of public expenditure – a service fragmentation by private interests. This is the case for health and education, housing, pensions, probation, rail, the Post Office and local government.[8]

Why have New Labour taken this controversial and unpopular route to the delivery of public services? Writing in the *New Statesman*, two Labour MPs, John Cruddas and Jon Tricket recently provided a succinct explanation:

> After years in opposition and with the political and economic dominance of neoliberalism, New Labour essentially raised the white flag and inverted the principle of social democracy. Society was no longer to be master of the market, but its servant. Labour was to offer a more humane version of Thatcherism, in that the state would be actively used to help people survive as individuals in the global economy – but economic interests would always call all the shots.[9]

Stuart Hall, Emeritus Professor of Sociology at the Open University, argued that whilst the Labour government has retained its social-democratic commitment to maintaining public services and alleviating poverty, its "dominant logic" was neoliberal: to spread "the gospel of market fundamentalism", promote business interests and values and further residualise the welfare system[10].

New Labour and global neoliberalism – the "new reality" and the "logic of accommodation"

The early 1980s saw the rise of neoliberal globalisation through the world-wide abolition of capital controls, removal of trade barriers, and computerisation. This facilitated the freedom of movement of capital and goods and services across national borders. Heavy influence promoting this approach has come from the World Trade Organisation (WTO), the World Bank, the Organisation for Economic Co-operation and Development (OECD), the European Union and the World Economic Forum. However, it is now generally acknowledged that this reality has significantly eroded the capacity of the nation state to command its own destiny because governments must retain the confidence of international asset holders by whatever policy modification is deemed necessary[11,12], otherwise they face the risk of massive capital flight with potentially very serious economic consequences[13].

After four successive election defeats (1979, 1983, 1987 and 1992), Labour's social-democratic model of Keynesian demand-management economics, progressive taxation, extending welfare spending and redistribution was no longer seen as a practicable solution[14].

This was described as the "New Reality" by New Labour "modernisers" like Peter Mandelson and led to the jettisoning of traditional "Old Labour" social-democratic policies in favour of a variant of neoliberal Thatcherism[15].

This approach would accommodate the global financial markets by promoting economic growth through the introduction of business-friendly supply-side policies aimed at freeing up markets and expanding choice, ensuring economic stability for the private sector's planning environment, strict financial management and control of public expenditure, the defeat of inflation, privatising state-owned enterprises and premises, privatising the provision of a vast array of public services, and remodelling the state's internal operations along business lines (New Public Management)[16]. This was inherently unpopular with the centre left and left, and has therefore been described as the "logic of accommodation"[17].

Thus the Labour party understood that achieving the trust of investors and market credibility was crucial to their election hopes. In opposition in the early 1990s, the Labour party went on the "Prawn Cocktail offensive" to convince the City that Labour were "the party of business". Labour's political risk premium* went from 2% in 1992 to 0.5% in 1997, thanks mainly to the promotion of policies such as the Private Finance Initiative (PFI)[15].

The abolition of the Labour party's constitutional Clause IV further appeased the City, by denouncing nationalisation and emasculating the power of the unions and the policy-making ability of the annual Labour party conference. For many commentators, this symbolised the end of Old Labour and the start of New Labour. Thus, the 1997 Labour election manifesto stated:

> In economic management, we accept the global economy as a reality and reject the isolationism and 'go-it-alone' policies of the past.

Whilst in power, Labour further achieved the trust of investors and market credibility by reducing the capacity of government to steer economic policy by a strategy of "depoliticisation". This took two main forms: firstly, the control of interest rates was transferred to the Bank of England's Monetary Policy Committee; and secondly, a binding framework of rules governing fiscal policy, designed to tie all government departments to rigorous expenditure limits, was adopted. In his Mansion House Speech in 1997, Gordon Brown said that for a government to succeed it has no option but to "convince the markets that they have the policies in place for long-term stability."

Professor Anthony King described the Blair government as the "first ever Labour government to be openly, even ostentatiously pro-business"[18]. Thus, the New Labour leadership had been "converted" from tolerating private enterprise to promoting it actively: a significant political U-turn.

---

* Political risk premium: this is the additional interest that investors take into account for political parties in power and is a measure of how business friendly they are.

New Labour's change in direction for health-care policy and the English NHS

Labour's 1997 election manifesto was opposed to privatisation of clinical services within the NHS. However, we now have a policy agenda promoting a market-driven approach to health-care delivery with active encouragement of the private sector to deliver clinical services in competition with NHS organisations, through the mechanisms of patient choice, plurality of provision, and payment by results. Thus, current government policy appears to be sympathetic to the World Trade Organisation's (WTO) General Agreement on Trade in Services (GATS), which aims to opens up service provision like health and education (which account for approximately 15% of GDP in most European countries) to direct multinational competition and ownership[19]. This is despite a statement in 2002 from the UK government that it would not take on WTO commitments that would compromise public service delivery via the NHS. This represents a major U-turn in health-care policy and it is therefore important to understand from a historical perspective how and why this happened.

Prudence and PFI

In Labour's first term in office, the 1997 white paper *The new NHS: Modern, dependable*[20] actually pushed the "divisive" internal market aside a little by recasting relationships between contractors onto a longer-term basis, and by consolidating local purchasing into primary care groups, abolishing GP fund holding in the process[21]. In addition, Labour opposed patient choice. Alan Milburn stated in June 2000 that "we are not prepared to trade off being free and fair, for efficiency and responsiveness to the demands of patients"[22].

Health policy at this stage was about continuity and incremental changes, not radical reform. This was essentially a Fabian approach and the role of the private sector was extremely limited, with the word "private" hardly mentioned in policy documents[4]. The only real evidence supporting a neoliberal approach to health-care delivery at this time was the Private Finance Initiative (PFI), which has been a key long-term attribute of the government's broad political strategy[23].

The PFI was the brainchild of Tory MP David Willetts and was introduced by the Major government in 1993, although very few schemes actually went ahead. It was initially bitterly opposed by frontbench and backbench Labour MPs, but most were eventually "converted" to the ideology of PFI to the extent that the 1997 Labour party manifesto promised to "overcome the problems that have plagued the PFI". This U-turn came about because the PFI enabled public capital spending projects to be undertaken without adding to the Public Sector Borrowing Requirement (PSBR), thus keeping public borrowing "off balance sheet". This allowed continued public service investment whilst still conforming to the Treasury's strict fiscal rules, a key part of the government's "prudent" economic strategy. It also helped New Labour to win the confidence of financial and business institutions. The NHS Private Finance Act of July 1997 removed the last doubts that the private sector had about the PFI and paved the way to billions of pounds worth of contracts.

Gordon Brown's acceptance of PFI was a deliberate attempt to distance the Labour party from the past[24], upholding its new found reputation for "sound finance", whilst at the same time building an unprecedented "vote winning" number of new hospitals and schools. He wooed financiers in 2000 when he was quoted as saying that they would be investing in "core services which the government is statutorily bound to provide and for which demand is virtually insatiable. Your revenue stream is ultimately backed by government. Where else can you get a business opportunity like that?"[25].

However, the PFI has been highly controversial and the criticisms are well documented elsewhere, mainly through the work of Professor Allyson Pollock and colleagues. Further problems are likely with the introduction of international financial reporting standards (IFRS) to the public sector, which could put billions of pounds worth of PFI deals back on the balance sheets. According to the Audit Commission, in the case of the NHS, "reclassification of PFI assets will potentially have significant financial implications for individual organisations". If current rules are not amended, NHS trusts would have to pay not only the annual service charge for their PFI buildings, but also an annual capital charge on top[26]. Unsurprisingly, the Treasury has managed to delay introduction of the IFRS until next year.

An important effect of PFI has been the significant recruitment of private-sector business advisors/consultants into the big tent of government e.g. Partnerships UK and the NHS Commercial Directorate. People who were not neutral referees but interested players were located centrally within the decision-making process. By 2007, the Commercial Directorate had a staff of 190, of whom just eight were civil servants, the other 182 being recruited from the private sector [27].

The road to privatisation, marketisation and consumerism

In keeping with strict fiscal policy, the first two years also saw Labour keeping to Tory spending plans. Unfortunately, the continued chronic underinvestment resulted in the winter crisis of 2000 and prompted Tony Blair to appear on the BBC's *Breakfast with Frost* show and famously promise that UK health spending would match the EU average within five years. The highly ambitious ten-year NHS Plan[28] was announced soon after and Gordon Brown commissioned Derek

Wanless to report on the financial state of the NHS. The report concluded that between 1972 and 1998, the cumulative underspend on the NHS compared to EU average spending was £267billion[29]. A massive injection of money was delivered to the NHS increasing GDP spend from 5.6% to 9.4%, but strings were attached in the form of a performance-driven managerialist assessment framework, which included a "target culture" and a new ratings system for NHS Trusts[30].

The subtitle of the NHS plan, "A Plan for Investment, a Plan for Reform", is important because it suggested that the government wanted something in return for its money ("Investment") i.e. significant changes to the way the NHS operated ("Reform"). A pivotal moment came when Alan Milburn signed the NHS Concordat with the Independent Healthcare Association in November 2000, which stipulated that the private sector should be considered alongside NHS bodies as potential providers of clinical services. At the time Milburn, explained to the *Guardian* (30 May 2001) that the private sector would only be used to increase the capacity of the NHS and this was "not about introducing a mixed economy into healthcare". However, by 2002, the plans for a market-driven approach to health-care delivery had become clear. In the document *Delivering the NHS Plan: Next steps on investment and reform*, it was stated that increased patient choice was to be accompanied by a market for health care. Moreover, Alan Milburn told the Health Select Committee that as long as care and treatment were freely provided by the NHS, whether it took place in a private-sector hospital or an NHS hospital was frankly a secondary consideration.

Since then, the private sector has played an ever-increasing role as the government took to the mantra of "what matters is what works". There would be "no ideological barriers" to NHS modernisation and this was born out with the publication of the *NHS Improvement Plan* in 2004, which prompted former Director of Strategy for the Department of Health, Professor Chris Ham, to state in an interview with the *Financial Times* that:

> The foundations have been laid for the complete transformation of health care delivery. We are shifting away from an integrated system, in which the National Health Service provided virtually all care, to a much more mixed one, in which the private sector will play an increasingly major part. The government has started down a road which will see the NHS increasingly become a health insurer.[31]

Choice, competition and diversity are now creating a patient-led consumerist health-care market in the English NHS, resulting in the most radical departure from previous Labour policy[32]. Two recent Labour Secretaries of State for Health provide further evidence for the increasing privatisation and marketisation agenda. Patricia Hewitt said that "no arbitrary targets should be set for limits on one provider or another"[33]. Following placement of an advert in the *European Journal* by the Department of Health Commercial Directorate inviting expressions of interest in managing the purchase of clinical services from health-care providers in the UK, Frank Dobson said: "If this is not privatisation of the Health Service, then I don't know what is".[34]

The decision to open up the NHS to the health-care market has led to a recent rash of policy initiatives, which has attracted much criticism from across the political spectrum and within the health-care sector. Politicians are at the bottom of the MORI veracity index and it is therefore of no surprise that the government has started using influential members of the medical profession (who rate at the top of the MORI veracity index) to promote their policy agenda.

The drivers of the health-care market

The "choice" agenda is about turning patients into consumers. Choice, accompanied by Payment by Results (PbR), is the main driver for market-driven health care and privatisation, and is seen as a mechanism to increase institutional efficiency, overcome producer/provider interests and empower the public. PbR (or more accurately payment by activity) has been described as the reform "which makes everything else possible"[35].

To make "choice" work, the NHS needs to provide reliable and relevant information to patients to help them make informed market choices between hospitals and clinicians etc. This information is made available through the obsessive data collection of the performance management framework of audits, inspections, monitoring and evaluation. Crucial to this whole process is the National Programme for IT (NPfIT) with its Choose and Book system and the Extended Choice Network (ECN), which allows patients to choose the hospital to which they want to be referred. The Extended Choice Network is essentially a national choice menu (for England) containing all Foundation Trusts and accredited Independent Sector providers. Unfortunately, NPfIT has been plagued with problems and the Public Accounts Committee (PAC) of the House of Commons issued a damning report, which concluded that despite a probable expenditure of £20 billion, "at the present rate of progress it is unlikely that significant clinical benefits will be delivered by the end of the contract period"[36]. The Chairman of the PAC claimed NPfIT "is the biggest IT project in the world and it is turning into the biggest disaster"[37]. However, it is obvious that the government's choice agenda can only work with a successful IT system in place and this may explain why Tony Blair appeared to rush through NPfIT and is probably the main reason why this expensive debacle has not been shelved[38].

Another important development is the step towards privatisation of practice-based commissioning (PBC) through the Framework for procuring External Support for Commissioners (FESC). This is backed by Lord Darzi's *Our NHS, Our Future* report, which suggests there should be "extensive use within every SHA of the new Framework for procuring External Support for Commissioners (FESC)". Fourteen private companies have now been approved (see Box 1) to support PCTs in their "world class commissioning" role, but it is clear that some of these firms are also health-care providers and that there are obvious potential conflicts of interest. However, the uptake of FESC has been very poor so far[39].

Box1: FESC Approved Firms

Aetna Health Services (UK) Ltd
AXA PPP Healthcare Administration Services Ltd
BUPA Membership Commissioning Ltd
Partners In Commissioning
Dr Foster Intelligence
Health Dialog Services Corporation
Humana Europe Ltd
KPMG LLP
McKesson Information Solutions UK Ltd
McKinsey & Co, IncUK
Navigant Consulting, Inc
Tribal Consulting Ltd
UnitedHealth Europe Ltd
WG Consulting

Other initiatives aimed at promoting market-based health care and increasing privatisation

A detailed discussion of the full range of initiatives and policies promoting the marketisation of the NHS is outside the scope of this article, but the following list provides plenty of examples:

1. Independent Sector Treatment Centres (ISTCs). Please refer to the recent article by Pollock and Godden in the *BMJ* for a detailed analysis[40].
2. ICATS (Integrated Clinical Assessment and Treatment Services) – these units act as intermediate steps between primary care and secondary care, but importantly have power to refer on to ISTCs.
3. Privatising GP services through Alternative Provider of Medical Services (APMS).
4. Darzi polyclinics, which are likely to be built and run by the private sector, although some Foundation Trusts may build and run polyclinics to ensure a guaranteed supply of referrals.

5. Unbundling of primary care. Services are being broken up into saleable commodities. GPs provide core services which can be "topped up" either by GPs or private providers.
6. Privatisation of NHS logistics (sold to DHL (Novation)), Oxygen supplies, pathology services (£1 billion over 5 years), ambulance services, and offshore medical secretaries.
7. Advertising of health services.
8. Independent sector use of the NHS logo. Private companies providing services as part of the Extended Choice Network can now use the NHS logo (http://www.nhsidentity.nhs.uk/ExtendedChoiceNetwork/index.htm).
9. Individualised health accounts/vouchers. This is clearly another ploy to promote the market by encouraging patients to become consumers.
10. Top up fees for new drugs and technologies. The recent Richard's review has suggested that patients should be allowed to top up their NHS care in the private sector.

Conclusion

It is clear that the government is pursuing a market-driven approach to healthcare delivery in the NHS (in England) with increasing use of the private sector. There are no signs that the new Prime Minister is going to reverse this process, and in fact we are actually seeing policies with greater emphasis on privatisation through the introduction of polyclinics and new GP health centres that will almost certainly be procured and delivered by the private sector. This should come as no surprise when considering the importance Gordon Brown placed on the neoliberal agenda to ensure economic stability. In addition, when he was Chancellor of the Exchequer, Brown had significant control over public services through the Public Service Agreements and Public Spending Reviews. Hence, much of New Labour's health policy over the past decade has his fingerprints all over it. Those hoping for a slow down in the pace of change are likely to be disappointed.

The late Robin Cook summed up this situation, shortly before his death:

> The history of social democracy can be expressed as the struggle to set limits to the market and to define those areas where priorities should be set by social policy rather than commercial forces. Yet this government is dismantling the barriers that its predecessors had erected to keep those commercial forces off the public-service turf.[41]

References

1. International Chamber of Commerce, *The Benefits of services trade liberalisation*, Policy Statement Document 03/210, September, Paris, ICC, 1999
2. Dobson, F., 'Foundation Trusts and the new health service market: What Future for the NHS?', speech to Catalyst fringe meeting at TUC Congress, 9 September 2003
3. King's Fund, *An Independent Audit of the NHS under Labour 1997–2005*, King's Fund, 2005
4. Driver, S. and Martell, L., *New Labour*, Polity Press, 2006, p.120
5. Hinchcliffe, D., *On the Record*, BBC Radio, 24 June 2001
6. Shaw, E., *Losing Labour's Soul? New Labour and the Blair Government 1997–2007*, Routledge, 2007
7. 'Doctors stick the knife into Labour', Epolitix.com, 13 April 2005, http://www.epolitix.com/latestnews/article-detail/newsarticle/doctors-stick-knife-into-labour/
8. Meacher, M., http://www.michaelmeacher.info/weblog/2007/03/
9. Cruddas, J. and Tricket, J., 'How New Labour turned toxic', *New Statesman*, 6 December 2007
10. Hall, S., 'New Labour's double shuffle', *Soundings*, 2003
11. Helleiner, E., *States and the re-emergence of Global Finance: from Bretton Woods to the 1990s*, Cornell University Press, 1994, p.173
12. Shaw, E., *Losing Labour's Soul? – New Labour and the Blair Government 1997–2007*, Routledge, 2007, p.161
13. Garrett, G. and Mitchell, D., *Globalisation and the Welfare State*, 1999, available at: http://www.yale.edu/leitner/pdf/1999-04.pdf
14. Shaw, E., *Losing Labour's Soul*, Routledge, 1997, p.10
15. Leys, C., *Market Driven Politics: Neoliberal Democracy and the Public interest*, Verso, 2003
16. Hay, C., *The Political Economy of New Labour: Labouring under false pretences?*, Manchester University Press, 1999, p.29
17. Cerny, P.G. and Evans, M., *Globalisation and public policy under New Labour*, Policy Studies, vol.25, no.1, 2004
18. King, A., 'Tony Blair's First Term' in: King, A., ed., *Britain at the Polls, 2001*, 2002
19. Pollock, A. and Price, D., 'Globalisation? Privatisation!', *Healthmatters*, issue 41, Summer 2000, pp.12–13
20. Secretary of State for Health, *The new NHS: Modern, dependable*, London, HMSO, 1997
21. Greener, I., 'The three moments of New Labour's health policy discourse', *Policy and Politics*, vol.32, no.3, 2004
22. Bosely, S., 'Controversial health list ranks UK 18th in world', *Guardian Unlimited*, 21 June 2000
23. Greenaway, J., Salter, B. and Hart, S., 'The evolution of a "Meta-Policy": The Case of the Private Finance Initiative and the Health Sector', *British Journal of Politics and International Relations*, 2004, 6 (4)
24. Keegan, W., *The Prudence of Mr Gordon Brown*, Wiley, 2003
25. Gordon Brown, quoted on *File on Four*, BBC Radio 4, 2004
26. Audit Commission, *IFRS Briefing paper: Managing the transition to international financial reporting standards*, 2007
27. Timmins, N., 'Private Sector role in pioneering healthcare scheme to be slashed', *Financial Times*, 15 November 2007
28. Secretary of State for Health, *The NHS Plan – A plan for investment, a plan for reform*, London, HMSO, 2000
29. Wanless, D., *Securing Our Future Health: Taking A Long-Term View*, HM Treasury, 2002
30. Greener, I., 'The three moments of New Labour's health policy discourse', *Policy and Politics*, vol.32, no.3, 2004, p.308
31. Timmins, N., 'Election 2005', *Financial Times*, 19 April 2005
32. Robinson, R. and Bevan, G., *Economic ideas and political Constraints: 15 years of health policy reform in the UK*, LSE Health and Social Care, 2002
33. Department of Health, Speech by Patricia Hewitt MP to the Institute for Public Policy Research, 19 September 2006
34. Frank Dobson, quoted in *Guardian*, 30 June 2006
35. Timmins, N., 'Use of Private Healthcare in the NHS', *BMJ*, 331, 12 November 2005

36. House of Commons, *Public Accounts – Twentieth report*, 26 March 2007, available at: http://www.publications.parliament.uk/pa/cm200607/cmselect/cmpubacc/390/39002.htm
37. Hope, C., 'Patients won't benefit from £12 billion IT project', *Telegraph*, 18 April 2007
38. Collins, T., 'Secret Downing Street Papers revealed Blair rushed NHS IT', ComputerWeekly.com, 18 February 2008, available at: http://www.computerweekly.com/Articles/2008/02/18/229447/secret-downing-street-papers-reveal-tony-blair-rushed-nhs.htm
39. Mitchell, P., 'What a mess', *Health Investor*, April 2008
40. Pollock, A. and Godden, S., 'Independent sector treatment centres: evidence so far', *BMJ*, 2008; 336: 421–4
41. Robin Cook, quoted in *Guardian*, 17 June 2005

CHAPTER 9
Combating health inequalities amidst the credit crisis

Dr Onteeru Reddy
Public Health Nutritionist, UK, working in Public Health, NHS Berkshire West[1]

Introduction and background

Alan Johnson, then Secretary of State for Health, said in a speech three years ago:

> In 1937, Attlee wrote that the aim of socialism should be… "to see that every family in the country has a house with electric light and power for cooking, central heating, refrigerator and plenty of floor space… one in fact that is well furnished with everything that a modern housewife needs."
>
> But although everyone is now much better off in absolute terms, inequality has flourished – as the gap between those at the top of society and those at the bottom has widened, across many areas of national life, including health.
>
> Since the 1930s, despite the creation of the NHS, massive social reforms and unparalleled scientific advances, the gap in mortality between professional and unskilled men has more than doubled. There can be no more chilling form of

---
1   The views expressed in this article are the author's own and do not in any way represent those of his employer.

inequality than someone's social status at birth determining the timing of their death.

The nation's health has improved massively since the introduction of the NHS. But still a man living in Manchester is likely to die almost nine years before a man living in the Royal Borough of Kensington & Chelsea. Infant mortality amongst low-skilled workers is almost twice that amongst professionals. And, for every stop on the Jubilee line between Westminster and Canning Town, life expectancy goes down by one year.

(Johnson, 2007)

The credit crisis and its impact on health

This impact is likely to grow in the current financial crisis. The 'Britain Under Pressure' report commissioned by Friends Provident warns that the credit crunch could have a dramatic impact on the nation's health (Medical News Today, 2008; Friends Provident News, 2008; Montia, 2008).

The report suggests that almost 29 million people in the UK, or nearly two-thirds of adults, feel more stressed, less fit, less healthy and more prone to illness than they did three years ago. The report, which is a joint venture with the Blood Pressure Association, found that 56% of respondents were spending less on food, with 15% cutting back on fresh fruit and vegetables. A further 16% said they expected to reduce spending on fresh fruit and vegetables in the next six months. 21% of respondents were not using gyms as often as in 2008. 7% admitted they had been drinking more alcohol since the onset of the credit crisis, and 9% anticipated a rise in alcohol consumption during the next six months. Worries about the economic situation left 19% sleeping less and 15% working longer hours.

According to Professor Graham Macgregor of the Blood Pressure Association, "the effect on lifestyles of the credit crunch plus a lack of concern over long term health is putting the nation at risk of a rise in blood pressure rates" (Medical News Today, 2008; Friends Provident News, 2008).

In February 2008, a team of social epidemiologists from the University of Cambridge published what it claimed to be the first study into the relationship between a banking crisis and mortality. According to the research, the stress created by a global banking crisis could kill thousands of people around the world. High-income countries such as the UK and US might see a 6.4% rise in deaths from heart disease, whereas in low-income countries mortality rates could increase by 26% (Montia, 2008; Stuckle et al., 2008).

The NHS is not immune to the impact of other wider economic consequences, like high commodity prices, high and variable fuel prices, food prices and the low value of sterling affecting most other businesses nationally. The NHS will feel the recession, trying to balance a rising demand while also trying to find savings. For NHS managers, in common with the rest of the country, challenging times are ahead.

Economic impact of the credit crisis

NHS income could be under threat from the Treasury (Appleby, 2008). NHS employment costs could go up due to increases in national insurance and VAT. NHS pensionable age and contributions could be affected in future. A further economic downturn could increase the demand and pressure on the NHS as a consequence of greater fuel and income poverty, reduction in pension funds and pensions and increased ill health and mortgage repossessions.

Apart from the pressures on NHS funding, "the combined effect of the credit crunch and recession on the population's health and wellbeing will increase ill health and demand on healthcare services" (Appleby, 2008).

Creative approaches to deal with the crisis

Both commissioners and providers will need to increase the focus on the 'better care, better value' indicators in a way that maximises health gain and improves productivity. NHS organisations can no longer depend on historical budgets and go on over-spending because deficits pile up year upon year, making it harder each year to reach a balance; there is a very strong link between the best financial management and the best standards of patient care (Ham, 2009).

We could adopt creative approaches:

- Early identification of issues and providing help to organisations with the biggest problems.
- Share best practice; get better care for people with better value for money. More health promotion and prevention; better support in the community for people with long-term conditions; more personal, flexible and local services.
- Joint strategic working partnerships between primary care trusts in each region to help each other with joint funding and saving opportunities. Encourage savings rather than spending.

The focus therefore should be on prioritising basic health care, cutting down costs, achieving savings and improving productivity.

New innovative partnerships

In the NHS, voluntary and community sectors, social care and local government could work together to provide services to the community in areas of neglect and need.

For example, self-help groups such as Calorie Killers, which is supported by the FAB Project and the Braunstone Community Food Project, offer a model where different agencies backed by government investment join up to secure better health for hard-to-reach communities (Calorie Killers, 2009).

According to the respected Psychiatric Morbidity Survey (2000) one in six of us could be diagnosed as having depression or chronic anxiety disorder, which means that one family in three is affected. Many of these people remain on incapacity benefits as they are unable to seek work. In previous recessions, we have seen the number of people on income support benefits rise, so tackling this is one element of action being taken to prevent this happening again (Centre for Economic Performance, 2006).

About one in three of the 1.3 million people claiming long-term incapacity benefit in the UK have a mental health problem, mostly mild to moderate depression. Improving Access to Psychological Therapies (IAPT) has the potential to save the economy millions of pounds by helping people with mild to moderate depression to get back into employment, and off incapacity benefit. The two pilots – one in Doncaster, South Yorkshire and the other in Newham, East London – were announced in May 2006. The two sites were chosen because they serve very different demographics with different health needs, and they offer different treatment models such as community-based, voluntary-sector-led, and employer-led (Government News, 2006).

Such an investment could help to provide more training for staff in primary-health-care teams, helping them to recognise mental health problems early as well as to develop the public's skills in managing their mental wellbeing as a life skill. Complementary services like increased availability of debt advice and family counselling would enable the NHS to support people back to work.

There are conflicting reports about the impact of the economic downturn on disadvantaged people in the labour market and the numbers of people on incapacity benefits. However, the government seems determined to act to prevent people falling into long-term unemployment.

Conclusion

The current credit crisis is probably the worst economic crisis and recession since the Great Depression. However, the overall impact of the downturn on the NHS needs to be watched. There is a debate about the extent of cuts the Department of Health and the Treasury are likely to pursue over medium to longer terms.

We need to ensure that, throughout the NHS, there are the right incentives for continuous improvement, innovation and better value for money, moving from a provider-led NHS to a patient-led NHS. "Patient choice saves patients' lives" (Ham, 2009).

"Europeans have been too slow to do a fiscal stimulus. But the human suffering is going to be much greater on the other side of the Atlantic because Europeans don't lose their health care when they lose their jobs… When Americans lose their jobs, they fall into the abyss." Hence we should continue to provide universal health care. "This is exactly the time when the importance of having a decent social safety net is driven home to everybody" (Bradley et al., 2009).

Strategic partnership, working between the NHS, local government, voluntary and community sectors and social care, targeting the neediest, with proper utilisation of social marketing strategies, will be the key to success.

References

Appleby, J. (2008) 'The credit crisis and health care', *BMJ, 2008*, 337:a2259, available at: http://www.bmj.com/content/337/bmj.a2259.full

Bradley, B., Roubini, N., Soros, G., Krugman, Ferguson, N., et al. (2009) 'The Crisis and How to Deal with It, *New York Review of Books*, 56, 10

Calorie Killers (2009) 'FAB Project and the Braunstone Community Food Project', Braunstone Health & Social Care Centre, Leicester City PCT, available at: http://caloriekillers.co.uk/component/content/frontpage

Centre for Economic Performance (2006) *The Depression Report: A New Deal for Depression and Anxiety Disorders*, Mental Health Policy Group, London School of Economics and Political Science

Friends Provident News (2008) 'Credit crunch hits the nation's long-term health, says Friends Provident', available at: http://www.friendsprovident.co.uk/common/layouts/subSectionLayout.jhtml;jsessionid=FWLJJPSRXEF5CCWCDYYCFGAKYIPDIIWA?pageId=fpcouk/SitePageHTML%3APress+Release+Display+Page+Rebranded+Media&repositoryItemId=fpcouk/pressreleases%3Afppr08092008creditcrunchhealth&pageNum=1

Government News (2006) 'Doncaster Talking Therapies Pilot sees 1,000 in just three months – Rosie Winterton celebrates success', available at: http://www.gov-news.org/gov/uk/news/doncaster_talking_therapies_pilot_sees_1000/58268.html

Ham, C. (2009) *Learning from the best: What the NHS needs to do to implement high quality care for all*, NHS Institute of Innovation and Improvement, available at: http://www.hsmc.bham.ac.uk/news/pdfs/Learning_from_the_Best_Final_PDF.pdf

Johnson, A. (2007) 'The Healthy Society', Speech in the House of Commons, 12 September, Department of Health Speeches, the National Archives, available at: http://webarchive.nationalarchives.gov.uk/20100509080731/http://www.dh.gov.uk/en/MediaCentre/Speeches/DH_078397

Medical News Today (2008) 'Britain Under Pressure – The Blood Pressure "Ticking Time Bomb"', Hypertension web news, available at: http://www.medicalnewstoday.com/articles/120733.php

Montia, G. (2008) 'Credit crisis impacts the health of the nation', *Daily Insurance Industry News, Insurance Daily*, available at: http://www.insurancedaily.co.uk/2008/09/11/credit-crisis-impacts-the-health-of-the-nation/

Psychiatric Morbidity Survey (2000) available at: http://www.statistics.gov.uk/downloads/theme_health/psychmorb.pdf

Stuckle, D., Meissner, C.M., Lawrence, P. and King, L.P. (2008) 'Can a bank crisis break your heart?, *Globalization and Health*, 2008, 4:1, available at: http://www.globalizationandhealth.com/content/4/1/1

CHAPTER 10
'Save our hospital' campaigns in England
Why do some hospital campaigns succeed?
A preliminary exploration

Sally Ruane
Deputy Director of the Health Policy Research Unit, De Montfort University, Leicester

Introduction

Over the past few years, English health policy has been dominated by the reconfiguration of health services. This has involved the centralisation of some hospital services into fewer, larger units (including some maternity and paediatric services and accident and emergency (A&E) services) on the one hand and the transfer of some other hospital services into the 'community' on the other. This is undermining many district general hospitals (DGHs) across England and, partly because of the reduced local access which can result and partly because there are significant problems with the 'evidence base' for these policies, they have been and are being contested by the establishment of numerous local 'save-our-hospital' campaigns. Many of these exhibit great creativity and imagination but, to date, there has been limited academic interest in them.

This paper examines a small number of save-our-hospital campaigns in England. Some of these campaigns have succeeded in achieving their objectives; the others have not. In three cases, the outcome remains uncertain at the time of writing. This paper highlights a number of campaign features and seeks to compare and contrast factors which may have contributed to a campaign's success or failure.

The paper is based on preliminary research for a bigger project investigating popular campaigns to save hospital services[1]. This preliminary research draws overwhelmingly on internet sources, particularly the websites developed specifically to support and promote the campaign and forms part of an audit exercise to ascertain where across England save-our-hospital campaigns have been mounted. The picture presented here, therefore, has been put together from internet sources and does not benefit from the greater detail, subtlety and nuance possible when interviews with key activists or direct observation, participant or otherwise, are undertaken. The internet search revealed thirty-six campaigns which have been undertaken in recent years or are currently being conducted. This paper draws on eight of them. These limitations should be borne in mind as a significant qualification to the analysis offered.

Background

The reconfiguration of hospital services currently underway is one of the most extensive redesigns of health services since the founding of the NHS. In recent years, some 60 reconfigurations involving 'core' services such as accident and emergency (A&E), inpatient paediatric and maternity units have been envisaged (Carvel, 2006). The concentration of these services into fewer, larger units and the downgrading of some district general hospitals have provoked a number of popular protests. Whilst campaigns share a local focus and principally defensive character, preliminary research suggests they vary in terms of membership, scale, capacity, success in popular engagement, political flavour and overall objectives. While some studies of local protests exist (e.g. Mandelstam, 2006), a thorough-going comparative analysis does not.

Reconfiguration proposals and the centralisation of hospital services are ostensibly being driven by a number of factors, some of which are within the control of local health bodies and some of which are not. These include a range of government policies such as *Care Closer to Home* and strengthened commissioning (Department of Health, 2003; 2004; 2006). In addition, local reconfigurations are shaped by a belief that better health care can be provided in fewer, larger units; staffing pressures arising from the effects of the *European Working Time Directive*, *Modernising Medical Careers* and from recruitment difficulties; changing morbidity patterns with an increase in chronic conditions (such as diabetes, obesity and asthma) considered to be more appropriately treated in the community; developments in medical technology such as telemedicine; and revised staffing guidelines in some areas such as maternity services (e.g. see Nicholson, 2006; Academy of Medical Royal Colleges, 2007;

---

[1] I am particularly indebted to Dr Kathryn Jones, Health Policy Research Unit, De Montfort University.

Farrington-Douglas and Brooks, 2007). Last, but not least, severe financial constraints arising from a combination of local factors and national policies are shaping service redesign in some areas. Those arguing for reconfiguration include not only politicians but also some major professional groups such as the Royal College of Surgeons (RCSEng, 2006).

However, reconfigurations are proving highly contentious. Along with resistance from local residents in some areas, challenges to the official justifications for such reconfigurations have been made by academics and professionals (e.g. Byrne and Ruane, 2007; CEM and BAEM, no date). Questions arise, therefore, as to the characteristics and strategies of the campaigns which emerge as well as the use they make of evidence and argument and these themes are explored in discussion below about how successful and failed campaigns differ. It is not even clear to what extent these campaigns should be conceived of as 'pressure groups' or 'social movements' about which there exists a considerable literature (e.g. Grant, 2000; Byrne, 1997). The term 'protest politics' seems to fit better. This is a vaguer and broader term, encompassing spontaneous protestof limited life-span through to more structured, complex and enduring campaigns (see Jordan and Maloney, 1996; Ridley and Jordan, 1998). Perhaps where the current research differs from much reported in that literature concerns its comparison of similar campaigns addressing similar causes.

The reconfiguration process and where power lies

The decision-making process relating to the reconfiguration of hospital services and the withdrawal of major services from one location and their transfer to another is a rather long drawn-out affair because health service planning is very complex. We do not intend here to describe this in detail but instead draw attention to some of its key features. There is usually a period of several years between the moment when discussions begin within the local (up to county-wide) health service regarding changes to hospital provision and the point at which services are actually closed or reorganised. During this period, a campaign can take off (and perhaps fizzle out). The process is likely to entail the formulation of options, a process in which there may be some 'public involvement' and there will be a formal public consultation exercise on specified options set out in a public consultation document produced by the relevant health service body. It is important to note that the formal public consultation exercise, which typically lasts three-to-four months, forms only a limited part of a much broader and longer process. It is this broader and longer process which offers the context for the campaign. We know of no instances where an NHS body has withdrawn its proposals for reconfiguration on the basis of a lack of public endorsement secured through the formal consultation exercise. Such a withdrawal has sometimes occurred, however, as some campaigns here demonstrate, as a result of a more widely waged and sustained local battle.

The public are not, therefore, formally empowered to halt the determined efforts of the local NHS to change services; they can only be *consulted* when a substantial change is proposed. The only formal checks on the power of NHS bodies are the action of the Secretary of State (in fact, even this is not the case with Foundation Trusts which are regulated by Monitor) or the action of the courts, following a judicial review (for instance, where a court rules that the local NHS body has undertaken inadequate public consultation). In order to trigger the involvement of the Secretary of State, a campaign must secure a decision by the local Health Overview and Scrutiny Committee (HOSC) (or relevant joint HOSC where affected health services cover several local authority areas) to refer the NHS decision to the Secretary of State. A HOSC has a duty to oversee and scrutinise the local health service and has the power to refer to the Secretary of State where it is convinced that a health service decision is not in the best interests of the local health service or where it considers that the consultation undertaken by the NHS has not been adequate in terms of content, time allowed and ability of affected individuals and groups to participate. Typically, a HOSC will invite local NHS personnel to make presentations and answer questions at HOSC committee meetings in order to describe, explain and justify policy and practice. Where a major change of service is proposed and being consulted on, the HOSC may also invite members of the public and interested groups to submit evidence or opinion direct to the HOSC. It might even organise a dedicated day or two-day inquiry in which key protagonists can offer oral evidence.

As a campaign can hope to exert little influence via the formal public consultation exercise undertaken by the NHS itself, it must aim to persuade the HOSC to refer the NHS decision to the Secretary of State. The Secretary of State then has the option of requesting the Independent Reconfiguration Panel, a national body, to conduct its own investigation into the local decision and to make recommendations to the Secretary of State. At the end of that process, which can take many months and which offers a new space for campaigning and a new audience (the Panel) for campaign messages and evidence, the Secretary of State makes a decision as to whether the NHS can proceed as it had hoped or must develop new proposals. All the successful campaigns considered in this paper persuaded the relevant HOSC to refer; the Sussex campaigns whose outcome remains uncertain also persuaded the HOSC to refer. The failed campaigns did not persuade the relevant HOSC to refer.

Use of internet sources and structure of the paper

This paper focuses on a limited number of possible explanations for the success of some campaigns and the failure of others. These are first, the range of specific campaigning methods such as use of petitions, marches and public rallies. The second explanation investigated is the use of evidence and clarity of argument presented by the campaign. Finally, we examine the campaign's relationship to its environment and key actors within that environment. This part is divided into three aspects: first, the relationship to different constituent parts of the local population whose interests the campaign claims to be safeguarding; second, the relationship to other save-our-hospital campaigns in the region; and, third, the relationship to the local medical profession.

But first, it is necessary to say a few words about the methods used and the evidence offered in this paper. As mentioned, above this forms part of a larger study of save-our-hospital campaigns. The evidence presented here is drawn from an early scoping exercise in which the internet, along with other approaches, was used to identify the existence of current or relatively recent hospital campaigns in England. By relatively recent, we refer principally to campaigns during New Labour's second and third terms in office during which period, large-scale hospital reconfiguration has become more systematically pursued. The methods upon which this paper is based, therefore, consist of the analysis of the internet presence of the campaign. To a large extent, this is its own website presence and the content of that website. To a lesser extent, it involves the results of pursuing various internet 'leads' from the campaign website: such as following up the related documentation produced by the relevant health service bodies (Strategic Health Authority (SHA), Primary Care Trust (PCT) or Hospital Trust) or newspaper coverage or local authority HOSC papers or the websites of local members of parliament (MPs). This search of other websites has not attempted to be comprehensive but rather has been undertaken on a 'need to' basis. Thus, the main thrust of the evidence presented here comes from campaigns' own websites and their conscious self-presentation. The observations made in this paper have not been checked with the campaigners themselves.

The dual role of the campaign website as both method and data should be acknowledged and, inevitably, there are significant limitations to this. Most obviously, if this window on the campaign is scant and thin (as it is, for instance, in the Save the QE2 campaign in Welwyn), the campaign itself appears thin. By contrast, a well-maintained website offers a wealth of data relating to the campaign. Although it is not possible to be absolute about this, it is not unreasonable to suppose that a weak website may suggest a lack of campaign capacity while a rich, multifaceted and informative one may suggest strong campaign capacity.

Another limitation is that this method does not give much voice to views which challenge the campaign's perspective or understanding of the facts. Nor does it permit more than a partial picture to be portrayed: for instance, the absence of some parties from mention on the campaign website might possibly be interpreted as an indicator that that party was not perceived by the campaign to be playing a key role in local efforts to save the hospital (although even that could be questioned) but could certainly not be taken as evidence that that party was not involved at all. In addition, the full range of alliances and their complexity are difficult to ascertain without interviews or discussions with key campaign actors, in other words, without evidence obtained through the involvement of 'human participants'. Nor can gaps in the campaign website be filled.

In addition, the campaigns selected for analysis here were not chosen because they were in some way representative of all save-our-hospital campaigns with a website presence. Instead, they were selected because they include both successful and failed outcomes and because they were conducted in diverse regional contexts.

So, there are some significant limitations to the data presented here and the arguments developed as explanations of campaign success or failure should be seen as preliminary and tentative and requiring further research.

It is also worth diverting briefly to make some observations about hospital campaigns. Although, we refer to campaign outcomes, this should not necessarily be taken to imply that the campaign has come to an end. At the time of writing, all of these campaigns retain a campaign website and update it at least every few months and in some cases much more frequently, with the exception of the Support the Princess Royal which removed its campaign website at some point between February and June 2009. Some campaigns remain 'on alert' (our phrase, not theirs) (such as the Support St Richard's) because hospital reconfiguration is ongoing and the IRP's investigation has been suspended but not at the time of writing withdrawn. Some campaigns continue with a broader outlook, drawing public attention to other health service reforms to which they object (such as the contracting out under 'alternative provider' contracts of GP surgeries in Hastings). One campaign, which pre-dated by several decades the struggle of the 2000s to retain a local hospital, continues even though the hospital has now been closed down (Dacorum Hospital Action Group in Hemel Hempstead, set up in 1974). So save-our-hospital campaigns are not necessarily 'bounded' in terms of time or scope – or, at least, these boundaries are blurred.

The campaigns

The campaigns chosen fall into three geographical areas:

Keep the Horton General (Banbury, Oxfordshire)
Close major services (inpatient paediatrics, maternity and A&E) and transfer from Banbury to Oxford 23 miles away. Campaign started 2006 and concluded successfully following Independent Reconfiguration Panel (IRP) investigation in 2008.
http://www.keepthehortongeneral.org/

Hands off The Conquest (Hastings, East Sussex)
Began 2006; initially A&E and maternity; then just maternity but campaign was prepared to defend all 'core' services. Threat was to centralise in either Hastings or Eastbourne. Concluded successfully with retention of services on both sites in 2008 following IRP report.
http://www.handsofftheconquest.org.uk/

Save the DGH (Eastbourne, East Sussex)
Began 2006; initially A&E and maternity; then just maternity but campaign was prepared to defend all 'core' services. Threat was to centralise in either Hastings or Eastbourne. Concluded successfully with retention of services on both sites in 2008 following IRP report.
http://www.savethedgh.org.uk/

Support the Princess Royal (Haywards Heath, Mid Sussex)
Campaign launched August 2006 after Strategic Health Authority's (SHA) *Creating an NHS Fit the Future* proposed several options, each of which involved downgrading at least two Mid/West Sussex hospitals. Proposals for downgrading lifted at least temporarily following merger of Worthing and Chichester hospitals. MP confident of success, January 2009.
http://supportprh.org

KWASH (Keep Worthing and Southlands Hospitals) (Worthing, West Sussex)
Began 2006; threatened with loss of major services following *Creating an NHS Fit for the Future*. W. Sussex Health Overview and Scrutiny Committee (HOSC) referred 2008; IRP investigation suspended when merger talks (with Chichester) announced autumn 2008.
http://www.kwash.org

Support St Richard's (Chichester, West Sussex)
Began 2006; threatened with loss of major services following *Creating an NHS Fit for the Future*. W. Sussex HOSC referred 2008; IRP investigation suspended when merger talks (with Worthing) announced autumn 2008.
http://www.supportstrichards.co.uk/

Save the Hemel / Save Hemel Hospital (Hemel Hempstead, West Hertfordshire)
Ongoing campaign but proposal to close maternity and special baby care 2001 (closed 2002). SHA *Investing in Your Health* (2002) proposed consolidation of major hospital services on two county sites (in West Herts either Watford or Hemel); proposed to be Watford 2006. Two local campaigns with unclear relationship between them. Hospital effectively closed March 2009.
http://www.savehemelhospital.com/
http://www.savehemel.com/

Save QE2 / Hospital SOS (Welwyn Garden City, North Hertfordshire)
SHA *Investing in Your Health* (2002) proposed consolidation of major hospital services on two county sites (in North Herts initially Hatfield, then Stevenage). Campaign launched 2005 to safeguard major services. 2007 – HOSC declares consultation flawed but refuses to refer. 2008 – campaigners decide against judicial review and terminate campaign in failure. The two websites reflect a change in the title of the campaign rather than two different campaigns.
http://www.savetheqe2.com/
http://www.hospitalsos.com/

In this chapter, the campaigns will be referred to by place (e.g. Hemel rather than Dacorum Hospital Action Group) unless the precise name of the campaign is important.

Possible factors in explaining success or failure

(1) General campaigning methods

It is not unreasonable to suppose that it might be possible to distinguish the successful from the unsuccessful by their overall campaigning methods: for example, their use of petitions, marches, stunts, use by the local MP of Prime Minister's Questions and so forth. It is possible to identify a large number of specific methods from the websites and some of these are accompanied by a short narrative account and/or photographs. The following list shows some of the methods identified:

Petition
Leaflet/poster
March
Rally picnic and/or family event
Vigil
Stunts
Filmed ambulance trip
Sponsored bike ride or walk
Walk/lobby of Westminster or Whitehall
Meeting with PM
Seeking sponsorship from local businesses
Attend NHS meetings
Submit written response to consultation
Submit views to HOSC
Make use of local media
Local MP makes speech in parliament
Publicise high-level/celebrity support
Write to professionals for views
Use website to report news updates, post pictures, invite personal stories, advertise events and invite personal actions, provide copies of petition, poster etc.

In practice, however, many of these methods or devices were used by many or all campaigns and were no predictor of outcome. The methods appear to be the bread and butter of hospital campaigning. For instance, all campaigns used petitions and public events, all campaigns made use of the local media and all campaigns took their demands to Westminster in some form or another. The majority of campaigns, including successful and unsuccessful ones, staged stunts (such as hands-around-the-hospital, a bed push carrying signed petition sheets), reported the views of professionals explicitly supporting the stance of the campaign and made use of a logo.

It appears the use of specific methods does not itself allow a determination of which campaigns will succeed and which will not.

(2) Use of evidence and clarity of argument

Use of evidence should not be seen as the same as the clarity of argument offered. Clarity of argument requires coherence, logic and consistency. It can be put forward – and be persuasive – without any accompanying evidence. The compiling and presentation of evidence is another matter and requires not merely awareness of key arguments but also access to 'facts'. We expected at the outset that the use of evidence might be very significant in persuading both public and decision-makers about the rightness/worthiness of a campaign but there are significant differences in the use of evidence among successful campaigns.

The Keep the Horton General campaign in Banbury was the most 'cerebral' of the campaigns studied here and was selected for this comparison partly because of this. Its website shows that it collated, analysed and presented masses of evidence, especially quantitative evidence. It offered evidence relating to specifics of the local situation, including: travel times by car and by ambulance (included video) between Banbury and Oxford (to show how much longer it would take patients to reach a hospital); statistics on how often GPs are told there is no acute capacity at Oxford and so must refer to Horton; statistics on how many children from all hospitals are referred to Horton because of lack of capacity in Oxford; and information relating to population growth and immigration in the local area. All these items of evidence were presented to demonstrate that the capacity provided by the Horton was essential.

As well as compiling statistics relating to the specifics of the local situation, the Banbury campaigners also drew on wider debates within health care and health policy. These included national debates, reports and policy development relating to the wider national discussion on the future of District General Hospitals (DGHs); the safety of midwife-led units and desirable distance from consultant-led units, quoting the Royal College of Obstetricians and Gynaecologists and the Academy of Medical Royal Colleges on this. Campaigners quoted the Children's Surgical Forum report (RCSEng, 2007) which criticises the drift of children's surgery away from DGHs and linked this explicitly to the local NHS proposals which did not resist this drift. Campaigners addressed issues raised by Tooke's review of medical training (Tooke et al., 2008) and quoted the then Secretary of State for Health, Alan Johnson, when he stated that 20 miles was a bit far for a woman in labour to travel. They also invoked wider, more generic policy arguments where it was useful to do so: for example, on choice.

But perhaps as significant is the way in which this evidence is used. Statistical information is presented in a more simple form on the website for general consumption – i.e. for use by all members of the public accessing the website – but is also, in one document which was submitted to the IRP, embedded in a complex and sophisticated narrative of analysis, explicitly drawing out implications. It was used for the IRP in a way which demonstrates the knowledgeability of the campaign team and communicates that the campaign is founded upon reason and has solid foundations in fact.

The evidence makes reference to the views of professionals which adds to credibility. Evidence is also compiled in a way which requires and reinforces collaboration with other organisations in the community. For example, the

'SAVE OUR HOSPITAL' CAMPAIGNS IN ENGLAND

filmed ambulance trip between Banbury and Oxford required collaboration with the St John ambulance and the ambulance travel times were obtained through consulting the Central Ambulance Trust. Where wider policy debates are drawn on, they are applied to and interpreted for the local context.

Evidence was also used in a way which undermines the credibility of the hospital Trust by contrasting the facts with the Trust's claims and giving the impression that the Trust is not being honest. For instance, the Oxford Hospital Trust claimed that ambulances could reach the hospital in 'under 40 minutes' but the Central Ambulance Trust's figures on ambulance transfer times found that only a tiny proportion of ambulances reached the Oxford Hospital in under 40 minutes.

So the Banbury campaign approach was to give facts and draw out consequences. But its approach was also to do reputational damage to the Trust while enhancing its own status as (and implicit claim to be) accurate, honest, informative and dependable. It implied or stated explicitly that the Hospital could not be trusted to play by the rules; could not be trusted to manage resources and be able to cost plans appropriately; and could not be trusted to state the facts accurately or make accurate claims. It used the Healthcare Commission's rating of the Trust as 'weak' in its use of resources and the Trust's approach to the post-consultation phase and manipulation of public involvement, especially the Trust's publication of the medical reports before that of the (critical) Stakeholder Panel, as further evidence.

As well as providing arguments and evidence on the website and at public meetings, the campaigners wrote formal reports and responses, for instance to the HOSC and to the IRP and they participated in the deliberations of the Stakeholder Panel and the composition report. Arguments used include the fact that the Oxford Hospital Trust had a staffing crisis and might not be able to cope with A&E whilst Horton was fully staffed; that the proposed reliance on community nurses was flawed because of gaps in provision and the absence of recruitment plans; that services should be organised for patients and not for staff; and the 'domino effect' (that once some services were removed, others would follow because of the inter-dependencies of many hospital services). The website suggested a number of arguments members of the public might use in their letters to the IRP. In presenting evidence, campaigners demonstrated their own ability to reason and claimed medical and public opinion were united.

By contrast the unsuccessful Hemel campaign gave less emphasis to evidence. Limited wider arguments and evidence were used. For example, reference was made to the Academy of Royal Medical Colleges report and to the Sheffield research on ambulance times to justify keeping A&E (Nicholl et al., 2007). Figures relating to PCT per-capita-funding differences between

Hemel Hempstead and the towns represented by members of the government were used to argue that Hemel was under-funded and to imply that the Department of Health was partisan in its allocation of resources. Generally, though, the campaign made use of scant statistical evidence.

More local arguments were used but generally without statistical back-up. One set of arguments rested on favourable comparisons with the Watford Hospital to which services are expected to transfer. Hemel's hospital was described as a modern and maintained facility whilst Watford General needed expensive repairs. Hemel was described as having a good road system whilst Watford was very congested, especially on (football) match days. Additional arguments included: the fact that Watford did not have sufficient bed capacity to take on the provision of A&E services for both towns; that there was no provision for extra paramedics; that savings per head would be small relative to loss of service; that Hemel Hempstead is the largest town in the county of Hertfordshire; that bureaucracy could be cut to make savings; that some Hemel facilities had received recent investment which would be wasted were the hospital to close, including the birthing unit and the stroke unit. Campaigners also argued that they paid their taxes and correspondingly wanted their services, and even that loss of services affected the right to life and human rights.

However, although the Save the Hemel campaign makes limited use of statistical evidence, it does make use of a different kind of evidence. It requests that members of the public send in their personal stories. Although these were not presented on a dedicate webpage (as they were in some other campaigns), they did seem to be taken up on a news updates page which related evolving developments. Most powerfully, these included individual tales of the difficulties of accessing the Watford General in a reasonable time because of heavy traffic, match-day congestion and police diversions and these were used to create the impression of nightmarish difficulty and threats to life.

Despite the different use of evidence and more modest use of quantitative evidence in comparison with the Banbury campaign, in common with the Banbury campaign, the Hemel campaign attacked the reputation of the NHS Trust. The Trust board was depicted as incompetent and failing, with examples given of previous errors of judgement; and there were repeated calls for the Trust board to resign (including by other local actors such as MPs). The 'Fact or Fiction' leaflet of the Trust was marred by typing errors which created confusion and the website created the impression of Trust chaos. Campaigners implied that the Trust lacked local independence and that a report commissioned by the Trust on closing the Hemel hospital could not be seen as credible since it had been authored by someone who formerly worked for Neil Kinnock and was described in the *Mail* as a 'spin doctor' for Labour. Campaigners claimed that the public response to public consultation has been ignored.

However, it is difficult to sustain any conclusion that successful campaigns made greater use of quantitative evidence while failed campaigns relied more on personal stories or anecdotes. In terms of its use of evidence, the Save the DGH (District General Hospital) campaign in Eastbourne was more similar to the Hemel campaign than to the Banbury campaign. Like Hemel, the Eastbourne campaign provided some limited quantitative evidence but used argument more and, like Hemel, it made use of individual stories to convey the need to retain local hospital services.

In Eastbourne's case, the website presentation of quantitative evidence is largely confined to the videos of speeches addressing a public rally held at one point in the campaign. There is a much stronger deployment of evidence through the personal stories and perspectives of individuals invited to email the campaign via its 'Your Stories' and 'Guestbook' entries. These included stories of lives saved by the proximity of the local hospital where they would have been lost, authors claimed, had the distance to travel been any greater; of the wonderful service provided by staff at the hospital, of the meaning of the services to those who had suffered health problems or lost a baby. These could themselves be considered evidence: not statistical evidence or overview evidence, but experiential evidence. Many of these stories are very moving and it could be argued that they represented a more emotional approach to making the case which, while possibly less impressive to some audiences, might have been an effective way of connecting to the local population. Again, the compilation of evidence became part of the process of engaging with potential supporters. This personalised approach may work better with members of the public than the use of statistics. This story approach also created space for other visitors to the website to contribute, offering their own evidence. For instance, one contributor exhorted the campaigners to continue since the closure of local services in his home town (not Eastbourne) had had, in his view, disastrous results and the people of Eastbourne needed to avoid this happening to them.

The principal collation of evidence is to be found in a document entitled *Option 5: Saving Lives*, drawn up in conjunction with the Hands off the Conquest campaign in Hastings as an alternative scenario to the options offered by the NHS Trust for public consultation. This document resembled an NHS document, bearing the trademark blue, and put forward the case for retaining services in both Hastings and Eastbourne using argument and evidence. The document based its case on three principles: safety (the importance of timing; that there was no shortage of trained consultants nationally; and that size of unit is not linked to safety); accessibility (the need for capacity and patient choice); and affordability. Intriguingly, this document is not directly linked from the Save the DGH website.

Excess demand in relation to capacity was illustrated by the case of a mother who, on 1 June 2007, had to travel out of county and go to Tunbridge Wells to have her baby since every single East and Mid Sussex maternity unit was full. This was used to illustrate the argument that Eastbourne capacity was required. The campaign used a video of a car journey between Hastings and Eastbourne and reported the results of a national survey of drivers which found that the A259 Hastings–Eastbourne road was the ninth 'most challenging' in Britain. Campaigners pointed out that the population of Eastbourne and surrounding districts had increased and that thousands more houses were expected to be built. They claimed that the number of local births had risen in the previous two years.

The Eastbourne campaign relied more on argument than on statistical evidence. Like Banbury, they quoted Alan Johnson's reference to 20 miles as too far to travel. They argued that it was their NHS and they paid for it, suggesting they were entitled to their services; that local services were essential to saving lives and that removing local services threatened lives since, in childbirth, having the right technology in the right place at the right time was critical; that caesarean sections need to be carried out within 30 minutes where the distance between Eastbourne and Hastings took 45 minutes; that the loss of some service would lead to the loss of other services (the 'domino effect'); and that cuts to service were to save money and not to improve health care.

Like the other campaigns, some of the arguments are used by the campaigners to discredit the NHS Trust, particularly in relation to not investigating ways of retaining local services and in relation to running a 'sham' consultation since key decisions had been taken prior to canvassing the public for their views.

(3) The campaign's relationships with wider environment

What may be more significant in terms of explaining success or failure – or contributing to success or failure – is the campaign's relationships with the wider environment. There are three aspects to this that we will explore here:

- Generally, breadth of the campaign in terms of reaching out to, engaging with, or drawing into action or at least sympathy, different sections of the local community.
- Specifically, relationship with other save-our-hospital campaigns.
- Specifically, relationships with health professionals and stance of health professionals.

Relationship to local community – the extent to which the campaign draws on and reaches a wide range of different groups

The character and extent of local engagement are not always easy to see from the website and the alliances created, their subtlety and their evolution over time are best retrospectively investigated through conversation with participants on either a one-to-one or small-group basis. In particular, absences should be interpreted with care.

One issue to consider is how best to measure engagement and reach. We have used a number of indicators to gain an impression of the success with which a campaign has connected to the local population whose interests it claims implicitly to represent. These are: numbers of people recorded as signing petitions or participating in public events such as marches and rallies; participation in the 'Your Story' pages of campaign websites; the diversity of participants in the campaign, include cross-(political)-party involvement; sponsorship by local businesses; and coverage or even backing from local media.

The invitation to submit individual stories or guestbook entries works to some extent to draw in patients, relatives, even members of staff. It can be used to share experience from elsewhere and to allow staff to speak anonymously. The stories allow members of the public to be involved and to be heard, and they reflect back life and death experiences to the public in which the local health service played a critical role. On the 'Story' page of Save the DGH in Eastbourne, the alleged bullying of staff at the local NHS Trust was revealed which, the anonymous writer suggested, accounted for the difficulty staff experienced in speaking out honestly on the issue of configuration, patient safety and access to services.

Another indicator is the number of those attending rallies and marches and other public events. Twelve hundred people turned out for the biggest march in Bognor's history and 15,000 participated in the public march and protest in neighbouring Chichester, both in support of St Richard's Hospital. A joint petition for West and Mid Sussex secured 129,000 signatures and in Worthing 7,000 attended a public rally. In Hemel, where the campaign to save hospital services failed, a Hands-Around-the-Hospital stunt was attended by 'thousands' and a 15,000 signature petition was submitted to the House of Commons in 2006.

Another dimension is the diversity of individuals who are mentioned as involved in the campaign, including evidence of cross-party support. Most campaigns recognised the need to try to develop this support and state explicitly on the website that members of all major parties support the campaign. In Welwyn, where the campaign failed to save hospital services at the QEII, the website tries to signal the cross-party direction of the campaign. The 'taskforce' was reported to consist of representatives from all the major political parties, the borough council, health experts and union members. However, beyond the taskforce and at grassroots, it is difficult to discern more deeply rooted cross-party support for the campaign. The two websites belonging to the campaign are hosted by the local Conservative MP, Grant Shapps, and his role is very prominent, with the websites featuring pictures of him and quoting speeches or statements by him, but not by anyone else. His role is so dominant that we have gained the impression that the campaign was used to promote him and that this might have made retaining cross-party support difficult and might even point to a more fundamental difficulty: namely, that the campaign was principally a one-man show. Certainly, it is difficult to get any sense of the campaign's being rooted in the local population – a helicopter-filmed public rally in 2007 being the exception rather than the rule. A newsletter produced by the local Keep our NHS Public group points to very different starting points of the representatives from different parties and this also may have contributed to a difficulty in holding the campaign together. The campaign does not seem to have made much of a mark, judging by local media coverage, but again, this is difficult to be certain of without interviewing those involved.

In successful Eastbourne, the website lists committee members and these include representatives from all major political parties, Churches Together, a former Hospital Trust Non-Executive Director, representatives from local business, a solicitor, the local Anglican Bishop, a representative of the maternity services liaison committee, consultant obstetrician, a local business representative and former leader of the borough council and the current leader of the borough leader.

Some campaign websites listed or made reference to local sponsors, mainly local businesses. Again, this not only indicates possible sources of funding or publicity but also signals the willingness of this section of the local community to be associated with the campaign. The Support the Princess Royal (Haywards Heath) and Eastbourne websites listed dozens of supportive businesses and organisations while the Hemel campaign lists nine and Welwyn does not identify any. The Worthing campaign identifies Worthing First, an association of local businesses, as a supporter.

The stance of local newspapers and other media is particularly significant, since it is unlikely that these will want to align themselves with an unpopular campaign. Local media can either give publicity to campaign events or they can go one step further and positively champion a campaign. Newspapers are mentioned specifically as supporting the campaigns in Hastings, Eastbourne, Chichester and Haywards Heath. Newspapers could be an important indicator of breadth of local support: not only will they not want to back an unpopular campaign but they might also be expected to give preferential treatment to the major institutions of the area (major employers, council etc.). The Banbury campaign makes specific reference to the 'huge amount of support' given by the *Banbury Guardian*. These campaigns all succeeded in retaining local services, at least to date. The failed campaigns of Welwyn and Hemel do not seem to have enjoyed any particular relationship with local media although the helicopter-filmed rally at Welwyn was reported sympathetically on the local BBC news.

Another indicator of local recognition and support is the willingness of celebrities to be associated with the campaign. Many of the successful campaigns enjoyed celebrity support. In Chichester, local residents, Patrick Moore, Keith Richards and Patricia Routledge, supported the campaign; in Haywards Heath, Dame Vera Lynn exhorted the public to continue to defend their services; in Hastings and Eastbourne, Jo Brand, Sir Paul McCartney and Nigel Havers supported. We cannot find internet-based evidence that the campaigns in Hemel or Welwyn received celebrity support.

Where the campaign originates or how it emerges may also reflect and shape its relationship to the local community. It is possible to contrast the emergence of the campaigns in Hastings and Eastbourne from the pre-existing, local respective Friends of the Hospital groups on the one hand with the establishment of the Save the QE2 in Welwyn apparently single-handedly by the local Conservative MP on the other. In the former, campaign leaders may already have been knowledgeable about local hospital and health issues and about processes of decision-making and the decision-makers themselves. They may have acquired a degree of credibility and trustworthiness among hospital users. The dominance of campaigns by a particular MP might be evident from the character of the website. Mike Penning's failed campaign in Hemel was clearly on his own website. However, the dominance of this MP was significantly attenuated since a campaign to save the Hemel was also undertaken by the Dacorum Hospital Action Group (DHAG) although the relationship between the MP and the Action Group is unclear. This Action Group had been established in the 1970s and has been campaigning without interruption since then. It is difficult to imagine that this Action Group has no presence in the town. However, the campaign seems very associated, possibly overly associated, with one person, Zena Bullmore. The 'About Us' page of the website is actually about Zena herself. The website does not list other campaign members. The Action Group successfully organised methods of public engagement, including stunts, petitions and a march to parliament but it is difficult to get a sense of the channels or mediating institutions through which it connects to the local population.

In Welwyn, the impression is gained of the dominance of a single MP. The impression given by the failed Welwyn campaign is that it always had a second objective, that of promoting the incumbent MP, Grant Shapps. This might have strained cross-party relationships and made cross-party unity difficult to maintain.

In Worthing and Chichester, where local campaigns succeeded in persuading the HOSC to refer but where the IRP investigation was suspended following merger talks between the two Trusts (i.e. where it isn't really clear whether to classify these as successful or unsuccessful campaigns), the campaigns were run, not in opposition to, but from *within* the two affected hospitals. This gave wonderful access but may make holding out against closures in the context of merger impossible to sustain.

Relationship to other save-our-hospital campaigns
Here again, there is significant contrast amongst campaigns, ranging from very close collaborative or joint campaigning, through collaboration on specific events and tactics to campaigning in isolation from other campaigns.

Collaboration was strong or very strong in Sussex. It was at its strongest between the campaigns in Hastings and Eastbourne where the threat faced was loss of services at one of the two hospitals and transfer to the other. Each campaign website provides a link to the other on its home page and one has a button on the left from which to link to the other from any page on the website. Both of these campaigns emerged from pre-existing Friends of the Hospital groups and it is supposed that the two women chairing these campaigns, who remained in contact with one another throughout, knew each other before the respective campaigns were launched. There are even joint events such as a march and rally in 2007 and joint open letters and frequent reference to each other's campaign: for instance "Both Hastings and Eastbourne stand together and both of us have been through thick and thin" (Liz Walke, campaign leader, November 2007, public speech). Equally significantly, as mentioned above, the two collaborate to produce an additional option which is released at the time of the formal public consultation exercise – *Option 5: Saving Lives*. Through close collaboration, the campaigns demonstrated a strong belief that they must resist divide and rule at all costs and this persisted even when the local (Hastings) Labour MP (the only Labour MP involved in any of the campaigns described in this paper – all the others being Conservative) abandoned the campaign stance of a two-site option and declared his willingness to support an NHS decision favouring transfer to Hastings. In addition to this very close collaboration, the Eastbourne campaign referred to and listed many hospitals facing downgrading, including links to their websites and to a wide range of campaigning websites such as those of Community Hospitals Acting Nationally Together (CHANT) and Keep Our NHS Public (KONP). It even has a webpage entitled 'Other Hospitals'.

There is less close collaboration but nonetheless a collaborative approach among the campaigns of Mid and West Sussex (Haywards Heath, Chichester and Worthing). They use similar tactics (such as rallies and vigils) and joint tactics in relation to a petition, a list of General Practitioners (GPs) opposed to the reconfiguration proposals and a trip to Westminster. Importantly, across East, Mid and West Sussex, there is a swathe of Conservative MPs who appear to have worked closely together, discussing and planning with each other, and who seemed to provide some kind of network. Obviously, this is likely to have made coordinated action more possible. Unlike the campaigns in Hasting and Eastbourne, the campaigns of Haywards Heath, Worthing and Chichester seem very strongly identified with their local Conservative MPs.

By contrast in Hertfordshire, there are no campaigns in Stevenage or Hatfield for the Welwyn campaign to link with or in Watford or St Albans for the Hemel Hempstead campaign to link up with. Moreover, despite the fact the both Hemel and Welwyn have Conservative MPs, there does not, from internet sources, seem to have been any collaboration or communication over campaigning between them. It is possible that as both of these MPs had been elected only in 2005 that they did not know each other well – but this is speculation.

Relationship to local professionals and, specifically, the stance of medical professionals on campaign

The last feature we wish to compare and contrast of these campaigns concerns the relationship of the campaign to the medical profession, specifically the degree of collaboration between the campaign and the local medical profession.

In Hemel, there is little sense of professionals being engaged in the campaign. There is no contribution from them to the website apart from one action involving a helicopter flyover, where nurses were waving at a helicopter camera. There are no links to documents they have submitted as part of the reconfiguration process. In Welwyn, the only evidence of involvement by any health professionals from the website is a subtitle on a website video stating 'staff and unions' over a picture of two women speaking during a rally. Who the women are, which staff association or trade unions they represent and what they say are not included in the video.

By contrast, in the Sussex campaigns and in Banbury, professionals are very involved and have a fairly high profile. In Sussex, campaigns wrote to local GPs asking for views and then listed their names on the website when they replied that they did not agree with proposals. As a result, a list of 200 GPs opposed to the reconfiguration proposals was drawn up in Chichester, Worthing and Haywards Heath and this list was presented to the Prime Minister. The filmed ambulance trip to measure the travel time between Worthing and Brighton was undertaken by a local doctor. Video footage on the Worthing campaign website emphasised lack of support by professionals for the proposals. At one stage, the point is made that only one member of the medical profession (the then chair of the Professional Executive Committees) was known to *support* the proposals. The Mid and West Sussex campaigns staged a trip to Westminster using a wheeled bed stacked with petitions and letters demonstrating opposition of both public and clinicians.

The Support St Richard's campaign in Chichester stressed in defence of their services that the relationship of GPs to hospital consultants was excellent. Good prior relationships might have made collaboration around defending the local hospital easier to organise. Some GP letters are on the website with their concerns spelt out – specifically, quality of patient care; unproven costings; the expense of moving services; damage or disruption to good professional relationships; and the observation that some community services can only function in context of a DGH. It should be noted also there was some competitiveness among GPs from Worthing and Chichester. Certainly the very close collaboration between campaigns which characterised Hastings and Eastbourne was not quite so evidence in Mid and West Sussex.

This can be seen in the responses of the campaigns to the proposals. In Sussex, a response to the document, *Creating an NHS Fit for the Future*, was commissioned from two hospital consultants. The response from Hasting and Eastbourne was a joint one, again drafted by members of the medical profession, and took the form of an additional option for service configuration, the two-site option.

In Mid and West Sussex there is strong medical opposition to the proposals for reconfiguration. In Hastings and Eastbourne, there is mixed medical opinion and a report by a medic at the Hospital Trust that staff were being bullied into silence (this appeared as an emailed message on the Eastbourne website) but enough collaboration with oppositional MPs to put together an alternative option. In Hemel and Welwyn, there is little evidence of a professional stance reported on the websites. There was an open letter written by GPs of Hemel Hempstead raising concerns about cuts to local services. This carefully worded letter calls for novel ways of utilising the Hemel site and for a slow down in the pace of reconfiguration rather than explicitly stating a preference for retaining all major services at Hemel. In other words, it was a letter which damaged the reputation of the local NHS management but did not explicitly support the stance of the local save-our-hospital campaign. However, the hospital in Hemel suffered numerous setbacks during the period of the campaign, including press reports in late 2006 describing the Trust as financially in an irrecoverable position; a Healthcare Commission report in 2007 condemning the Trust as weak on both financial and quality of service ratings; an Audit Commission in 2007 rating the financial management of the hospital as inadequate; Health and Safety Executive involvement following a breach of regulations, also in 2007; and repeated criticism of the Trust board and calls for resignations. Although the DHAG use this criticism to step up their own complaints about the mismanagement of the local hospital Trust, the effect of these criticisms is probably to undermine the ability of the Trust to operate across multiple sites rather than to reinforce it.

Discussion and conclusion

The limited character of the data was discussed earlier in this paper and so the reader will not be surprised that the brief conclusions outlined here are tentative and speculative. We have tried to work 'from the data' rather than from pre-formed theories or hypotheses. The tentative conclusions from this exploration of the data will inform later data collection and more detailed analysis. Discussion of influence and effectiveness in the pressure group and social movement literature often highlights the difficulties of measuring these concepts (e.g. Whiteley and Winyard, 1987; Coxall, 2001). By contrast, effectiveness is fairly straightforward in the current research since there is only one outcome of importance: the closure or survival of the disputed services. However, this does not mean that explaining it is easy. Some of the group attributes included in theoretical discussions of effectiveness are not even known from the data collected here, such as financial resources, internal organisational structure or educational level and other membership characteristics. However, some variables which appear in the literature may have some application, such as the importance of unity and sanctioning capability (see Grant, 2000, for example).

It is difficult to expect pointers towards success or failure simply from the specific devices or methods used by campaigners. The use of the internet, of marches, rallies, involvement of the media, petitions and so forth is very widespread. Additionally, it is not at all clear that the amount of evidence and careful use of evidence are critical to success: the picture is more complicated than this. Instead, it may be more useful to consider the capacity of the campaign as a whole and in particular its engagement with certain sections of the population and key protagonists as better indicators of success.

Public involvement in a formal NHS consultation exercise is unlikely to have much influence on NHS decision-making. It is certainly unlikely to reverse or halt NHS proposals although it may help shape modest details of implementation. However, community campaigns *can* be successful in doing this, where they 'take' in the local community so that sufficient political pressure is brought to bear on the local NHS decision-makers and sufficient damage done to their reputation such that the legitimacy of their leadership becomes irreversibly undermined. It is no coincidence that several of the affected NHS bodies saw the forced resignations of leading personnel. At the same time, this damage must not point to the non-viability of the hospital itself. The reputational damage to the West Herts Trust in Hemel Hempstead was enormous but indicated chronic problems with the hospital itself, not simply problems in its leadership: quality of care, financial management and health and safety matters were all officially rated as poor. Ironically, the campaign's highlighting of these signs of leadership failure simultaneously drew attention to fundamental weaknesses in the institution itself. The attacks on the reputation of NHS decision-makers in Banbury, Hastings and Eastbourne did not imply fundamental flaws in the hospital care itself and in Chichester the high standards of the hospital were contrasted with the quality of decision-making by the primary care trust.

It is difficult to measure the degree to which a campaigns 'takes' in the local community. Here we have suggested a number of indicators such as evidence of cross-party political support, numbers of local residents participating in events, the willingness of celebrities to be associated with the campaign and local press coverage and support. It may be that the less overtly political a campaign is, the more its general appeal. It is difficult to be sure of this. It was noticeable, from the photos and video recordings of rallies and marches, that the self-identification of supporters by party or trade union label was minimal or non-existent. Placards often appeared to be home-made or produced by the campaign rather than by supporting groups.

Some features of campaigns, such as participation in wider events, most markedly in Banbury, may point to activities which in themselves are not decisive or even contributory to success but instead indicate campaign 'capacity': the amount of time, energy, connectedness and ability to process and act on information amongst campaign activists as well as their number.

Despite an energetic and unflagging campaign in Hemel, it was difficult to get a sense from internet sources of how the campaign was grounded in the local community. It was strongly associated with one individual (or with two, if you count the local MP; but even here it wasn't clear how the MP's campaign dovetailed, if at all, with the Hospital Action Group campaign). Both the failed Hemel and Welwyn campaigns shared this characteristic of having campaigns strongly associated with single individuals. However, after that the two campaigns differed in many ways: the Hemel Action Group had existed since the 1970s and campaign around the threat to the hospital's future was a continuation of another and earlier campaign. The Action Group continues to exist although the hospital doesn't. In Welwyn, the campaign was set up by the new local MP but disappeared after a brief period with little trace. The website of the Hemel campaign is informative and entertaining; the website for the Welwyn campaign contains almost no information at all.

By contrast with these, the campaigns in Hastings and Eastbourne emerged from pre-existing Friends of the Hospital groups and the campaigns in Worthing and Chichester were run at least in part from the hospitals themselves with significant 'insider' and 'establishment' participation. In these last campaigns, the threat came from outside the hospital Trusts – from the primary care trust. In Eastbourne and Hastings, the threat came from the hospitals Trust itself and consequently the outspokenness and involvement of health workers was partial and muted.

Effective collaboration with sympathetic members of the medical profession does seem to be an important factor in success, perhaps a condition of it. In Hastings and Eastbourne, medical opinion appears to have been split but the campaigns had enough high-quality participation from medics to make the campaigns work. Endorsement by the medical profession appears to have a legitimation function: it appears to legitimise the stance of the campaigners. Other health professionals, especially nurses and midwives, might also confer some legitimacy but this appears to be less significant. Intriguingly, the Chief Executive of the NHS, David Nicholson, seems to have arrived at similar conclusions. In an interview with the *Guardian* in autumn 2006, he declared that in the process of securing the roughly 60 hospital reconfigurations he envisaged across England, persuading the clinicians and then having the clinicians persuading the public would be essential (Carvel, 2006). And this approach also became a key feature of the 'Darzi reviews' which spread across England from 2007.

Collaboration with other campaigns also appears to be useful and may be critical. All of the Sussex campaigns concerned hospitals whose fates were bound up with each other: one hospital could gain at another's expense. It was in this context that campaigns collaborated. In Hastings and Eastbourne where there was a clear zero sum game between the two, the ability of the two campaigns to trust each other, and especially of the two women heading them up to trust each other, may have been one of the most decisive factors in their success. The Hastings campaign clung to this mutual trust, two-site approach even where the local MP broke ranks and admitted he would settle for a one-site configuration providing it were in Hastings. It is difficult to imagine that this trust could have been established and then maintained throughout the period of the campaigns (several years) without the individuals involved knowing each other.

Resisting divide and rule, securing proper grounding in the local community and acquiring the legitimacy conferred by medical expertise may be more significant features of a successful campaign than use of evidence or the precise selection of methods. Sanctions typically involve pressure groups being able to orchestrate blockades, disruption and non-cooperation – an example being the ability to get a workforce to strike. The campaigns examined here have not attempted these kinds of sanctions. However, perhaps it is not far-fetched to suggest that the successful ones have wrought reputational damage on the responsible NHS authority such that the relationship of that body with the population it is supposed to serve reaches a critical point. At this point, the ability of the NHS body to claim it is responsive to that population becomes unconvincing and the body – or more likely, its leadership – effectively loses the confidence of the public. It is possible that this moment becomes decisive when the leader's peers or superiors consider that confidence to have been lost. This concept of sanctioning capability is worth further exploration in the context of these campaigns.

References

Academy of Medical Royal Colleges (2007) *Acute Health Care Services: Report of a Working Party*, London: AMRC

Byrne, D. and Ruane, S. (2007) *The Case for Hospital Reconfiguration – Not Proven*, London: Keep our NHS Public

Byrne, P. (1997) *Social Movements in Britain*, London: Routledge

Carvel, J. (2006) 'Plan for wave of closures of NHS services', *The Guardian*, 13 September

CEM and BAEM (no date) *Seven Myths about Emergency Medicine*, London: College of Emergency Medicine and British Association of Emergency Medicine

Cox, B. (2001) *Pressure Groups in British Politics*, Harlow: Pearson Education

Department of Health (2003) *Keeping the NHS Local: A New Direction of Travel*, London: Department of Health

Department of Health (2004) *The Configuring Hospitals Project Evidence File: Part One*, London: Department of Health

Department of Health (2006) *Our Health, Our Care, Our Say: A New Direction for Community Services*, London: Department of Health

Farrington-Douglas, J. and Brooks, T (2007) *The Future Hospital: the Progressive Case for Change*, London: IPPR

Grant, W. (2000) *Pressure Groups and British Politics*, Basingstoke: Palgrave

Jordan, G. and Maloney, W. (1996) *The Protest Business*, Manchester: Manchester University Press

Mandelstam, M. (2006) *Betraying the NHS: Health Abandoned*, London: Jessica Kingsley Publishers

Nicholl, J., West, J., Goodacre, S. and Turner, J. (2007) The relationship between distance to hospital and patient mortality in emergencies: an observational study, *Emergency Medicine Journal*, 24: 665–8

Nicholson, D. (2006) 'Letter to MPs', *Gateway*, No.7,409, http://www.dh.gov.uk/prod_consum_dh/idcplg?IdcService=GET_FILE&dID=122724&Rendition=Web (accessed December 2007)

RCSEng (2006) *Delivering High-Quality Surgical Services for the Future*, London: Royal College of Surgeons in England

RCSEng (2007) *Surgery for Children: Delivering a First Class Service*, London: Royal College of surgeons in England

Ridley, F. and Jordan, G. (1998) *Protest Politics: Cause Groups and Campaigns*, Oxford: Oxford University Press

Tooke, J. et al. (2008) *Aspiring to Excellence: Findings and Final Recommendation of the Independent Inquiry into Modernising Medical Careers*, MMC Inquiry, London: Aldridge Press

CHAPTER 11
Reducing senility to 'bare life'
Are we heading for a new Holocaust at mid-twenty-first century?

Dr Andrea Capstick

*Bradford Dementia Group, Division of Dementia Studies,
School of Health Studies, University of Bradford, UK
a.j.capstick@bradford.ac.uk*

Introduction

> The tradition of the oppressed teaches us that the 'state of emergency' in which we live is not the exception but the rule. We must attain to a conception of history that is in keeping with this insight…. The current amazement that the things we are experiencing are 'still' possible in the twentieth century is not philosophical. This amazement is not the beginning of knowledge, unless it is the knowledge that the view of history which gives rise to it is untenable.
>
> (Benjamin, 1940: 248–9)

The German–Jewish critical theorist Walter Benjamin (1892–1940) wrote these lines shortly before his death in exile whilst fleeing from the agents of fascism. They seem particularly relevant to a healthcare policy conference with the title 'Condition Critical' taking place almost 70 years later. In this paper one of the things I hope to do is outline how Benjamin's concept of the permanent state of emergency relates to health and social care provision for older people with dementia today.

Benjamin believed that the Holocaust came about because of the 'amnestic' view of history as an unbroken, linear process of scientific achievement, including the belief in human perfectibility. He suggested that in order to see history stripped of this ideological myth of progress, we need to wake from a collective 'dream history'; from our usual somnolent acceptance of surface appearances (Cohen, 1993: 5). Similarly it can be argued today that the twentieth-century 'dream history' of linear progress away from a never-to-be-repeated Holocaust is a myth. My strong claim in this paper is that present-day demographic panic related to the economic 'burden of care' for an ageing population is leading to proposed solutions analogous to the ideological killing of psychiatric patients, the physically disabled, Jews and other victims of Nazism in the mid-twentieth century. Such 'solutions' are fuelled by media propaganda, the profit motives of what has been described as the 'medical-industrial complex' (Bond et al., 2004) and a reductive, medicalised, biological determinist model of the cognitive changes of ageing.

Biological determinism

Nazi programmes of ideological killing were based on a biological determinist concept of human life in which individual physiology and genetic makeup (as opposed to environmental conditions or social welfare) were held to be responsible for 'defects' connected with mental health, social behaviour or 'race'. The eradication of certain groups on the basis of their assumed hereditary taints or innate inferiorities was rationalised by Nazism. The dominant view of dementia today is, similarly, the biological determinist one of an inexorable disease process in the individual brain, which is ultimately terminal, and in which the progression of 'symptoms' such as memory loss, language impairment and disordered behaviour are solely the result of localised brain damage.

This is the model of dementia which is used to support calls for assisted suicide or passive euthanasia for those diagnosed with the condition. Such calls are dangerous; not because we should question the moral right of any *individual* to opt for euthanasia if fully informed of his or her prognosis and able to make a decision on that basis, but because they bring much nearer the prospect of the *wholesale* elimination of older people simply because they have become dependent and unproductive. Although those who advocate euthanasia in the case of people diagnosed with dementia invariably take a biological determinist view of the condition, there are other models such as the psycho-social model popularised by Kitwood (1997) under the flag of 'person-centred dementia care', and the social constructivist model (e.g. Harding and Palfrey, 1997). If dementia is considered from such alternative perspectives, calls for euthanasia are untenable.

From biopolitical life to bare life: constructing dementia as a 'living death'

Agamben (1999) notes that in Nazi Germany Jews and other Holocaust victims were reduced to the condition of 'bare life'. Unlike ordinary citizens with rights, who are granted the status of 'biopolitical life', the victims of the Nazis were reduced to a condition of mere physiological existence. This could not be achieved in one move, however: as the 1930s progressed, Agamben points out, Aryans were first distinguished from non-Aryans, non-Aryans transformed into Jews, Jews into deportees, deportees into prisoners and prisoners into those under sentence of death. Only when no further degradation was possible and a condition of 'bare life' had been arrived at did this process of categorisation end.

In a radio broadcast entitled *Education after Auschwitz*, Adorno (1970) suggested that we need to build awareness of the links between civilisation and barbarism for the very reason that "the fundamental structure of society and its members, which brought it [Auschwitz] on, are today the same" (cited in Rothberg, 2000: 49). Adorno insists that Auschwitz was *not* a single aberration that can be dismissed in the post-Second-World-War world as something never to be repeated; rather it was a logical conclusion of the Enlightenment notion of human perfectibility and progress through science. He saw an urgent need to educate the post-war generations to anticipate and prevent the continuation of these myths which are so evident today in society's response to the cognitive changes of ageing.

Following Agamben, it might now be argued that in the case of dementia, pseudoscientific means have been used to construct a category of 'others' in which the cognitively intact are first distinguished from the mildly cognitively impaired; the mildly cognitively impaired transformed into those who have dementia; those who have dementia transformed into those with 'Alzheimer's'; those with Alzheimer's into the terminally ill; and the terminally ill into the 'already dead'. The media play a significant role here, with their penchant for sensationalist representations of dementia as 'the death that leaves the body behind'. See, for example, the recent report 'A living death' in *The Times* newspaper (17 March 2008) on the diagnosis of the author Terry Pratchett with a form of dementia.

It is well-established that psychiatric patients were the first victims of the 'final solution'. Conservative estimates suggest that more than 70,000 psychiatric patients, including those with 'senile diseases' whose lives were considered by doctors to be 'not worth living', were gassed or killed by lethal injection (Strous, 2007). Covert euthanasia (for example, through starvation and failure to treat infections) was also common, and the true number of deaths is incalculable (von Cranach, 2003). As late as 1943, 'selections' at Auschwitz-Birkenau were still being made on the basis of age and physical fitness, rather than whether deportees were Jewish. The relatively healthy were sent to the labour camp at Auschwitz (where their life expectancy was three months) and the very young, the old and the physically or mentally incapable straight from the trains to the adjoining death camp at Birkenau.

In recent years major biomedical research efforts and funding have been dedicated to the pursuit of genes for Alzheimer's disease. These research projects are justified to the lay population by suggestions that once such genes are identified they can then be eliminated. In reality, however, there is no clear evidence of a genetic basis for late-onset dementia. The belief that dementia is hereditary is just one of the misconceptions that have arisen from the over-extension of the disease category 'Alzheimer's disease'. As initially described by Kraepelin (1910), this was a rare pre-senile form of dementia, later discovered to be familial in a minority of cases. Fox (1989) provides a detailed account of the subsequent extension of the disease category to take in ever-increasing numbers of older people. Fox notes that this extension of the disease category was not carried out for scientific reasons, but in order to create what one of its proponents described as a 'health politics of anguish' and thus attract increased publicity and funding. In the process, Alzheimer's disease was transformed from a rare condition affecting, exclusively, people under the age of 65, to the fourth-most common cause of death in older people, after cancer, heart disease and stroke.

There is a direct line of descent between the pre-Second-World-War German eugenics programme and the post-war and genomics projects of the former Allies. Franz Kallman, who argued in pre-war Germany for the sterilisation of the relatives of people diagnosed with schizophrenia, continued to advocate this programme with enthusiasm following his arrival in the USA in 1936. In 1938, Kallman wrote that schizophrenics were:

> a source of maladjusted crooks, asocial eccentrics and the lowest type of criminal offenders. Even the faithful believer in... liberty would be much happier without these... I am reluctant to admit the necessity of different eugenic programmes for democratic and fascistic communities... there are neither biological nor sociological differences between a democratic and a totalitarian schizophrenic.
> (quoted in Rose et al., 1984: 208)

Kallman went on to become president of the American Society for Human Genetics, and US sterilisation programmes for the mentally ill and 'morally depraved' continued in some US states until the 1970s. In spite of the often-grandiose claims of the Human Genome Project, no new mechanisms have been identified since then that enable individual genes to be eliminated without also eliminating the individual alleged to carry them.

Demographic panic and propaganda

Historically, discrimination has almost invariably been accompanied and fuelled by demographic panic, based on the idea that an undeserving or unproductive group of people are consuming more than their fair share of national resources. On a surface reading, policy documents on dementia today invariably stress the humanitarian project of research into prevention or cure, and the improvement of care services. Read against the grain, however, they often reveal an overriding concern with what has been heralded for many years now as the 'rising tide of dementia' and its material implications for the mid-twenty-first-century economy.

The recent Dementia UK report commissioned by the Alzheimer's Society (Knapp et al., 2007) carries on its front cover the following words, prominently displayed:

> *By 2025 one million people in the UK will have dementia*

> *Dementia costs the UK over £17 billion per year*

This major report runs to 189 pages, but the two 'factoids' selected for emphasis are the number of people affected (too many) and the cost of their care (too much); there seems to me to be a strongly implied 'already' lurking beneath that second line. The blue front cover of the report bears an image that resembles surging waves, or perhaps steeply ascending lines on a graph. Knapp et al. (2007) estimate that around 700,000 people in the UK currently have dementia, but go on to suggest that prevalence may be up to three times higher than this figure, due to underreporting. Projections suggest that, due to the ageing of the population, prevalence could reach 1.7 million by 2050. MacDonald and Cooper (2007) report that currently around 50 per cent of all people with dementia in the UK live in care homes and that present provision will need to double over the next 30 years in order even to maintain the status quo. The authors suggest that we are on the cusp of a national crisis of care provision.

The metaphor of the 'rising tide', as applied to dementia, can be traced back to the title of an article on the demographics of dementia by Ineichen (1987) published in the *British Journal of Psychiatry*: 'Measuring the rising tide. How many dementia cases will there be by 2001?' This title is almost certainly, however, a conscious or unconscious reference to the much earlier 'scientific racist' text *The rising tide of color against white world supremacy*

(Lothrop Stoddard, 1920). This metaphor, of a tidal wave that will engulf society due to the over-representation of a particular group, has no doubt passed into common parlance in such a way that it need not be used with any overtly discriminatory intention and I am not suggesting here that Ineichen did so. The point remains, however, that the image of a society 'swamped' and overrun by non-productive older people who are about to bankrupt it has echoes of earlier racist and fascist propaganda.

In 2008 the bioethicist and former UK government advisor, Baroness Mary Warnock, suggested in an interview for the Scottish church magazine *Life and Work* that "if you're demented, you're wasting people's lives – your family's lives – and you're wasting the resources of the National Health Service". Warnock goes on to advocate, not only voluntary euthanasia for people with dementia who, she suggests, have "a duty to die" but also that there should be specialists who are licensed to "put down" those whose lives are a burden to others: "That's the way I believe the future will go" (Warnock, 2008). Here there appear to be covert assumptions about social class, as well as age and infirmity, since it is NHS patients who are particularly singled out for being wasteful and undeserving, rather than those who have been able to make private provision for their health care in later life.

Similarly, writing in an academic journal of bioethics, Cooley (2007) suggests that those diagnosed with dementia should commit suicide immediately, so that their relatives are not left having to make the decision to terminate life when the person in question is no longer capable of doing so. These authors' understandings of what it means to be 'demented' are, however, clearly based on a biomedical model in which alleged symptoms of dementia are attributed solely to a disease process in the individual brain. From this standpoint both diagnosis and prognosis are taken to be precise sciences, whilst environmental factors and human responses are considered to play no role in the onset or progression of the condition. Also lacking from these pronouncements is any proper consideration of historical precedents, or of the failure of post-war social reforms to provide decent standards of living in old age for those have contributed to the public purse by means of direct and indirect taxation throughout their adult lives.

Countering 'neuropathic ideology'

Kitwood (1997) coined the term 'neuropathic ideology' to describe the determinist biomedical model of dementia, with its assumption of a straightforward, linear, causal association between biological defect and symptom expression. This is an ideology, it might be added, that distracts our attention from the fact that diagnostic procedures, abusive care regimes, social stigma, post-traumatic stress and iatrogenic illness can all both create the appearance of dementia, and precipitate its onset, in older people.

So, for example, the most widely used diagnostic screening test for dementia, the Mini-Mental State Examination (Folstein et al., 1975) has been found to have an 86 per cent false-positive rate in people over 75 (White et al., 2002). Ballard et al. (2008) report that neuroleptic drugs, initially developed to treat major psychoses in younger adults, are inappropriately prescribed to 45 per cent of older people in care homes and lead to a significant deterioration in verbal fluency and cognition, both of which are considered to be symptoms of dementia. People prescribed such drugs were twice as likely to die during the course of Ballard et al.'s five-year study as those who were not. This study also found that people in care homes who are deemed to have dementia, whilst often having received no formal diagnosis, are routinely sedated so that they can be dealt with by untrained staff.

Earlier diagnosis is leading to increasingly blurred boundaries between mild cognitive impairment (MCI) and dementia. Although mild cognitive impairment (MCI) is currently estimated to progress to 'full blown' dementia in only one-in-three cases (Fleischer et al., 2007), US studies are beginning to appear which conflate MCI and Alzheimer's disease. The demand for increasingly early diagnosis of 'Alzheimer's' thus appears, in many cases, to be leading to a tentative and provisional diagnosis – as 'MCI' – of what may well be part of a continuum of normal age-related memory impairment experienced to some extent by all older people. In the process, however, a climate of fear is created in which the most transient example of 'memory lag' provokes images of terminal decline. Fear of not being able to remember may, indeed, become a self-fulfilling prophecy, since anxiety has been reported as one of the most significant factors in predicting whether those diagnosed with MCI ultimately go on to develop dementia (Palmer et al., 2007). In an article on stigma and Alzheimer's disease, Scholl and Sabat (2008) report on a number of studies which suggest that people who have low confidence and self-esteem are likely to perform poorly on standard cognitive-screening tests.

Social amnesia: forgetting as a societal disorder

The quality of life enjoyed by people diagnosed with late-onset dementia today varies considerably, but it is characterised in general by high levels of segregation and social invisibility (Bond et al., 2004). In long-term care settings, high levels of sensory deprivation – known to cause sleep disturbance, loss of concentration, confusion, and disorientation in time and space – are common (Cohen-Mansfield, 2005). Typically, also, once admitted to formal care, a person with dementia will be moved several times, and these moves will usually be to successively more controlling or medicalised environments (Baldwin and Capstick, 2007). Here it might be argued that people with dementia are already being ghettoised; their journey through the care system takes place out of sight, and largely out of mind, of the rest of the population.

Care services for people with dementia might thus be considered an example of what was termed by Rousset (1946) "the concentrationary universe": a system of social organisation which is at one and the same time, unthinkable and yet everyday. Primo Levi commented that "the Lagers [a general term for camps of various kinds – labour, concentration, extermination] constituted an extensive and complex system which profoundly compenetrated the daily life of the country" (Levi, 1989: 15) whilst simultaneously remaining hidden or unnoticed by the population at large. Arguably the Lagers themselves could not have been conceptualised at all had we not already had slavery, workhouses, prisons, asylums and the factory system of production.

In a similar way, the various types of care setting where older people live out their final years are present in every community, although the worlds within them are generally kept out of public view, enabling the population as a whole to carry on as though nothing is happening. Within care homes it is not unusual for people to be deprived of personal possessions and dignity. As one practitioner commented about his own workplace, "You do not often see jewellery worn, other than rings. Glasses and dentures are often missing; usually slippers not shoes are worn" (Capstick, 2008).

The theory of social amnesia advanced by Jacoby (1996) suggests that the "disorder of forgetting" is located less in the individual brain than in society as a whole, in the collective denial and wilful repression of things that are already known. He suggests that the erosion of links between past and present, and the increasing tendency to mistake novelty for progress, mean that the lessons of the past are not learned; history repeats itself, albeit in changed circumstances. Social amnesia is "a general syndrome... society has lost its memory... the inability to think back, takes its toll on the ability to think at all" (Jacoby, 1996: 3–4).

Whilst the case of people diagnosed with dementia may be only one example of a "lesson not learned from history" it is a demographically urgent one for

European societies to pay attention to now. It is characterised by pseudoscientific and ideological arguments chillingly unchanged *nach Auschwitz*, to use Adorno's term for the post-war world (Adorno, 1977). Ironically, too, the former Holocaust survivors, prisoners of war, and combat veterans, the civilians involved in bombing raids, war work and mass evacuations, are now the very at-risk generations for late-onset dementia. Here we are not dealing with two separate populations but one. Benjamin's permanent state of emergency has afflicted not only their formative years but also, now, their old age as they enter into increasingly marketised care systems, and the shadow of the 'medical-industrial' complex.

References

Adorno, T.W. (1970) 'Education after Auschwitz', cited in Rothberg (2000)
Adorno, T.W. (1977) *Gesammelte Schriften in Zwanzig Banden* [Collected works in 20 volumes], cited in Rothberg (2000)
Agamben, G. (1999) *Remnants of Auschwitz: The witness and the archive*, New York: Zone Books
Baldwin, C. and Capstick, A. (2007) *Tom Kitwood on dementia: a reader and critical commentary*, Maidenhead: Open University Press
Ballard, C., Lana, M.M., Theodoulou, M., Douglas, S. and McShane, R. (2008) 'A randomised, blinded, placebo-controlled trial in dementia patients continuing or stopping neuroleptics (the DART-AD Trial)', *Public Library of Science Medicine*, 5 (4): 76
Benjamin, W. (1940) 'Theses on the philosophy of history', in *Illuminations* (1999, trans. Zohn), London: Pimlico, 245–55
Bond, J., Corner, L. and Graham, R. (2004) 'Social science theory of dementia research: normal ageing, cultural representation and social exclusion', in Innes, A., Archibald, C. and Murphy, C. (eds) *Dementia and social inclusion*, London: Jessica Kingsley Publishers
Capstick, A. (2008; unpublished EdD thesis) *'I'm wondering now if I'm the only person who remembers': using film and narrative biography to resist social amnesia in dementia studies*, Manchester Metropolitan University
Cohen, M. (1993) *Profane Illumination: Walter Benjamin and the Paris of surreal revolution*, University of California Press
Cohen-Mansfield, J. (2005) 'Nonpharmacological interventions for persons with dementia', *Alzheimer's Care Quarterly*, 6 (2): 129–45
Cooley, R. (2007) 'A Kantian moral duty for the soon-to-be-demented to commit suicide', *American Journal of Bioethics*, 7 (6): 37–44
Fleischer, A.S., Sowell, B.B., Taylor, C., Gamst, A.C., Petersen, R.C. and Tal, L.J. (2007) 'Clinical predictors of progression to Alzheimer disease in amnestic mild cognitive impairment', *Neurology*, 68: 1,588–95
Folstein, M.F., Folstein, S.E. and McHugh, P.R. (1975) 'Mini-Mental State: a practical method for grading the cognitive state of patients for the clinician', *Journal of Psychiatric Research*, 12: 189–98
Fox, P. (1989) 'From senility to Alzheimer's disease: the rise of the Alzheimer's disease movement', *Millbank Quarterly*, 67 (1): 58–102
Harding, N. and Palfrey, C. (1997) *The social construction of dementia: confused professionals*, London: Jessica Kingsley Publishers
Ineichen, B. (1987) 'Measuring the rising tide; how many dementia cases will there be by 2001?', *British Journal of Psychiatry*, 150: 195–200
Jacoby, R. (1996) *Social amnesia: a critique of contemporary psychology*, London: Transaction
Kitwood, T. (1997) *Dementia reconsidered: the person comes first*, Buckingham: Open University Press

Knapp, M., Comas-Herrera, A., Somani, A. and Banerjee, S. (2007) *Dementia UK: Report to the Alzheimer's Society*, London: Personal Social Services Research Unit, London School of Economics/Institute of Psychiatry, King's College London

Kraepelin, E. (1910) cited in Berrios, G.E. (1995) 'Dementia. Clinical section', in Berrios, G.E. and Porter, R., eds, *A history of clinical psychiatry: the origin and history of psychiatric disorders*, London: Athlone, 52–61

Levi, P. (1989) *The drowned and the saved*, trans. Rosenthal, New York: Vintage

Lothrop Stoddard, T. (1920) *The rising tide of colour against white world-supremacy*, Montana: Kessinger Publishing Company

Macdonald, A. and Cooper, B. (2007) 'Long-term care and dementia services: an impending crisis', *Age and Ageing*, 35: 16–22

Palmer, K., Berger, A.K., Monastero, R., Winblad, B., Backman, L. and Fratiglioni, L. (2007) 'Predictors of progression from mild cognitive impairment to Alzheimer disease', *Neurology*, 68: 1,596–602

Rose, S., Lewontin, R.C. and Kamin, L.J. (1984) *Not in our genes: biology, ideology and human nature*, Harmondsworth: Penguin

Rothberg (2000) *Traumatic realism*, Minneapolis: University of Minnesota Press

Rousset, D. (1946) *L'univers concentrationnaire*, Paris: Pavois

Scholl, J.M. and Sabat, S.R. (2008) 'Stereotypes, stereotype threat and ageing: implications for the understanding and treatment of people with Alzheimer's disease', *Ageing and Society*, 28: 103–30

Strous, R.D. (2007) 'Psychiatry during the Nazi era: ethical lessons for the modern professional', *Annals of General Psychiatry*, 6: 8

The Times (17 March 2008) 'A living death', London: Times Group Newspapers

von Cranach, M. (2003) 'The killing of psychiatric patients in Nazi Germany between 1939–45', *Isr. J. Psychiatry Related Science*, 40 (1): 8–18

Warnock, M. (2008) 'A duty to die?', *Life and work*, October 2008, Church of Scotland

White, N., Scott, A., Woods, R.T., Wenger, G.C., Keady, J.D. and Devakumar, M. (2002) 'The limited utility of the Mini-Mental State Examination in screening people over the age of 75 years for dementia in primary care', *British Journal of General Practice*, 52: 1,002–3

CHAPTER 12
The impact of the media on health policy
Case studies from England and the UK

(Opening presentation at the conference)

John Lister

This conference at Coventry University, called by the International Association of Health Policy in Europe, is as far as I have been able to establish the first ever conference to link health policy with the role of the media. Everyone I have discussed it with has said "what a good idea": there is an immediate recognition of the connection between the two issues.

How can most people get information on health services and developments in health care? Few people have any first-hand access to information, and most of that will be very local. Virtually everyone is dependent upon media sources for what knowledge they have, and this has to be transmitted by health journalists, few of whom have any specialist training.

If we look at the circulation figures this becomes even more obvious. In Britain, the publications of the specialist health press – the *British Medical Journal*, the *Health Service Journal*, the *Nursing Standard*, *Nursing Times* and other even more specialised titles – have a combined circulation of fewer than 100,000 weekly. (Although obviously, some increase their reach through online publication; but again, this is mainly to a specialist reading audience of health professionals and academics).

By contrast, the mainstream national newspapers have an estimated readership of over 20 million daily, plus many more accessing online and broadcast news, and many more reading local newspapers. Many magazines, especially those aimed at women, also cover health issues, although in general this is from a more individualised, lifestyle and human-interest standpoint[1].

Why is reporting of health care especially important?

Health care is a major factor in every major national economy and on a world scale: it is possibly the biggest global industry, with a turnover of more than $5 trillion and 59 million employees, and touching the lives of tens of millions more, who supply goods or services to health providers, or who make use of the services of health systems. Health spending accounts for one dollar in six in the US economy (the US, with 5 per cent of the world's population, spends 40 per cent of the world's health budget) and upwards of 7 per cent of the GDP of most advanced economies[2].

The scale of this spending, the size of the health workforce, and the even larger numbers of people whose health depends upon the various health-care systems mean decisions about them are inevitably very political. Again health care has the highest political profile in the wealthiest countries, where 87 per cent of global spending takes place – much of the funding flowing through public-sector or social health insurance budgets, or in other ways influenced by government. The continued controversy in the USA over President Obama's fairly minimal and belated health reforms underlines the fact that the sensitivity over health policy can reach well beyond the centres of government and the users of health services into the boardrooms of powerful insurance companies of hospital corporations.

Health care and its accessibility to those who need it more is also massively a social issue. Everyone is at least from time to time potentially interested in their own health, but many are also drawn in by 'human interest' angles on health care, examining the plight of particular individuals or groups, or may be worried over potential epidemics or other heath issues, and seek information and reassurance.

The rapid rate of technical and scientific advance in health care (and all of the decisions on priorities which are implicit in the investment of money and human resources) is also important for understanding the present situation and future challenges of health care and health systems. Priorities need to be decided upon: resources are almost inevitably rationed, whether explicitly through excluding certain costly and/or ineffective treatments, or (in the USA and many other countries which lack universal health coverage) implicitly rationed by price – excluding the poor and uninsured. However, amidst the

---

1 Figures from National Readership Survey, http://www.nrs.co.uk
2 Lister, J. (2008) *Globalization and Health Systems Change,* Globalization and Health Knowledge Network, WHO Commission for Social Determinants of Health

progress and scientific breakthroughs there are also major problems (the most notorious still being Thalidomide in the 1960s[3]), questionable techniques and ineffective 'cures'. For too many who face poor and inadequate treatment there are also questions of negligence and incompetence, whether at the level of professional clinicians or management and systems: news reporting and debate of these issues helps to maintain a level of scrutiny and accountability in services which historically have been the preserve of a medical hierarchy and its closed professional circles. Other issues which can usefully be aired in media reports include the discussion of the design of buildings and systems: are they user friendly? And lobby groups and campaigners, especially those warning of huge unresolved problems in the poorest developing countries, need the weight of the media to force drug companies and other powerful institutions to explain who controls the research agenda, and whose interests current research is designed to meet.

All of these aspects help to make health, health care and health systems a natural topic for media coverage. However, they can also work to limit the focus and extent of coverage:

- **Economics:** the economic power of health providers as potential advertisers (often among the largest local employers) and their political connections and influence can result in a deferential approach from editors and journalists, especially at local level, who are often reluctant to challenge or confront them.
- **Politics:** health-care systems tend to be complex, with varying levels of local and democratic accountability – if any; and in the UK, especially rapid "reforms" have left many editors and journalists out of date and lacking any critical view. Neoliberal and pro-market assumptions are seldom challenged in the media, despite the fact that there is no evidence that they are shared by most of the target audience. In England, government public relations departments, and regional and local organisations pump out a regular stream of "news" and statements, often arguing a contentious point of view as if it were simply a statement of fact. Lazy journalists or weak editors, without any alternative point of view or depth of knowledge, often simply echo or even reprint these press releases to deliver one-sided coverage that leaves readers lacking basic information. Even experienced health reporters can be reduced in this way to delivering little more than a bland summary of government's professed policy aims, with no clear critique and little attempt to find any cogently argued balancing views.

---

3   *Time* magazine (1962) 'Medicine: The Thalidomide Disaster', Friday, 10 August 1962, available at: http://www.time.com/time/magazine/article/0,9171,873697,00.html#ixzz0yUnWVy9z

- **Social:** the quest for the headline-grabbing media story can lead to misleading information receiving high prominence, while subsequent corrections are downplayed or ignored: perhaps the most obvious example of this was the hue and cry over the MMR vaccine on the basis of flawed research in 1998 – fuelled by populist right-wing press, and limply answered elsewhere. This is not simply a problem in the overtly right-wing press. For example, the *Guardian* in 2001 ran the ambiguous headline "Study claims MMR vaccination is safe" – effectively reinforcing fears among those already convinced that it was not[4]. The vacillating coverage of the panic over swine flu, forcing governments in Europe into spending billions on dubiously effective vaccines and anti-viral medicines is another example, with some newspapers like the right wing *Daily Mail* managing to indulge in populist anti-government rhetoric at each stage – with screaming headlines warning of large-scale loss of life, castigating ministers for their dilatory response one week, and furious headlines complaining that money had been wasted and the whole "pandemic" exaggerated a few weeks later.
- **Technical:** where health systems are chaotic or weak, such as in the USA, health journalists tend to hide behind an increasing level of technical and "scientific" reporting, focused on new cures, new drugs, and human-interest stories, but giving little coverage to the campaign for a more rational and efficient system, such as single-payer health insurance. This can be clearly seen in the predominant subject matter of email discussions of the main US professional body, the Association of Health Care Journalists[5]. The focus on technical issues can be to the detriment of any more political and rounded understanding of issues, as shown by a packed workshop session on the financing of health care at the AHCJ conference in Seattle in 2008, which was eager to hear the figures on soaring health costs into the mid century… but almost unanimously resistant to discussing how the wasteful costs of the system might be reined in through a 'single payer' system. Of course, one limitation of news coverage focused on very technical aspects of health care is that relatively few health reporters are scientifically trained: this leaves them very dependent upon PR from drug companies and hospitals, while individual 'experts' have to be located to provide any critical view. Some of these experts in turn prove to have an agenda which may skew their comments – the net result being that the news audience again is left with less than reliable information, claim and counter-claim.

---

4   *Guardian Society* (staff and agencies) (2001) 'Study claims MMR vaccination is safe', Friday 12 January 2001, available at: http://www.guardian.co.uk/society/2001/jan/12/health1
5   Available to members only at: http://www.healthjournalism.org/list/html/ahcj-l/

The quality and depth of the journalism covering health issues is also affected by general pressures on the news media: the thinning out of news rooms by employers seeking short-term gains at the expense of long-term quality in their product has left fewer staff to keep up with the news, often with little or no time to investigate behind stories and check out a rising tide of sophisticated PR – or to investigate the curious silences and changes of emphasis which often tell a lot about what is happening.

Websites, competing against each other for audience share, have more effectively introduced 24-hour rolling news than the rather tedious and repetitive TV equivalents – and in doing so, have reduced the time allowed to turn around a fresh story from a press release. BBC webpage staff are under instruction to get stories processed and up on the web inside five minutes of receiving the first email, and to check details afterwards. This makes it impossible to seek out any alternative take on the story: often there is not even time to check out the main contact at the bottom of the press release.

Nick Davies' book **Flat Earth News**[6] and the National Union of Journalists' "Stand up for Journalism" campaign have helped to expose the phenomenon of 'churnalism' in which under-resourced newsrooms recycle unchecked press releases as 'news'. The pressure on staff means that many have to remain as generalists rather than focus on developing the more specialist knowledge which takes time to build up, but which would then allow a more independent and critical stance towards assertions, many of which hang on tenuous evidence, if any.

One example, from the BBC Radio 4 *Today* programme, was the news item that there had been a ten-fold increase in numbers of NHS patients being treated in private hospitals. The web version of the story begins "Patients going private on the NHS. Thousands of patients a month are using a government reform to get what is effectively private treatment paid for by the taxpayer…"[7]. Further down the article it reveals that the 3,500 patients a month who have made this choice "still represents less than 1% of overall non-emergency treatment". It does not spell out that the NHS treats 6.5 million elective cases a year, compared to just 44,000 who were invoking their new right to choose private hospitals (or compared to a minimal 4,000 or so the year before). Nor does it mention that the average cost of these NHS-funded operations in private hospitals is just £2,000 per patient[8], suggesting only the most minor operations are going to non-NHS hospitals.

---

6 Davies, N. (2008) *Flat Earth News*, Chatto and Windus, London
7 Triggle, N. (2008) 'Patients going "private" on NHS', 2 December, available at: http://newsvote. bbc.co.uk/mpapps/pagetools/print/news.bbc.co.uk/1/hi/health/7742363.stm?ad=1
8 3,634 of these operations apparently cost just £7.6 million, according to the same article.

This type of reporting effectively bolsters up and lends credibility to controversial government policies, suggesting that the trend is far more significant than it really is. The exaggerated view reaches millions of people in the UK and worldwide, most of whom will see or hear only the opening few lines and not have any way of putting the story into context.

Another symptom of the general weakness of local and national reporting is the tacit acceptance of the growing cult of secrecy among NHS Foundation Trusts, which were allegedly established to make themselves more accountable and responsive to local people. The *Health Service Journal* has found that less than a quarter of the 30 Foundation Trusts it surveyed meet in public, and less than a third publish their Board papers[9]. A survey in 2008 had also revealed that over 40% of Foundations only held directors' meetings behind closed doors, with the public excluded: but where has this been challenged in the local or national press?

Why have local, regional and national news editors and reporters allowed themselves to be excluded in this way from discovering anything other than the content of an occasional PR handout from many of the largest and best resourced hospital Trusts in the country? One reason may well be that too few journalists these days would think of scrutinising the board papers of FTs or other NHS bodies even if they received them.

- They may well not have time to work on a task which will not always necessarily generate a story;
- Many also lack the experience and expertise to single out potential stories and separate the rhetorical padding and PR spin from the newsworthy content;
- Even fewer local (and very few national) journalists look at the wider picture across the NHS, so hardly any of them are in any position to make a comparison between local developments and the wider picture across the NHS.

Yet of course NHS and Foundation Trusts are major organisations, each in many cases turning over hundreds of millions of pounds each year, and responsible for delivering a range of vital services to local communities – which have no direct voice in shaping what is done, or checking on the standards of health care they and their relatives receive.

A failure to report local events within Trusts and Primary Care Trusts means that even controversial policies often cannot be challenged or subjected to any real public debate. Occasionally policies emerge from behind this wall of silence to be put into the public domain for "consultation": by this time the decisions have already been largely taken, and the consultation is a meaningless

---

9   West, D. (2009) 'Private board meeting risks spelled out', *HSJ*, 2 April

formality – but even then some local news coverage fails to develop a serious critique, or challenge the prevailing secrecy.

Another very significant example of this has been the hyper-secretive process of negotiating and signing **Private Finance Initiative** contracts for building new hospitals and facilities (PFI). Pleading "commercial confidentiality", the NHS Trusts refuse to divulge any of the details before these contracts worth hundreds or millions or even billions of pounds are signed – but often continue to resist publication of potentially embarrassing details on the cost and implications of the new plans long after the negotiations are complete and the deal has been signed.

Occasionally the news media will play a role in helping to draw out some of this information – as with the recent BBC Merseyside phone-in debate between me and the chief exec of the Royal Liverpool Hospitals Trust on its plan for a £477m PFI scheme: but the deferential approach meant that every question went first to the NHS boss, who filled up the lion's share of the time with long and evasive answers, and very few sharp questions were aimed at him by the programme's presenter.

In this way, PFI deals totalling £11 billion have been signed or are now close to conclusion, involving over 100 NHS Trusts in deals costing £62 billion over the next 30 to 40 years[10]. Precious few of these have been subject to any serious local scrutiny or debate by the media, which has generally been too happy to accept the local Trust's word for it that the deals are affordable and value for money.

Only when it becomes clear that this is not the case, and that the repayments are unaffordable, or the situation of local services is changed, are some local newspapers and broadcasters forced, after the event, to take stock of problems – financial or technical – arising from PFI hospitals, which could have been foreseen and challenged in advance. National coverage is if anything even more superficial, containing little explicit debate on the investment of billions, with payments to drag on for a generation to come.

One excuse for not giving more detailed coverage to issues such as PFI and to the repeated and increasingly bizarre reorganisation and restructuring of the NHS is that the issues are said by editors and some journalists to be "too complex" for the wider public to understand. Almost any debate on PFI is punctuated by reminders that we must "keep it simple" for the audience, and not "throw confusing statistics around"; while NHS managers, put on the spot by the use of simple but embarrassing case studies of PFI schemes that have gone horribly wrong, hasten to make the discussion more confusing – by using statistics or claiming that the example is inappropriate.

---

10 HM Treasury, 'PFI Signed Projects List', available at: http://www.hm-treasury.gov.uk/ppp_pfi_stats.htm

The resistance to serious debate is greatest on the restructuring of the NHS, which now runs hand in hand with the drive towards a competitive market in health care and the controversial privatisation and fragmentation of services. Even back in 1999, in a feature article for the middle class and relatively well-informed readers of the *Guardian*, health correspondent David Brindle introduced a discussion of the government's reorganisation of primary care services with an apology:

> Few people outside the health service ever understood the Conservatives' internal market, its separation of 'provider' hospital and community trusts and the 'purchaser' health authorities having been confused by the addition of voluntary GP fundholding. ...
>
> It is highly unlikely that tomorrow's changes will be followed any more closely. If anything they are more complicated still...[11]

The article, which went on to discuss the establishment of Primary Care Groups, confined itself to quoting doctors and their concerns: but it was not followed up by any serious discussion of the process by which, within two years, all of the PCGs had themselves been replaced by bigger Primary Care Trusts, in which the influence of GPs was effectively minimised.

In 2005, the Primary Care Trusts themselves came up for a new round of "reform", facing merger into fewer, larger units in a policy to create a new market in health care: NHS Chief Executive Sir Nigel Crisp issued a circular in July 2005 entitled "Commissioning A Patient-Led NHS"[12]. This sparked an unexpected level of publicity and political anger, with widespread fears of fragmentation and privatisation. In October 2005, it was the *Guardian*'s John Carvel who entered apologetically into the discussion:

> Much of the talk among NHS folk at fringe meetings and in the bars of Brighton was about [Health Secretary Patricia Hewitt's] plans to change the size and functions of primary care trusts (PCTs) – the local organisations that hold the health service in England together. A word that came up surprisingly often was "bonkers".
>
> Many patients may not even know the 300 PCTs exist, but they are the organisational bedrock of the service. Their

---

11 Brindle, D. (1999) 'Up for grabs', *Guardian*, 31 March
12 Lister, J. (2008) *The NHS After 60: for Patients or Profits?*, Middlesex University Press

annual budget is worth about £45bn, which is three-quarters of total NHS spending.[13]

The argument over these changes rumbled on into 2006, when (no thanks to the *Guardian* or its low-key coverage of the issues) Patricia Hewitt was forced by the weight of opposition to put the proposal to hive off PCT services to private or social enterprise providers on hold, and even apologise to the health unions for the way it had been handled. Fortunately the instincts of the public had, on this occasion, coincided with the fears of many local politicians that they might be held responsible for unpopular changes, and the lack of adequate analysis in the news media was compensated by other forms of communication.

But since 2008 we have seen a renewed attempt to force through the same changes – under a different label, and without any high-level press coverage or public consultation. The plans to create a new market in primary care and community health services has been incorporated into the confusingly named project of "World Class Commissioning", for which the literature at national and local level is written in completely unreadable jargon[14]. Most of it appears only on websites, but the occasional leaflet has been produced. The key point has been smuggled in as number ***seven*** in a list of eleven "competencies" against which PCTs' performance is to be measured: this seventh competency is the extent to which a local PCT acts to "stimulate a local market" in health care.

Despite its importance and the recent experience of public anger on this question, not a single press release on this programme has been produced by the Department of Health, and little or no news has appeared about it in the national or local press. Journalists and their editors are clearly as confused or nonplussed by the publicity material as the wider public. Rather than explaining the issues at stake, they have opted to ignore the issue and focus on other things.

In addition there is a further plan to drive through the fragmentation and privatisation of PCT services – worth an estimated £11 billion a year, and employing around 250,000 staff, all of them currently on NHS contracts, and standing to lose their pension rights and other important rights at work. This plan is called "Transforming Community Services"[15].

Details are contained in a 112-page document published in January by the Department of Health – but which again has not been publicised at all. There

---

13 Carvel, J. (2005) 'Feeling the Pressure', *Guardian*, 5 October
14 Lister, J. (2009) 'A Health Workers' Guide to World Class Commissioning', UNISON Eastern region, available at: http://www.healthemergency.org.uk/workingwu/Healthworkersguide.pdf
15 Lister, J. (2009) 'Don't let them turn our health care into a market', *Eastern Eye*, UNISON Eastern Region

has been no press release or attempt to ensure press coverage. Ministers and DoH bureaucrats obviously realise that their plan is at best controversial and at worst hugely unpopular, so they have attempted to minimise any discussion.

In addition to this, the government has also decided to establish yet another body to drive forward the involvement of the private sector in NHS provision, and offer aggrieved private companies a forum through which they can complain if they feel themselves to have been unreasonably excluded from any local "health market". The new "Cooperation and Competition Panel" published extensive and highly contentious consultation documents on its website in January, which in theory marked the opening of a three-month consultation. They make clear that the implications of the new panel and the policy it embodies are far-reaching, opening a space for many more private providers to force their way into a new "market", in which services are paid for by the taxpayer – from the NHS budget.[16]

But yet again there were no press releases issued, and no attempt to ensure the proposals were featured in the press. The government's tactic worked: with the exception of a couple of mentions in the specialist *Health Service Journal* and three articles I wrote for the *Morning Star* newspaper, there was no national press coverage to alert the wider public, health workers or local politicians to the controversial changes taking place.

To promote ONE major national initiative without any publicity might be seen as an oversight by the media: but to promote THREE closely related national initiatives, aimed at establishing a policy known to have been highly unpopular a couple of years earlier, with absolutely zero coverage in any of the mainstream press can only be a deliberate concealment of information from the public.

Editors and journalists have allowed this situation to occur: the biggest privatisation process ever to hit the NHS is being pushed through with no press comment or public consultation. Primary Care Trust bosses, knowing that the policy is unpopular, have argued that to switch from public-sector to private-sector providers would not change services for patients – and therefore does not need to go to consultation. But they are not being challenged on this by local or national news media.

And of course, with no public awareness, the possibility of mounting any kind of campaign to prevent these changes is largely excluded.

We can also conclude that it is no accident that media coverage of primary care services, and in particular of GPs, in the same recent period has switched from the early widespread concern at the problems in recruiting and retaining sufficient GPs to focusing on the increased salaries and reduced workload which GPs secured in the 2003 contract.

---

16   Lister, J. (2009) 'Pulling the wool over your eyes', *Morning Star*, 18 March, available at: http://www.morningstaronline.co.uk/index.php/news/content/view/full/73155

Ministers clearly hope that demonising GPs as money-grabbing and lazy (for accepting a contract which was welcomed by health ministers and by much of the media in 2003) helps to undermine the consistent opinion-poll figures which show that 84 per cent of the public have strong trust in their GP, and the huge popular support for the BMA's campaign in 2008 against the imposition of "polyclinics". Undermining this bond with GPs on NHS contracts helps to open up space for profit-seeking commercial companies such as UnitedHealth to take over local GP contracts, with government targets of privatising 15 per cent of GP services[17].

So what are we to conclude?

We know that both local and national press are under pressure from owners and management seeking to maximise profits and scaling back the investment in skilled and experienced staff. We know that this means that few journalists ever get to read the key policy material, or probe the detail behind the press releases they receive from NHS organisations.

But they don't have to settle for saying nothing. They could always call on expert help. There are people who can help them to fill in the gaps in knowledge, if the journalists will simply seek out advice. In this conference and in university departments up and down the country, there are health policy experts who have a more developed and critical view of the policies and who have some idea of the total lack of any evidence to support market-style reforms.

There are campaigners and campaigns such as Health Emergency, Keep Our NHS Public, the Politics of Health Group, and others which have a developed critique of some of these policies and have a variety of spokespeople able to explain these in simple terms to a wide audience.

And although all of my examples have been taken from England and the UK media, the same is very much true of international health policy, where bad decisions go without scrutiny, and poor policies are applied without debate. Our government is expensively represented in the World Bank, the WHO and the EU, but no reports ever come back on the debates and the decisions that they have been involved in, which also shape the health and health care of countless millions. The world's biggest industry is among the world's least accountable to the public, at local, regional, national and global level.

Of course the media does not shape health policy directly: but the angle of coverage, the extent to which a policy issue hits the wider public agenda and becomes known to a wide audience IS shaped very much by the media.

---

17 Lister, J. (2008) *The NHS After 60: for Patients or Profits?*, Middlesex University Press

That's why we need to look to improve the training and expertise of health journalists, fight for increased staffing levels and resources for newsrooms, and develop a more sophisticated and ambitious press and publicity operation for health unions and the campaigns and organisations seeking to stem the tide of market-style reforms that are threatening to swamp public-sector health care in England and elsewhere.

CHAPTER 13
Talking drugs at the captain's corner
An analysis of a pharmaceutical industry conference

Marisa de Andrade
Institute for Social Marketing (ISM),
University of Stirling

Introduction

Pharmaceutical companies are legally required to put shareholders' interests first and to maximise business revenue. In its pursuit for profit, industry has been accused of being unprincipled and using immoral practices to achieve this goal: "Corporate social responsibility [CSR] or anything that reduces profitability in the long term violates the corporation's fiduciary duty to its shareholders and leaves it vulnerable to a civil lawsuit" (Lexchin, 2006, pp.20–1). Consequently, the public rhetoric on CSR, public 'education' and patient-centredness is being challenged.

Furthermore, "[L]obbying is an enormous international industry" used by the drug industry that has been "regarded with suspicion and even outright mistrust by journalists and the wider public" (McGrath, 2006, p.67). The extent to which this massive undertaking may not necessarily result in public good is not easy to assess, as studies in the field "have always been hampered by difficulties with unveiling the detailed stories behind the political masks" (Haug and Koppang, 1997, p.245). Documenting lobbying strategies is regarded by some to be "as difficult as writing authoritatively about the practice of espionage" (Stanbury, 1988, p.305).

Lobbyists and other key stakeholders collaborate in pharmaceutical advocacy, but discerning their intentions is a challenge without having direct experience of the thinking behind these public positions. Participant observation at industry conferences is therefore an ideal approach for examining the conflict between internal discourses (discussed by drug companies behind closed doors) and external discourses (the messages conveyed to the public through the media and other communication channels).

Industry symposiums provide opportunities for 'networking' and debating best practices in corporate communications. They attract several stakeholders, who collaborate during communicative processes. These include PR experts; lobbyists; members of patient advocacy groups; media representatives and academic researchers. Patients are excluded from these elite, high-level meetings, and are expected to trust that communication strategies discussed in private are socially responsible and in their best interest.

From a corporate perspective, the notion that social responsibility is good for PR and therefore good for business is not a new one (see Golden, 1968, for example). Bernays defined PR as "the practice of social responsibility" (Grunig and Hunt, 1984 in Clark, 2000, p.368) and more recently Clark (2000, p.368) has suggested that PR and CSR have "similar objectives; both disciplines are seeking to enhance the quality of the relationship of an organization among key stakeholder groups. Both disciplines recognize that to do so makes good business sense."

It follows that if PR is simply a tool used by corporations to "manipulate public opinion and perceptions" (see Beder, 1999; Miller and Dinan, 2000; and Stauber and Rampton, 2001, for examples), then CSR may be nothing more than "faux altruism" (Hastings and Lieberman, 2009, p.74) at the expense of the public.

At industry seminars, representatives from lobby groups strip off their "political masks" (Haug and Koppang, 1997, p.245) to engage corporate delegates and share political communication strategies that are executed on behalf of companies. The forum is not only used as a platform to discuss numerous case studies illustrating effective dissemination techniques and focused PR campaigns that if successfully applied by companies will ensure that they "always achieve... public relations goals" (Pratt, 1994, p.292), but also encourages an open, honest debate about industry practices. This is important as it has been determined that there are "disparities between what many lobbyists said [say] in public and private" (Dinan, 2006, p.64).

Equally significant is how the media report health stories that may lead to negative publicity for pharmaceutical companies. Working on the assumption that deadlines drive the news agenda (Gandy, 1982) and journalists prefer to consult reliable, readily available sources rather than searching for unknown alternatives (Tanner, 2004), company press offices cultivate mutually beneficial working relationships with media representatives. Often working closely with PR firms to "manage messages" that are circulated to the media, internal and external media consultants selectively present news items that are in companies' best interests (Corbett and Mori, 1999, p.229). The outcome has been described as "passive", "unaggressive" reporting (Schwitzer, 1992; McManus, 1990).

Drug companies also communicate with the public 'through' patient advocacy groups that are sometimes dependent on financial aid from pharmaceutical firms for survival, but insist they remain impartial (House of Commons (HoC), 2005, pp.74–7). There are more than two hundred patient organisations and support groups operating in the UK seeking to "influence healthcare policy for the benefit of patients", and the government has stated that often it does not know what funds or support in kind patient groups receive from industry (HoC, 2005, p.74–7). A HoC Health Committee report (2005) on *The Influence of the Pharmaceutical Industry* concluded that legislation limiting funds from the industry to these groups would be disadvantageous to patients and that patient groups are "funded by companies' charitable arms, rather than by companies themselves" (HoC, 2005, p.77). However, critics argue that objectivity on the part of the patient group is challenging if financial support comes from a pharmaceutical sponsor (see Mintzes, 2007 for example). Representatives from patient advocacy groups collaborating with companies on disease-specific awareness campaigns are also invited to attend and present at certain industry seminars.

This paper describes the aims and methodology of a case study of an industry conference and discusses the main findings under four headings: working with the media; public education, engagement and awareness; CSR; and political communication strategies.

Aims and method

The research aims to observe how pharmaceutical companies and other senior stakeholders in the market plan and execute their inter-relationships and communications; to gain firsthand experience of these relationships at work; and to acquire deeper insights into the meaning behind the public discourse of constructs like CSR, corporate affairs and public education.

A case study was selected as the preferred methodology to carry out a "holistic, in-depth investigation" focusing on issues "fundamental to understanding the system [elite pharmaceutical strategies] being examined" (Tellis, 1997). The empirical inquiry sought to examine relations in their "real-life context" as these "contextual conditions" were considered to be "highly pertinent" to the "phenomenon of study" (Yin, 2003, p.13). The participant-observation technique thus enabled attempts "to uncover the structures of meanings in social settings" by "becoming immersed in the group" (Kent, 2007, p.108). Ethnography, which has been described as the "truth serum of research", allowed for a "deeper" analysis of stakeholder relations and strategies (Kent, 2007, p.108).

Industry conferences organised by pharmaceutical corporations or private companies specialising in public health seminars attract several like-minded executives. Surrounded by corporate colleagues, key representatives from top multinational firms have the chance to discuss business strategies that would not typically be openly deliberated in the public domain. Obtaining access to these events and reporting on briefs and experiences, therefore, "brings a unique perspective" to industry "activities" and facilitates an analysis of "inner workings" of internal processes that are rarely seen "outside of litigation" (McHenry, 2009, p.943).

A prominent industry conference was identified and an attendance request sent to organisers, who replied with an offer of a press pass and the prospect of participating on a panel session dedicated to working productively with the media. Thus, primary research commenced with the chance to be a part of key e-mail and telephone conference exchanges in the run-up to the event. The two-day meeting allowed for the involvement, depiction and analysis of PR and communication tools used by industry in the promotion of licensed pharmaceuticals in an "ecological" context (see Sismondo, 2009).

Numerous pharmaceutical executives attended with the intention of meeting the "right players and partners" in corporate communications and sharing policies and experiences that would expand industry reputation management. As such, the perspectives of participants, presenters and panellists were examined more generally rather than concentrating on specific strategies used by individual companies and their corresponding representatives.

To reduce the potential of bias and "confirm the validity of the processes" (Stake, 1995), data triangulation was used after collecting information from other sources including conference literature, shared documents and informal interviews (Yin, 2003, pp.98–9).

Findings

Working with the media

One of the group panel sessions focused on working more efficiently with the media, with a view to discover which "key issues" and "agenda items" medical journalists were intending to report on in the subsequent year. These "key media professionals" were identified as stakeholders who "impact" on a company's "brand" and "reputation", and the session was described as an opportunity to learn about "what's most important to journalists when dealing with Pharma communicators".

Three journalists took part in the largely question-and-answer-based discussion, which was moderated by a director of international communications for one of the world's largest pharmaceutical companies. The direction and content of the session was considered in e-mail exchanges and a telephone conference in the run up to the summit. While the moderator claimed that he did not want to "influence participating journalists'" "actual contributions", he offered "a brief summary… on how to approach our [the] session, plus a few additional thoughts… to provide clarity and make it easy and comfortable for everyone."

It was suggested that the session commenced with "brief introductions" of the panellists and the moderator. "Key themes" were identified: the notion that industry representatives "wish to work more effectively with the media/with each other"; the opportunity for company delegates to meet "key media professionals (of different backgrounds/publications) who impact" on "brands" and "corporate reputation"; the prospect of "listen[ing]" and "discuss[ing] openly about things that work and things that don't in our [industry's] approach to the media"; the chance to "learn their [journalists'] current agenda and key focus issues re health and pharma over the next 6–12 months"; to find out more about "what's most key to journalists when dealing with pharma communicators and their agencies"; and to stimulate an "active audience participation and a lively discussion and dialogue" between the media and the industry.

Journalists were encouraged to start the first round of questions by outlining their professional background; the "type of stories" they "typically seek"; disclosing "what sources of information" they use "including calls to companies; alternative sources; online sources, blogs, [and] forums"; describing their "specific work situation" and how they effect "pressures, needs, timelines, etc."; and detailing their "expectations to press offices and agencies". The second interchange was to begin with journalists revealing their "top three mistakes in communicating with the media frequently made by press offices"; "what behaviours or actions" (or lack of these) were "really hate[d]" and how "these hinder[ed]… [journalistic] work"; how these traits have an impact on reporting and "affect… future work/relations with these companies/agencies"; and offer "suggestions to improve" media relations or provide a "wish list", while "bearing in mind also the specific agenda and pressures on companies". If time permitted, the moderator hoped to find out more about journalistic sources: "where do you go to 'discover' interesting story angles if not delivered directly by companies?"; discover the impact of "online sources/health bloggers/twitters etc." and the extent to which "they influence" agenda-setting; whether journalists get in direct contact with headquarters or local/regional offices when dealing with multinational companies; how media communications are different in Europe from the US; how journalists use "respective international networks in order to obtain news fast and beat [your] competition"; how press offices can "simplify" the life of journalists; and whether there are "win–wins" for industry and the media.

A fairly interactive discussion ensued on the day of the presentation, but feedback from attendees was mixed. Overall content and presentation was rated highly, but while some industry representatives found the exchange "useful", "insight[ful]" and "helpful", others thought journalists "did not provide content we [industry] didn't already know" and "seemed negative and not trusting of the industry."

Public engagement, education and awareness

In a presentation on PR in a changing market, a senior executive for a prominent pharmaceutical company described how important it was for industry to recognise the "changing role of stakeholders". Patient advocacy groups were accredited as stakeholders who "are influencing" areas such as patient compliance and prescription rates; access to pharmaceuticals; and clinical trial recruitment. It was noted that patient advocates are members of expert panels for regulatory and guideline-setting bodies such as the United Nation (UN) and the World Health Organization (WHO). Consequently, increased collaboration could aid a decline in drug prices and damaging publicity for the pharmaceutical industry.

The USA National Breast Cancer Coalition (NBCC) was used as a case study to illustrate the power of patient advocacy groups. The Coalition was established in 1991 and aimed to eradicate breast cancer by way of political activism and grassroots advocacy. According to a pharmaceutical executive, the NBCC managed – "through intensive lobbying efforts" – to secure funding from the US Department of Defense's (DoD) budget to finance breast cancer research. As a result, the US DoD Breast Cancer Research Program (BCRP) has funded over $2 billion in breast cancer research.

In order to illustrate further the shifting positions of stakeholders, attention turned to evolving interactions between doctors and patients. Whereas a "Client–Agent Model" was prominent in previous years, a shift towards a "Shared Decision Making Model" was noted. In the former, communication allowed the doctor alone to make a decision as the patient was a passive participant merely receiving "specific, packaged information". The latter paradigm sees the patient as being "active", engaged and knowledgeable enough to make choices about "risks and uncertainties". According to a drug company representative, these "new considerations" have to be taken into account alongside established communication strategies such as securing "robust publicity for key scientific studies" and continued dialogue with "expert influencers" or "KOLs" (key opinion leaders). Communication strategies for the future, therefore, have to be devised with the intention of creating relationships facilitating "two-way communication and dialogue for long term success".

It was also suggested that executives should exploit knowledge across networks through reputation management (Christopher and Gaudenzi, 2009). Trust and reputation would result in "stable relationships, favourability, and emotional attachment" which in turn would lead to "attraction, satisfaction, retention and better knowledge of stakeholders" – a win–win situation. For example, Novartis was involved in a pilot project with the National Institute for Health and Clinical Excellence (NICE) "to assess the extent to which advice by the Institute on the design and conduct of pre-marketing trials might be mutually beneficial" as discussed in a HoC Health Committee report in 2007–2008. The case was used to illustrate how "collaborative relationships are likely to be more satisfactory to the buyer than transactional relationships" as they lead to "increasing trust"; "raising performance"; the "heightening [of] communication"; and a reduction in "the perceived risk of the purchase decision".

The role of reputation was deemed important as "94 percent of consumers and 81 percent of industry stakeholders" think "that drug companies are too aggressive in promoting unapproved uses of their products" and that the "public believes the industry has put profits before patients, abandoning its original vision of improving human health" (PricewaterhouseCoopers, 2007). Therefore, in order to ensure that the "right reputation has favourable effects on customer commitment and purchase intention", companies were encouraged to foster "trust" in patients through "transparency", "accountability" and "objectivity". This could be realised by identifying "shared goals", "common values" and "professional interests" (Keh and Xie, 2009).

Companies were also told that they could "do more with less" by steering "patient behaviour through unbranded disease education"; "public health education"; and "working in partnership with patient advocacy organisations". Product PR was recognised as a means of gaining favourable reporting by the media; a rise in prescription rates and sales for specific brands; fostering "trust and credibility"; and altering "behaviour and attitude". This could be supplemented with Public Health Education Campaigns (PHECs), which were specifically constructed "to engage target consumers with important information and persuade them to have a discussion with their Health Care Provider about a symptom, a disease or a drug therapy". If "motivated patients" were convinced to approach their physicians who were "prepared" by a pharmaceutical "sales force", then a "more productive dialogue" would ensue and "successful outcomes" would result in new prescriptions.

A successful PHEC programme was described as one that consists of an "unbranded website" with "banner ads" and "keyword buying", along with the involvement of patient or physician organisations. The sales force would be notified, letters were sent to target doctors and additional reading material strategically placed in waiting and exam rooms. The effort would be complemented by PR, and bring local and global consumer marketing teams together.

CSR

CSR was identified as a way to add "value" to a company's "business strategy" and "engaging audiences" with messages. The construct was framed as an essential corporate element in a business context: "CSR is no longer nice to have but a way business is conducted" due to mounting "scrutiny and expectations from stakeholders regarding the role of (healthcare) business in society". Examples are the public's belief that health organisations should be accountable for making treatments accessible and shareholders' expectations for returns on their investments. Prospective advantages of CSR include an increase in share prices and a better reputation; reduced "regulatory burden[s]" and lower operational expenditures.

A pharmaceutical representative drew attention to an ever-increasing collective focus on neglected diseases (NDs), which had led to a consciousness of diseases of poverty, support from government and non-governmental organisations and a "desire" from industry to "contribute". While committing to research and development (R&D) in NDs can be perceived as philanthropic, it also secures additional corporate benefits: the opportunity to "contribute in a meaningful way while simultaneously promoting [their] sustainability and profitability"; reaping the rewards of "industry involvement in the global health arena" by getting "policy support" on regulatory and pricing issues for example, "avoid[ing] loss of public trust and goodwill"; "attract[ing] and retain[ing] highly motivated employees"; "develop[ing] new capabilities through partnerships"; and cultivating public–private partnerships as "a way to share and take advantage of respective competencies and areas of expertise".

A successful CSR campaign focusing on NDs, for example, creates a "win–win" situation for public–private collaborations by enhancing worthwhile relations with industry and "government, societies, researchers, [and] employees". CSR messages have to be communicated through various "online tools" such as websites, blogs and virtual tours of company research sites; pamphlets; conferences; and PR activities.

Industry was told to create the impression that it was "doing the right thing" by devising "proactive, high-fit CSR actions and communications". Competitive CSR positioning which was both "intrinsic (noble)" and "extrinsic (self-interested)" would secure "stronger relational benefits", "higher awareness" and elevate "loyalty and advocacy". Furthermore, companies were advised to ensure public relations/communications activities "balance R&D enterprise with [current] commercial activities"; "key CSR actions are well-positioned, visible, voluntary and valuable"; and "public and professional dialogue" is used "to build long-term networks (relationships) founded on shared healthcare goals".

Political communication strategies

A representative from a large pharmaceutical lobby group delivered a presentation on communicating in an increasingly politicised health-care arena. Corporate colleagues were enlightened with the "new" reality of health care in Europe in 2009: "Policymakers are a vital audience for the life science industry; political influence is here to stay in healthcare and what will shape the future; [and] the challenge of a policy-driven environment needs to be faced and embraced." Executives were encouraged to communicate with the policymakers through the lobby group as the European Commission (EC), the Executive Branch of the European Union (EU), "doesn't want to speak to individuals". By working with and through the organisation, pharmaceutical companies were told they could overcome the barriers the "government has put… in place to stop key opinion leaders from influencing policy".

"Who really matters" in health care and politics, according to the lobbyist, depends on who is asking the question as clinicians, patients, the government and patients all consider themselves to be of utmost importance. It was emphasised that some "bit players" in the political communication process think they are of greater consequence than they actually are: "Ptolomy argued that the universe rotated around the earth… some people still do". This patient-centred outlook, however, was misguided: "The Copernican view is the accepted reality; patients should ideally be at the centre of the universe… even if the perception of relative importance differs… the truth is perhaps more mundane and less altruistic… but we need to play the game". Industry representatives were thus advised to "follow the money" by influencing policymakers with a sense of urgency, as a "pressing political issue" of far more seriousness than "the credit crunch" loomed.

Health care, it was explained, is under "political pressure" as a growth in life expectancy facilitated by pharmaceutical advancements (extensive vaccination and disease screening programmes for example) puts strain on the industry. The "popularity" of long life, therefore, has "created its own problems" as "retirement age has not radically changed to reflect this increase". As the proportion of lifetime spent in retirement increases, so too does the cost of health-care provision. An untenable social model exists as this "problem" is coupled with a "fertility crisis" in Europe, which means that "funding coming into the social system from the workforce is not enough to sustain current levels of care".

The lobby group predicts that health care will suffer as the government finds a way to "pay for the grey" and is reminding industry that "the rules of the game are changing" and it needs to act by revising communication strategies.

Whereas industry had been "successful in meeting the needs of their priority stakeholders" in the past, the "uptake of new treatments" were "no longer driven through clinical opinion leaders". In addition, "new therapies" are now viewed as "potential financial burdens for budgets" rather "solutions". An advanced, politically motivated communication model was advocated, as "the nature, relative importance and influence of stakeholders has changed".

As "traditional" influences are no longer "effective", pharmaceutical companies are being advised to make themselves "part of the solution to what policymakers see as their challenges", and make their "therapy areas" both politically and clinically relevant. One of the organisation's strategies is to ensure industry "messages… resonate with a much broader range of stakeholders" and to "accept that many of these stakeholders have little knowledge of – or interest in – the clinical, data-driven language which we [industry] routinely use". Furthermore, the challenge, according to the lobby group, is to make certain that the pharmaceutical industry is not affected when these policymakers decide to "squeeze budgets".

Drug company executives were reminded that they "need to understand and accept policy drivers and empathize with the logic behind [their need to be cut back on spending]". This can be achieved by engaging with policymakers and those who influence them; and knowing and explaining "how their products impact policy delivery in areas outside of health" (through employment, competitiveness, social security, pensions and innovation, for example). When engaging with policymakers, the group's advice is to keep the message simple and memorable by "choosing the right channel for the right audience" and "a clear objective for their communications". "Brief, relevant and appropriate" messages should be constructed by choosing the "minimum level of understanding" that needs to be assumed. They should not be "too technical" or over-simplified as "no one likes to feel stupid or patronized". Moreover, the importance of "segmenting" the audience was emphasised: "What level of detail do they need? A desk officer will have different needs to a Minister; a patient group representative may know more about your area than you do… What will they do with the information?"

Subsequently, the industry was told to identify the "one or two core messages relevant to them [the target audience]", while maintaining an awareness about "what is being said about you [industry] externally". It was highlighted that "credibility is as important as ideology" and that some new stakeholders would be "idealistic". It was therefore important for industry to believe in the products it was selling in order to generate belief in them by the public; remember that "living up to expectations is at the core of reputation"; to "be realistic" on what is deliverable; to be "consistent" and "never, ever lie".

When constructing a message, industry representatives were first encouraged to identify whether their audience is politicians; patients and their representatives; opinion formers; clinicians; or the lay public. It would then be necessary to determine how the target audience fits into the industry's four "frames of engagement": high political; emotional; rational or common man. The reform of the National Health Service (NHS) in the UK was used as an example. If this issue was presented to politicians, a highly political approach was suggested. According to the group, a "big picture view" emphasising equality, universality, sustainability and solidarity as principles in health care should be accentuated. The same message would have to be tweaked if presented to patients, who would respond better to emotional messages that "speak to the right side of the brain". This would be the angle of choice if the message was being delivered to the "carer of a woman with Alzheimer's disease who was unable to gain access to treatment"; or "relatives of a dead relative for whom an ambulance arrived too late". Clinicians and opinion formers, for example, may respond better to rational messages "speak[ing] to [the] left side of the brain". They may engage in a debate on the reform of the NHS by deliberating on patients rights versus responsibilities. The common man, on the other hand, would be more interested in how the reform would impact on the lives of everyday citizens practically through waiting lists and times.

Attention was then shifted to the fact that Brussels "does 'do' healthcare". It was predicted that the EU will manage health care within ten years and partly already does. However, it is still imperative for industry to continue to be engaged at national and local levels. Communications have to be directed "at the right level – i.e. where the decisions you need will be taken!"

Part of the proposed communication strategy includes the need to connect "before you [industry] need[s] to". If senior company executives thought it was time to engage, it was "probably too late". And once the process of engagement had commenced, it needed to be maintained. Drug companies were told that they need to have an awareness of "what is being said, by whom and [to] have a response ready". Communications teams need to know how to disseminate "quick" and "effective" responses through appropriate communication "channels".

Finally, industry representatives were advised to "try your [their] best to be 'unreasonable'": "The reasonable man adapts himself to the world: The unreasonable one persists in trying to adapt the world to himself. Therefore all progress depends on the unreasonable man".

Conclusion

Prominent industry conferences attract representatives from influential companies, patient advocacy groups, PR firms, lobby groups, and the media and gaining access to them facilitates an understanding of key strategies used by industry to promote its products. Admission provides an opportunity to engage with various stakeholders both formally and informally in a structured environment, where concurring and cooperative pharmaceutical allies gather to share internal information. Case studies of industry "success stories" are outlined with a view to enlighten corporate colleagues who may be competitors on a case by case basis, but are essentially united in the quest to influence policymaking that will help the promotion and sales of products to the public.

As patients are deliberately excluded from these meetings, executives have the chance to discuss candidly communication strategies that may not necessarily centre round them. In effect, these seminars are used to share and elaborate on techniques that are used to persuade the public to believe the messages created by the industry.

Journalists are invited to take part in industry conventions so that symbiotic relationships between the media and industry can be nurtured or created. Official exchanges in the form of panel discussions provide platforms for informed debate. Collectively, pharmaceutical executives pose premeditated questions, the answers to which facilitate the crafting of superior media strategies. The intention is not to alienate journalists who may not be "trusting of the industry", but to try to discern why they hold beliefs that could negatively "impact" on a company's "brand" and "reputation". Information gathering exercises are used to find out more about how journalists operate on a daily basis. Despite claiming that formal, interactive panel sessions are not intended to be "influenced" by industry moderators, it is apparent that the discussion of specific "key issues" is on the agenda, issues such as the disclosure of traditional sources and the impact and use of online sources. Journalists' responses inform future media campaigns, thus evasive replies are of little use.

The attendance and contribution of patient advocacy groups is also valuable as these entities emerge as influential stakeholders who can help industry on a practical level, by reducing drug prices for example, and on a reputational level by constructing compassionate corporate images. While collaborating with these stakeholders is portrayed as a way of actively engaging with patients, this "two-way communication" process is framed as an essential business strategy to secure "long term success[es]". Knowledge sharing and the concept of the "informed patient" are described as trust- and reputation-building techniques, rather than patient-centred approaches to improve public health. CSR is similarly advocated as a way to promote patient allegiance and support. While certain industry representatives stress the importance of "shared healthcare goals", this contradicts the "more mundane and less altruistic" "truth" shared in other presentations that patients are not as important as they think they are.

Educational and public awareness campaigns are viewed as opportunities to persuade the public to go to their doctors and ask about treatments, which could lead to an increase in prescriptions and profits. Carefully selected "keywords" are strategically placed on "unbranded websites" so the line between educating and advertising is blurred. These practices are consciously discussed during private industry conventions, but are not communicated to patients.

There is evidence that some of the proposed political communication strategies are misleading to the public – for example, the lobby group's allusion to patients' belief that they "matter most" in health care, when in reality their needs are deemed relatively insignificant by political players during policy-making. While lobbying efforts create the illusion that patients are of utmost importance, it is apparent that the motivation behind this pretext is self-interested financial reward. The inevitability of a "Malthusian catastrophe" is used to justify a politically motivated communication paradigm shift*, where the focus is not on the science itself, but on the way in which it is presented to policymakers. Policies are devised by industry for industry rather than the public at large, and are directed at influential legislators. Potential benefits for patients are regarded as less important than the maximisation of company profits. Messages in accordance with business strategies are purposively created and propagated through the right channels so that target audiences, such as patients, do not challenge industry initiatives. On the contrary, the "emotional messages" that they receive are devised to assure patients that companies are acting altruistically.

In conclusion, an intra-elite communication network created by Big Pharma allows industry to collaborate with other stakeholders in the promotion of its products. These relations facilitate the construction of inter-related strategies and are thus central to pharmaceutical corporate affairs. Patients, on the other hand, are not privy to internal communications. While this may be an inevitable feature of corporate capitalism, it is of concern to public health.

Bibliography

Beder, S. (1999) 'Public participation or public relations?' in: B. Martin, ed., *Technology and Public Participation*, Wollongong: University of Wollongong, pp.169–92

Christopher, M. and Gaudenzi, B. (2009) 'Exploiting Knowledge across Networks through Reputation Management', *Industrial Marketing Management*, 38(2), 191–7

Clark, C.E. (2000) 'Differences Between Public Relations and Corporate Social Responsibility: An Analysis', *Public Relations Review*, 26(3), 363–80

Corbett, J.B. and Mori, M. (1999) 'Medicine, media, and celebrities: Media coverage of breast cancer, 1960–1995', *Journalism & Mass Communication Quarterly*, 76(2), 229–49

---

* While Malthus (1798) predicted that an exponential population growth coupled with limited agricultural resources would eventually lead to fundamental social changes, such as a decline in population which would usher in a state of misery, lobbyists expect a fertility crisis and other factors to stimulate similar disarray for the pharmaceutical industry unless political strategies are adopted to avert the situation.

Dinan, W. (2006) 'Learning Lessons? The registration of lobbyists at the Scottish parliament. A reply to Coldwell', *Journal of Communication Management*, 10(1), 55–66

Gandy, O.H.J. (1982) *Beyond Agenda Setting: Information subsidies and public policy*, Norwood, NJ: Ablex

Golden, L.L. (1968) *Only by Public Consent: American Corporations Search for Favorable Opinion*, New York: Hawthorne Books

Hastings, G. and Lieberman, J. (2009) 'Tobacco corporate social responsibility and fairy godmothers: the Framework Convention on Tobacco Control slays a modern myth', *Tobacco Control*, 18(2), 73–4

Haug, M. and Koppang, H. (1997) 'Lobbying and Public Relations in a European Context', *Public Relations Review*, 23(3), 233–47

House of Commons, Health Committee, Forth Report of the Session 2004–2005, *The Influence of the Pharmaceutical Industry*, accessed on 20 May 2008 from: http://www.publications.parliament.uk/pa/cm200405/cmselect/cmhealth/42/42.pdf

Keh, H.T. and Xie, Y. (2009) 'Corporate reputation and customer behavioural intentions: The roles of trust, identification and commitment', *Industrial Marketing Management*, 38(7), 732–42

Kent, R. (2007) *Marketing Research: Approaches, Methods and Applications in Europe*, London: Thomson

Lexchin, J. (2006) 'The pharmaceutical industry and the pursuit of profit', in: Cohen, J., C., Illington, P. and Shuklenk, U., eds, *The Power of Pills: Social, ethical &legal issues in drug development, marketing & pricing*

Malthus, T.R. (1798) *An Essay on the Principle of Population (As It Effects the Future Improvement of Society, with Remarks on the Speculations of Mr. Goodwin, M. Condorcet, and Other Writers)*, first edition, London: J. Johnson, in St. Paul's Churchyard

McGrath, C. (2006) 'The Ideal Lobbyist: Personal characteristics of effective lobbyists', *Journal of Communication Management*, 10(1), 67–79

McHenry, L. (2009) 'Ghosts in the Machine: Comment on Sismondo', *Social Studies of Science*, 39(6), 943–7

McManus, J. (1990) 'How local television learns what news is', *Journalism Quarterly*, 67(4), 672–83

Miller, D. and Dinan, W. (2008) *A Century of Spin: How Public Relations became the Cutting Edge of Corporate Power*, London: Pluto Press

Mintzes, B. (2007) 'Should patient groups accept money from drug companies? No', *British Medical Journal*, 334(7600), 935

Pratt, C.B. (1994) 'Hill & Knowlton's Two Ethical Dilemmas', *Public Relations Review*, 20(3), 277–94

Pricewaterhousecoopers (2007) *Recapturing the Vision: Restoring Trust in the Pharmaceutical Industry by Translating Expectations into Actions*

Schwitzer, G. (1992) 'The magical medical media tour', *Journal of the American Medical Association*, 267(14), 1,969–71

Sismondo, S. (2009) 'Ghosts in the Machine: Publication Planning in the Medical Sciences', *Social Studies of Science*, 39(2), 171–98

Stake, R. (1995) *The art of case research*, Newbury Park, CA: Sage Publications

Stanbury, W.T. (1988) *Business-Government Relations in Canada*, Scarborough, ON: Nelson

Stauber, J. and Rampton, S. (2001) *Trust Us, We're Experts: How Industry Manipulates Science and Gambles with Your Future*, New York: Penguin Putnam

Tanner, A.H. (2004) 'Agenda Building, Source Selection, and Health News at Local Television Stations: A Nationwide Survey of Local Television Health Reporters', *Science Communication*, 25(4), 350–63

Tellis, W. (1997) 'Application of a case study methodology [81 paragraphs]', *The Qualitative Report* [On-line serial], 3(3), accessed on 20 May 2010 from: http://www.nova.edu/ssss/QR/QR3-3/tellis2.html

Yin, R.K. (2003) *Case Study Research: Design and Methods*, third edition, Thousand Oaks, California: Sage Publications

CHAPTER 14
A brief historical review of the British press coverage of AIDS and its role as an educator in the 1990s

Danielle Cox
daniellecox@fsmail.net

Introduction

> "Were you aware in 1984 or 1985 that there was a fatal disease out there, called AIDS, and that you could contract it through sexual activity?"
>
> (*Philadelphia*, 1993)

In the UK many people were not aware of the disease until the mid-1980s as it had received little coverage in the press and this tended falsely to brand it a gay disease (BBC, 1981). Media coverage of the disease has evolved as knowledge and understanding have increased to form a more sympathetic coverage today.

This essay will look at three articles covering a particular HIV/AIDS-related event. Through analysing their content and linguistics, it will examine the levels of coverage offered by those three articles and whether or not they were representative of the research at that time.

The three articles chosen are from the late 1990s and represent a period of time during which public understanding had begun to turn, from considering HIV a death sentence to understanding it as a 'manageable' disease which can be treated and prevented although not yet cured.

To examine these articles successfully it is important first to look briefly at the history of HIV/AIDS in the UK. This will give the articles examined a context through which readers can evaluate the examples.

Historical context of media coverage

> "I'd heard of something. The gay plague, gay cancer, but... we didn't know how you could get it, or that it could kill you."
>
> (*Philadelphia*, 1993)

Between the first death from AIDS in the UK in 1981 and the end of 1982, there had been seven reported cases in the UK from what the American Centre for Disease Control had named Acquired Immune Deficiency Syndrome (AIDS). Its causes were not fully defined and in 1983 the *Mail on Sunday* was censured for writing an "alarmist" story when it informed its readers of the risk of contracting AIDS through blood transfusions, citing two cases of haemophiliacs who were known to have caught it in just that fashion. Over the next few years, despite the evidence to the contrary – including the deaths and diagnoses of haemophiliacs and drug users with AIDS – the papers still branded it as the "gay plague" and, in the *Sun*'s case, the "gay bug" (avert.org, 2009).

Media coverage became more common as the condition became more widespread and more people's lives were affected by the virus:

> In the beginning, with a few exceptions, the press slowly reacted to its presence, at first writing it off as an isolated disease of gay men. After 1985, however, coverage quickly expanded and gradually improved.
>
> (Killenberg, 2008, pp.299–300)

While much of the media continued to perpetuate the myths and panic surrounding the disease, a few papers began to take a more responsible attitude:

> [There is a] thin line between complacency and hysteria when dealing with AIDS. It is undoubtedly a serious disease which will probably kill 5,000 people by 1991. At present a vaccine looks a fairly far-off prospect... But equally AIDS is not a plague.
>
> (McKie and Timbs, 1985)

> The time when the average *Spectator* reader could think of the AIDS epidemic as being someone else's problem is past. The disease has spread beyond the high risk groups in which it started and is no longer confined to homosexuals, drug addicts, prostitutes and the victims of contaminated blood transfusions.
>
> (*Spectator*, 1986)

February 1986 saw the start of the government's first AIDS public-awareness campaign using full-page newspaper adverts – the same newspapers that were creating many of the public misconceptions. Over the next year, television and radio advertising campaigns as well as leaflet drops joined the government's media campaign to educate the public about AIDS (avert.org, 2009).

A popular figure, Freddie Mercury of the rock group Queen, announced that he had AIDS – then died the next day – appealing to the public and his fans to "join me, my doctors and all those worldwide in the fight against this terrible disease" (*Guardian*, 1991). The media had widely speculated about his condition prior to his announcement and it is possible the death of the hugely popular singer helped in following years to reduce prejudice in the media against AIDS. His death certainly inspired a tribute concert for AIDS awareness held at Wembley Stadium which raised around £20 million for AIDS charities. It also encouraged more famous UK faces, including British comedian Kenny Everett, to 'admit' that they had the virus and seek public understanding and support (fyne.co.uk, 2006).

Despite improved understanding and research into the condition, in 1989 the *Sun* ran a series of articles which flew in the face of the facts which were available; changing, ignoring and abusing the figures which were then available to run headlines including 'Straight Sex Cannot Give You AIDS – Official' and 'AIDS – The Hoax of the Century' (Randall, 1996, p.94).

Sensationalist stories about HIV and AIDS may have decreased since the 1990s began but they are still around – however, the tone has primarily changed, with most stories being about miracle cures, treatment breakthroughs and exaggerated progress. On 13 November 2005, the *Mail on Sunday* ran the story 'Miracle HIV-recovery man may have cure' (*Mail on Sunday*, 2005). The danger in these articles is in forming false hope for the sufferers and in encouraging them to switch from beneficial medicines to unproven quick cures.

In addition to stories of 'cures' and breakthroughs, exposés of fake cures and con-artistry came into prominence in the mid-1990s from vitamin pills being sold as a cure (Laurance, 1997) to inherited immunity to "the plague" helping people develop immunity to HIV (Butler, 2005).

Press coverage has not all been negative or sensational. *The Times* and the *Sun* endorse conservative political views on the economy although they sell to very different readerships; yet there was no common stance on AIDS amongst the Murdoch press, with each taking opposing sides of the argument. Where there is no forced point of view, the line the paper takes is decided by editorial viewpoint (Beharrell, 1993).

As public understanding of and treatments for the virus have improved, this editorial leeway has decreased. It is more difficult now for an editor to claim that non-drug-using heterosexuals *cannot* catch the disease; it is publicly understood that the risk to heterosexuals is real, although there have been fewer heterosexual cases of the disease than homosexual. An editor may dispute the validity of a medical claim within the paper but easy access to information with the expansion of the internet and 24-hour news networks has limited their capacity simply to deny that claim.

In the following three articles we shall see how – whether through bias, politics or simple opinion – this leeway can affect the way a news piece is portrayed.

Article analysis

> "The HIV virus can only be transmitted through the exchange of bodily fluids, namely blood and semen."
> (*Philadelphia*, 1993)

Here we look at three randomly chosen articles from 13 August 1999. It had just been announced that it was to become normal practice for all pregnant women to be offered HIV tests alongside the (then) standard tests offered. It had been suggested that these tests would become compulsory but at this stage they were voluntary.

The article headlines read:

'All pregnant women to receive HIV tests on NHS'
Paul Waugh, *Independent* (see Appendix 1)

'HIV tests plan to save babies: Mums-to-be targeted'
Shaun Connolly, *Birmingham Evening Mail* (see Appendix 2)

'HIV tests urged for mothers-to-be: Government acts to cut numbers of babies born with AIDS'
Sarah Boseley, *Guardian* (see Appendix 3)

These articles were published when research had reached a stage at which it was understood that it was not an automatic 'death sentence' for the baby whose mother was HIV positive. That it was possible, in many cases, to prevent the transmission of HIV from the mother to the baby through treatment during pregnancy; delivery by caesarean; and bottle feeding rather than breast feeding.

All three of these papers covered the subject with more sensitivity than had been seen in the 1980s and early 1990s.

Each paper offered an explanation for the government's decision to include HIV testing within the panoply of tests already being offered to expectant mothers. Though each article comes out in general support of the plan, and lists the main reasons behind it, those reasons are weighted differently in each article:

> *BEM*: "If women know they are infected then there is a chance they can reduce the risk of transmission from mother to baby from one in six to less than one in 20. It also means the women themselves can benefit from early treatments which are now on offer."
>
> (Connolly, 1999)
>
> *Independent*: "Of the 265 HIV-infected women who give birth every year, up to 50 babies are born with the virus, mainly because their mothers are unaware that they are infected."
>
> (Waugh, 1999)
>
> *Guardian*: "Modern interventions can cut the chances of a baby having the virus to less than 5%, but most infected mothers – 70% – do not find out they have HIV until their baby becomes ill and often dies."
>
> (Boseley, 1999)

The articles also make some attempt to address the concerns of those who may find themselves contemplating just such a test: discussing potential increases to life insurance premiums, confidentiality, possible treatments for mother and baby – including preventing the child from contracting the virus – and the support offered to those who find that they are HIV positive.

The ***Birmingham Evening Mail*** carries the minimum of facts – sharing the necessary information in a direct and straightforward manner. It lays the essential facts out in a plain and easy to understand fashion using strong language which conveys a sense of immediacy: "told to take HIV tests"; "would not be forced to give a blood sample but would be strongly advised to do so"; "standard medical procedure"; "too late to stop their babies being infected"; "insist"; "265 live births to HIV infected women" (Connolly, 1999).

There is also conflicting information contained within the article: "reduce the chances of passing on the virus by up to 20 times" and "reduce the numbers born with virus by two thirds".

The language used could create a very dark picture for those who are pregnant: phrases like "live births" can create the impression of still births being common in women with HIV (not accurate); "told to" seems to remove the choice of the pregnant woman while at the same time insisting the measures are not compulsory.

The *Guardian* uses more moderate terms than the *Birmingham Evening Mail*: "offered" and "recommend" replace "told", for example. It uses very emotive language throughout the article; for instance, supposition that the baby will be found HIV positive is inherent in:

> "What mother does not want to be screened for any condition which her baby could develop which is preventable?" she said. Without the test, "the baby will be delivered and then will not thrive, and then as part of routine investigations will be found to be HIV positive. ..."
>
> (Boseley, *Guardian*, 1999)

Guilt is also presupposed in the very emotive quote from a Dr Welch to persuade its readers that the test is essential and should be taken by all pregnant mothers:

> News that they are HIV positive is hard to come to terms with, "but what is harder is finding out your baby has Aids [sic] at three months".
>
> (Boseley, *Guardian*, 1999)

Also, the suggestion that this is a far more likely occurrence in British women than in women from other parts or Europe or America places additional pressure on pregnant women to conform to the new "non-compulsory" tests.

The article is littered with facts and figures, the most worrying one being that in London one in five pregnant women are HIV positive – though reassuring the rest of England that some areas have fewer than 1 in 5000 pregnant women testing positive.

The *Independent* article's opening lines do not follow the same pattern as the other two articles, initially not introducing the fact that the tests are to be optional; instead, it presents the information that "all pregnant women in England are to be given an HIV test under a Government scheme to reduce the number of babies born with the virus." It is not until half-way through the article that information is given.

This article clarifies the "live births" faux pas made in the *Birmingham Evening Mail* article by offering the information that "Of the 265 HIV-infected women who give birth every year, up to 50 babies are born with the virus". This article is not as figure heavy as that of the *Guardian* – nor does it contain as little information as the *Birmingham Evening Mail* – but it does attempt to illustrate each major point with a supporting statistic or additional piece of information.

Of these three articles, the *Birmingham Evening Mail*'s is perhaps the easiest to read but carries with it negative images and does not necessarily offer sufficient information when compared with the levels of information available at the time.

> Obviously, reporters must get the facts right. It is also vitally important for them to resist that urge – and the efforts of others – to exaggerate the importance of medical developments… reporters must proceed with caution and restraint.
> (Killenberg, 2008, pp.299–300)

History shows us that this is not always the case, but it is important to recognise that the press can only represent the facts as they are understood at the time.

> It is through the news media that highly specialised knowledge can be made accessible to much wider audiences through the public sphere. However… coverage of health and medical knowledge is frequently incomplete, oversimplified, partial, dependent upon a restricted number of powerful sources, or, in certain circumstances, sensationalised in a way that is associated with "health risk panics".
> (Manning, 2001, p.13)

While none of the articles can be said to be guilty of sensationalising the subject or inciting a "health risk panic", the statistics contained may have been a cause for concern for some of their readers.

Conclusion

> "Every problem has a solution. Every problem… has… a… solution."
> (*Philadelphia*, 1993)

Each of the articles manages to convey a distinct representation of the subject, despite using the same base information and source, using various language and content constructions. This potentially demonstrates each particular paper's stance towards the topic – although this would need to be examined in greater depth than this essay has been able to do.

Unfortunately it is not possible to say for certain that these articles are truly representative of the press coverage and the public understanding of the time as there would need to be a wider examination of the topic, but they could be classed as representative of this particular issue.

Perhaps then, what could be considered is whether or not each of the articles conveys the same basic level of information, the desired impression (i.e. that HIV testing for pregnant women is a good thing for both mother and baby) and whether it is suitable for their 'standard' readership – particularly as it is entirely possible that these and similar articles were the primary means for educating the public about this development. Yet as each of these articles includes and omits information found in the others, it is possible to criticise them as being incomplete; each appears to present the information in an impartial fashion but the phrasing discussed above does not wholly support this. Each is dependent upon a particular group of sources, with the same source – Tessa Jowell – being quoted in all three items.

While none of these articles claim to have a cure for AIDS or an answer for the infected mothers, they all create an optimistic picture for the unborn babies – contrasted with a very negative image of the future of the babies of non-diagnosed HIV-positive mothers. The new risks for babies with a mother undertaking HIV treatment and following the recommended guidelines is, respectively, 1 in 100, less than 5 per cent, less than 1 in 20. These figures do not match and prompt concern that the articles may be painting an overly rosy picture.

APPENDIX 1
'All pregnant women to receive HIV tests on NHS'

Paul Waugh, *Independent*, 13 August 1999

ALL PREGNANT women in England are to be given an HIV test under a Government scheme to reduce the number of babies born with the virus.

Tessa Jowell, the Health minister, will announce today that HIV screening is to be made available at every ante-natal clinic in the country, the *Independent* has learnt.

Ms Jowell will unveil the plans, to take effect within weeks, as a key part of her department's attempt to prevent the transmission of the illness.

Ministers decided to act after figures showed that the UK had one of the highest maternal HIV transmission rates in Europe, and one of the lowest identification rates among pregnant women.

Of the 265 HIV-infected women who give birth every year, up to 50 babies are born with the virus, mainly because their mothers are unaware that they are infected.

Ms Jowell's announcement will implement the recommendations of a group set up three months ago to find ways of reducing the problem.

The screening scheme, which will not be compulsory, will be available to all and will be offered alongside blood tests and other examinations currently offered.

There will also be measures to help those women who find they are carrying the virus.

Anti-retroviral drug courses will be offered during pregnancy, along with careful obstetric management and Caesarean sections. Once born, the babies should be bottle fed rather than breast fed. The combination of drugs,

Caesareans and bottle feeding reduces the chances of HIV transmission from one in six to one in 100.

Ms Jowell said: "With 50 babies born a year with HIV, it is tragic that most of their mothers don't know they have the virus before they give birth. In the majority of cases, transmission can be prevented once HIV is identified.

"There is no question of this being compulsory, but frankly what woman, who may have lingering doubts, is going to turn down a test which would make all the difference in the world to ensuring the right treatment?"

The scheme, which will also be accompanied by targets for numbers of women screened per year, follows similar projects in France and the United States, where mothers to be are routinely tested for HIV.

Britain has one of the highest rates of HIV among children and teenagers in the West.

Only a handful of clinics across the country currently offer an HIV screening service and the expert group, which was made up of paediatricians and public health officials, suggested that a comprehensive system should be created. The HIV blood test is simple and relatively cheap to carry out.

Anonymous surveys by the Department of Health found 195 cases of pregnant women with the virus in London, 56 in the rest of England and Wales and 14 in Scotland. Of those, 40 babies were born with the virus in London and 12 elsewhere.

London is the highest risk area, partly because of its large and cosmopolitan population, and a high number of drugs users. Glasgow, however, is seen as a "high prevalence" region due to widespread intravenous drug use.

While the scheme to be announced today only covers England, ministers hope it will be extended throughout the UK under powers devolved to the regional assemblies.

Fears about the levels of ignorance were confirmed when researchers found that in more than 70 per cent of cases the condition was undiagnosed until the baby was born.

The UK's HIV infection rates for adults are average for Europe, but the rate for mother-to-baby transmission is among the highest on the continent. Most worrying of all, the expert group found that while the number of Aids-infected babies under 12 months was dropping across the EU, it was rising in the UK.

Although anti-viral drugs are having some success, most children with HIV do not live beyond their teens.

Last night, a health department spokeswoman stressed that the tests were totally confidential and could not be released to insurance companies without a patient's consent.

The Government is due to publish a comprehensive HIV/Aids strategy early next year.

APPENDIX 2
'HIV tests plan to save babies: Mums-to-be targeted'

Shaun Connolly, *Birmingham Evening Mail*, 13 August 1999

ALL pregnant women are being told to take HIV tests in a radical move aimed at cutting the number of babies born with the virus.

Health Minister Tessa Jowell said that mothers-to-be would not be forced to give a blood sample, but would be "strongly advised" to do so and would have to make clear they were opting out of what will become standard medical procedure if they refused.

The action has been prompted by surveys showing that two thirds of HIV-positive pregnant women did not realise that they have the virus until after they had given birth when it was often too late to stop their babies being infected.

Medical experts insist that treatment with drugs, opting for a Caesarean delivery and avoiding breast feeding can reduce the chances of passing on the virus by up to 20 times.

Routine

Women will take the test along with more usual antenatal checks for rubella and hepatitis B.

In 1997, the last year for which figures are available, there were 265 live births to HIV-infected women.

This is a tiny proportion of the 600,000 babies born in the UK each year, but ministers believe routine testing could reduce the numbers born with the virus by two thirds.

Pregnant women are much more likely to be infected with HIV in inner city areas, where experts believe the problem is growing, than other parts of the country.

A Department of Health spokesman said: "There is going to be no element of compulsion in this at all.

"If women know they are infected then there is a chance they can reduce the risk of transmission from mother to baby by one in six to less than one in 20.

"It also means the women themselves can benefit from early treatments which are now on offer."

Local health authorities will be set targets on the take-up of the tests and Government hopes to move towards a 50 per cent test rate.

The move, however, could prompt concerns among some women who do not regard the virus as a significant hazard.

There could also be fears that taking an HIV test could affect life insurance premiums.

Great Ormond Street Hospital consultant paediatric immunologist Graham Davies said: "The case for HIV testing in pregnancy is now so strong that it should be made obligatory for all pregnant women to be given information about HIV transmissions and offered testing if they wish."

APPENDIX 3
'HIV tests urged for mothers-to-be: Government acts to cut numbers of babies born with Aids'

Sarah Boseley, *Guardian*, 13 August 1999

All pregnant women in Britain are to be offered and strongly recommended to have an HIV test as part of a government strategy to slash the numbers of babies born with the Aids virus.

Tessa Jowell, minister for public health, will today announce new targets for testing women in order to reduce the transmission of HIV from mother to baby. Modern interventions can cut the chances of a baby having the virus to less than 5%, but most infected mothers – 70% – do not find out they have HIV until their baby becomes ill and often dies.

Ms Jowell hopes the HIV test will become just another of the routine investigations all pregnant women undergo, but she stresses it will not be compulsory.

"What mother does not want to be screened for any condition which her baby could develop which is preventable?" she said. Without the test, "the baby will be delivered and then will not thrive, and then as part of routine investigations will be found to be HIV positive.

"There is a public health imperative that we begin to do better by these mothers and these babies."

Anti-Aids drugs given to women during pregnancy and to the baby for a few weeks after birth, together with delivery by caesarian section and bottle rather than breast-feeding can dramatically improve the baby's chances of being

HIV-free. The United States, France, Italy and Spain have cut the number of children with Aids through such methods, but Britain has not through ignorance of which women are infected.

High risk areas

HIV tests are offered by some health authorities to pregnant women but even in high risk areas uptake can be as low as 30%. There are far more people with the virus in some parts of the country than in others. In London, one in five pregnant women is HIV positive, while in some areas the ratio drops as low as one in 6,000.

King's College hospital, which draws its patients from the deprived boroughs of Lambeth, Southwark and Lewisham in south London, has succeeded in testing 90% of pregnant women. In this area, where 5% of the population are asylum seekers, including women who have been raped or abused in war zones, there is an urgent need to identify babies at risk.

"In England as a whole, most HIV positive people have been gay men," said Jan Welch, consultant in sexual health. "We are seeing a newer epidemic among people who are from or have links with parts where HIV is common in heterosexuals."

Refugees, she says, "are dealing with problems like grief, lack of money and the inability to speak English, and they may have HIV on top". To preserve their baby from infection, they must not breastfeed. "Bottle feeding requires sterilisation and formula milk and ideally not a kitchen shared with 10 other people."

If they are not breastfeeding, mothers-in-law want to know why. "A caesarian and bottle-feeding means they are HIV positive."

Most women are happy to have an HIV test as part of routine ante-natal screening. Those who are negative are informed by letter. Those who are positive are invited back to see an obstetrician. News that they are HIV positive is hard to come to terms with, "but what is harder is finding out your baby has Aids at three months," said Dr Welch.

Ms Jowell will tell health authorities to aim for an increased uptake of HIV testing to 50% of pregnant women by the end of 2000 and 80% by the end of 2002.

References

avert.org (2009) *History of HIV and AIDS in the UK 1981–1995*, accessed online 9/5/2009 at: http://www.avert.org/uk-AIDS-history.htm

BBC (1981) 'Mystery disease kills homosexuals', accessed online 9/5/2009 at: http://news.bbc.co.uk/onthisday/hi/dates/stories/december/10/newsid_4020000/4020391.stm

Beharrell, P. (1993) 'AIDS and the British Press', in J. Eldridge (ed.) *Getting the Message: News Truth and Power*, London: Routledge

Boseley, S. (1999) 'HIV tests urged for mothers-to-be: Government acts to cut numbers of babies born with AIDS', *Guardian*, 13 August, accessed online 9/5/2009 at: http://www.guardian.co.uk/uk/1999/aug/13/sarahboseley1

Butler, A. (2005) 'How plague can prevent HIV: Mystery solved in the battle to find a cure for AIDS', *Daily Post*, 10 March

Connolly, S. (1999) 'HIV tests plan to save babies: Mums-to-be targeted', *Birmingham Evening Mail*, 13 August, accessed online 9/5/2009 at: http://www.highbeam.com/doc/1G1-60166286.html

Cottle, S. (ed.) (2003) *News, Public Relations and Power*, London: Sage, p.9

fyne.co.uk (2006) 'Kenny Everett', accessed online 9/5/2009 at: http://www.fyne.co.uk/index.php?item=214

Guardian (1991) 'Queen Star Dies after AIDS Statement', 25 November, accessed online 9/5/2009 at: http://century.guardian.co.uk/1990-1999/Story/0,,112639,00.html

Killenberg, G.M. (2008) *Public Affairs Reporting Now: News of, by and for the People*, Oxford: Focal Press, pp.299–300

Laurance, J. (1997) 'UK vitamin pills sold as AIDS cure in Uganda', *Independent*, 27 July

Mail on Sunday (2005) 'First man in world to beat HIV virus', 13 November

Manning, P. (2001) *News and News Sources: A Critical Introduction*, London: Sage, p.13

McKie, R. and Timbs, O. (1985) 'Anatomy of Panic', *Observer*, 24 February

Philadelphia (1993) Movie/video release, TriStar Pictures, written by Ron Nyswaner, directed by Jonathan Demme

Randall, D. (1996) *The Universal Journalist*, London: Pluto Press, p.94

Spectator (1986) 'How AIDS Threatens All of Us', 15 November

Waugh, P. (1999) 'All pregnant women to receive HIV tests on NHS', *Independent*, 13 August, accessed online 9/5/2009 at: http://www.independent.co.uk/news/all-pregnant-women-to-receive-hiv-tests-on-nhs-1112303.html

Contributing authors (in order of appearance):

Dr John Lister, editor of this volume and organiser of the 2009 conference, is senior lecturer in health journalism at Coventry University, England. He has for 26 years been principal researcher and editor for *London Health Emergency*, a trade-union-backed pressure group in defence of the National Health Service in the UK, and opposed to privatisation, marketisation and cutbacks in spending. He has previously published books on global health reforms (*Health Policy Reform: Driving the Wrong Way?*, 2005) and the British NHS (*The NHS after 60: for Patients or Profits?*, 2008). John is a member of the Association of Health Care Journalists, the National Union of Journalists, and a joint Vice President of IAHPE.

Dr Alexis Benos is Professor in Social Medicine & Primary Health Care in the Aristotle University of Thessaloniki, Greece. He is elected president of the International Association of Health Policy in Europe (IAHPE) and is also active with People's Health Movement (PHM).

Nils Böhlke, born on 24 March 1979 in Hamburg, is a political scientist. He is currently working in the Institute for economical and social research (WSI) in the Hans-Bockler-Foundation, which is affiliated to the German trade union federation. In the Institute he is writing his dissertation about the impact of the privatisation of German hospitals on the employees and the industrial relations. In this context he is involved in the EU-funded PIQUE-project (Privatisation of Public Services and the Impact on Quality, Employment and Productivity).

Ian Greer has a PhD in Industrial and Labor Relations from Cornell University and is Senior Research Fellow at Leeds University Business School.

Dr Thorsten Schulten studied political science, economics and sociology at the University of Marburg and has worked in collaboration with the European Committee of Food Trade Unions (ECF-IUF) in Brussels, and then as freelancer for the Executive Board of IG Metall in Frankfurt, since 1997. He works with the WSI.

Elias Kondilis is a Psychiatry Registrar, holding a PhD on Health Policy and Economics. He is a Research Assistant in the Department of Hygiene and Social Medicine, Medical School, Aristotle University Thessaloniki.

Emmanouil Smyrnakis is a General Practitioner working in the National Health System and an Associate Lecturer in Primary Health Care with the Department of Hygiene and Social Medicine, Medical School, Aristotle University of Thessaloniki.

Stathis Giannakopoulos is a General Practitioner working in the Greek NHS.

He is an Associate Lecturer in Primary Care in the Department of Hygiene and Social Medicine, Medical School, Aristotle University of Thessaloniki and holds a PhD in Primary Care. He is a member of the International Association of Health Policy.

Theodoras Zdoukos is a General Practitioner working in the National Health System and active member of NHS Physicians Association.

George Nikolaidis, MD, MA, MSc, PhD was born in Patra, Greece in 1969. He studied Medicine and Psychiatry. He has a PhD, an MSc degree from KCL, University of London and an MA degree in "Psychoanalytic Studies" from the University of Sheffield. His scientific interests include a wide range of issues involving Public Health Sciences, Epidemiology, Health Policy and Politics, Health Services' Quality Assessment, Epistemology and Philosophy of Health Related Sciences, Philosophy of Psychopathology, Psychoanalytic Theory, Interpersonal Violence and Child Abuse and Neglect. From September 2005, he is Research Director of the Department of Mental Health and Social Welfare – Centre for the Study and Prevention of Child Abuse and Neglect of the Institute of Child Health in Athens, Greece.

Kayıhan Pala is Professor of Public Health at Uludag University in Bursa, Turkey. He has a PhD in Public Health and an MD in medicine. He is interested in public health areas including health policy & administration, health economics, and environmental & occupational health and safety.

Harika Gerçek, Uludag University in Bursa, Turkey

Alpaslan Türkkan, Uludag University in Bursa, Turkey

Hamdi Aytekin, Uludag University in Bursa, Turkey

Nilay Etiler is associate professor of public health at Kocaeli University in Turkey. After she graduated from the faculty of medicine, she worked as a general practitioner in several primary health care units of the Turkish Ministry of Health. Then she graduated as a public health specialist from Akdeniz University, Public Health Department. Her work currently focuses on healthcare reforms, immigrant health, and women's health and culture.

Betul Urhan, PhD is from Kocaeli University's Faculty of Economics and Business Administration, School of Labour Economy.

Öztürk Osman, MD is a General Practitioner, a member of Istanbul Medical Association and a former Executive Committee Member of the Turkish Medical Association.

Çerkezoglu Ali, MD is a Forensic Medicine Specialist and an Executive Member of the Turkish Medical Association.

Ağkoç Süheyla, MD is a General Practitioner, a member of Istanbul Medical Association and a member of the Turkish Medical Association's Committee for Health Policies.

Delia Alvarez and **Anton Saiz** are family physicians and members of Coordinadora Anti-Privatización de la Sanidad Pública de Madrid (CAS Madrid – http://www.casmadrid.org).

Dr Clive Peedell trained in medicine at the University of Southampton, England. He is now a Consultant Clinical Oncologist at James Cook University Hospital, Middlesbrough. He is a member of the National Council of the British Medical Association and of its Political Board.

Dr O.B.B. Reddy is a medical doctor with extensive training in internal medicine including cardiology, neurology, diabetology and specialisation in clinical nutrition. He has worked at grassroots level gaining primary care experience in India and the Maldives. He is the current PCT programme lead for obesity and diabetes at the NHS Berkshire West, since December 2008, prior to which he worked as a lecturer in Public Health at the University of Greenwich. His special interest is raising public health awareness about 'diabesity' [diabetes and obesity], bridging inequalities, linking services and providing a holistic, high-quality patient-centred care for the population.

Dr Sally Ruane is the Deputy Director of the Health Policy Research Unit, De Montfort University, Leicester. She has been researching privatisation in the NHS for 15 years and some of her work has been translated for use in Spain where she has addressed a range of audiences, particularly on the topic of the Private Finance Initiative.

Dr Andrea Capstick is a lecturer and MSc course leader in the Division of Dementia Studies at the University of Bradford, UK. She holds a professional doctorate in education, and is the co-author of *Tom Kitwood on dementia: a reader and critical commentary*.

Marisa de Andrade is a Doctoral Candidate at the Institute for Social Marketing (ISM) at the University of Stirling, completing a PhD on the communicative strategies used by several stakeholders during the promotion of licensed drugs. She has an MSc in Investigative Journalism at the University of Strathclyde with a focus on public health policy, and is a freelance journalist and broadcaster in Scotland.

Danielle Cox holds a BSc in Health Studies and an MA in Specialist Health Journalism. She has taught English and academic skills in four different countries but is currently putting her writing skills to use creating training materials and study aids for foreign Health and Social Care students in Birmingham.